SEARCHLIGHTS ON

CONTEMPORARY THEOLOGY

Other Books by Nels F. S. Ferré

SEARCHLIGHTS

ON

CONTEMPORARY

THEOLOGY

by

Nels F. S. Ferré

Abbot Professor of Christian Theology
Andover Newton Theological School

HARPER & BROTHERS, PUBLISHERS NEW YORK

To Roy Pearson
who, when my life was darkest,
gave his help and his hope

Contents

V

THEOLOGY IN EDUCATION

Preface and Acknowledgments

BOOKS are made or grow. This one grew. It represents my most recent thinking on many subjects, with a strong common core of the bearing of this thinking on contemporary theology, philosophy, social theory, biblical interpretation, and education. This volume, therefore, may be read as a whole or by sections. Many readers are concerned now with this interest and now with that, and grope for recent, relevant discussion of them. The present work lends itself easily to either use.

The intense interest in theological language may be temporary, but it certainly is contemporary. From personal observation while teaching in both Oxford and Manchester, I know how the Church has been hurt by a false approach to it in much of British thinking. And the toll is beginning to be taken in America. We need constructive conversation with the linguistic analysts, and on the whole question of theological language. John Hick and Willem Zuurdeeg have begun to use analysis and to formulate Christian thinking with reference to it. To a large extent Paul Tillich and Rudolf Bultmann must be interpreted with regard to their use of myth and symbol.

The first section is composed of the Adams Lectures at the First Methodist Church in Bloomington, Indiana. My thanks to the Rev. Benjamin Garrison and to the Trustees of the Foundation.

To inaugurate a new lectureship is an awesome responsibility. The Faith and Freedom Lectures at American University, Washington, D.C., put me in such a position for the sixth time. My foremost impression was the vision of those who made it possible for lectures to be given on so central a subject in the most strategic city of the world. My thanks to all those at American University and at the nearby Wesley Seminary who helped in launching the lectureship. What topic is more urgent in social theory than the relation between faith and freedom in its bearing on contemporary decisions? This material was also used in the Mendenhall Lectures

ix

at De Pauw University, a lectureship set up for the pastors of
Indiana as well as for the students of the university. This occasion
was filled with first-class theological interest. My thanks to President Russell J. Humbert and all connected with this important
undertaking. Once again these lectures were used for the Elva M.
Peel Theological Lectureship at the University Methodist Church
in Minneapolis.

By far the largest section of the book deals with contemporary
theology. The short parable of the castle of classical Christianity,
although less "scholarly" in tone than the rest, serves a real purpose
of preliminary orientation. Readers may rear at the sharpness, but
blinders are not for mature thinkers. The tracing of theology for
one hundred years as a background for contemporary intepretation
is largely American in scope. It was done as part of the one-
hundredth anniversary celebration of the Winthrop Club of Boston. In it American theology, however, is within the compass of
the larger scene of Protestant development. The treatment of
Tillich in this section as well as in the first should be seen in the
light of my fuller dealing with his thought in Chapter 11. The
statement on the future of theology in Chapter 12 is the most careful one I have made. The lectures on contemporary theology were
first given at Phillips University, and inaugurated the Caleb Davies
Lectureship. The reception these serious lectures on theology
received, especially from the undergraduate student body, still
astonishes me. The interest in theology in Oklahoma runs high!
Dean England and the faculty of the College of the Bible made
me feel thoroughly at home. Much of this material was also presented as the Crozer Lectures at Crozer Theological Seminary and
as the Moravian Lectures at the Moravian Theological Seminary.
What happy memories I have of both occasions.

The section "New Light on Old Problems" comprises discussion
of God's presence in nature and Christian experience, but especially in the Bible. The chapter on natural theology is my presidential address for the American Theological Society. That year,
the whole Society was dealing with natural theology. The concern
over this problem has increased even more after Karl Barth's
recent swiveling in his basic stance.

One of the main reasons for confusion and consequent dissipa-
tion of strength in the Church and in theological education is the
lack of a constructive Christian approach to the Bible that is
thoroughly open both to scholarship and to full faith. I was invited
to give constructive comments on the struggle among biblical
scholars over the principles for interpreting the Bible. The chapter

on hermeneutics represents more preparation and more hard work than any summation I have done of similar length. The treatment of the authority of the Bible bespeaks my basic attitude both to the meaning and to the use of the Bible for the contemporary Church. Some will feel that the two chapters differ in both perspective and attitude. Indeed, all sections and chapters in this book come at our contemporary problems from varying viewpoints and emotional involvements. Therefore, common themes appear several times, but always within differing contexts and circumstances. Such use of "searchlights" is the central meaning and motivation of the book. Lynchburg College asked me to give the Snidow Lecture on Christian experience. Leaders of fundamentalist sects fought to prevent my coming, but the college and the ministry of Lynchburg rallied quickly to the defense of the freedom of the Gospel.

The book concludes, I hope climactically, with higher education. During the next few years, denominations and national agencies will be concentrating on higher education. Since I wrote my book on the subject at the invitation of the National Council of the Churches of Christ in the U.S.A. and gave the Danforth Lectures at Boston University on the subject, I have been especially concerned with the question. The discussion of contemporary theology with respect to higher education I undertook at the request of the American Baptist Educational Committee, for its annual conference, and of the National Council on Religion in Higher Education as the opening lecture at its Week of Work. The general treatment of education and values I prepared as a lecture for Elmhurst College, and the chapter on the Church-related college resulted from an invitation to give an address at the one-hundred-twenty-fifth anniversary of Kalamazoo College.

The Adams Lectures and the Faith and Freedom Lectures are here published for the first time. Other chapters have appeared as follows: Chapter 7, "Can Classical Christianity Be Defended?" appeared as "The Choice before Us" in the Pulpit, January, 1957; in Episcopal Church News, Sept. 16, 1956; and in the British Weekly, April 19, 1956; Chapter 8, "Contemporary Theology in the Light of One Hundred Years," in Theology Today, October, 1958; Chapter 9, "The Rise and Role of Neo-Orthodoxy," in the Voice, January, 1959, and in the Moravian Theological Seminary Bulletin, Fall, 1959; Chapter 10, "The Meaning and Power of Neonaturalism and Existentialism" in the Moravian Theological Seminary Bulletin, Fall, 1959; Chapter 11, "Three Critical Issues in Tillich's Philosophical Theology," in the Scottish

Journal of Theology, September, 1957; Chapter 12, "Where Do We Go from Here in Theology?" in *Religion in Life*, Winter, 1956; Chapter 13, "Natural Theology and the Christian Faith," in the *Scottish Journal of Theology*, December, 1958; Chapter 14, "Notes by a Theologian on Biblical Hermeneutics" in the *Journal of Biblical Literature*, June, 1959; Chapter 15, "The Bible as Authority" in the *Asbury Seminarian*, Fall-Winter, 1959; Chapter 16, "A Definition of God in the Light of Twentieth-Century Knowledge," in *Religion in Life*, Autumn, 1958; Chapter 17, "The Nature and Power of Christian Experience" in *From Lynchburg College*, November, 1957; Chapter 18, "Contemporary Theology and Christian Higher Education" in the *Christian Scholar*, June, 1958; Chapter 19, "Higher Education and Values" in *Religion in Life*, Autumn, 1960; Chapter 20, "The Church-Related College and a Mature Faith" in *Religious Education*, March-April, 1959. My thanks to all concerned for having granted special permission to use this material and for the chance to present it to still wider circles.

The final typing of the manuscript was done by Mrs. Robert Suddath. My wife and I worked on the finishing touches together, and we have never felt more closely united by a common task. Two of my best critics have strongly urged the publication of this material, claiming that I communicate best by this kind of writing. Whether or not this be true, I send this book out with humble confidence that it will accomplish whatever work God has given me to do.

Nels F. S. Ferré

Newton Centre, Massachusetts
January, 1961

I

THE PLACE AND POWER
OF THEOLOGICAL LANGUAGE

Chapter 1

Myth and Symbol

THE contemporary world is almost pathologically concerned with the problem of communication. Frequently we hear that in the modern world communication has broken down. Certainly this is a fact. The question is, however, whether communication has broken down in the technical sense or has been destroyed because we are not sure about *what* we are communicating. Perhaps it is not only communication but faith that has broken down. Perhaps we fail in both faith and reason. It can be that we have come short of the kind of community that nourishes both faith and reason. Possibly this community itself has become alienated and estranged from its own source and reality.

Man may be unable to communicate because he is a stranger to himself and to God. Where there is no God, says Kierkegaard, there is no self.[1] Communication may also have been cut off because man has become a stranger to his fellow men. Thus, the concern about communication may be basically a concern about community, and the problem of community may itself be the problem of faith.

If this assumption be right, communication has broken down negatively because of fear, or even more fundamentally, because of anxiety about the self, about others, and about God. Faithlessness disrupts community and destroys communication. On the positive side, communication may have become impossible because the God that provided the unity of discourse for communication has been deposed as too small. There are deep drives of honesty that reject too narrow and too ignoble views of God. Maybe a deeper layer of reality in man is refusing outworn faiths, and arguments not truly adequate to authenticate real faith.

Positively and negatively, the question of communication may be the question of community in relation to faith. Linguistics, however, is a science in itself. We have no intention of starting

[1] A theme in *Sickness unto Death* (Princeton University Press, 1941).

3

a discourse on theological language and then shifting the investigation from communication in the religious realm to the question of community as such or to the question of faith. But we should, at the very beginning, keep in mind that the question of communication cannot be isolated, either from the person or from the community, or even from faith and reason as organized activities in ordinary usage on the part of individuals and communities. This chapter will be concerned basically with the question of symbol and myth, and their proper use in language. In this connection we shall consider in particular Paul Tillich's use of symbol and Rudolf Bultmann's use of myth.

I

By a linguistic symbol, I do not mean a sound or a written word that directly signifies a thing, a relation, or any property of the thing or of the relation. When a word stands for a thing, an event, a being, or for relations among these, that word is a sign and not a symbol if its signification derives from custom, convention, or from ordinary usage in a generally accepted manner. A reliable sign indicates directly or denotatively what is signified, what is intended. A sign, therefore, in this sense gives us literal language. A symbol is a sign used to indicate, within a context of common understanding, a reality not directly or literally designated but indicated, suggested, or represented by the sign. The distinction must never be made between a sign indicating some actual reality of a physical nature, and a symbol indicating meaning and not existence. Such a distinction is "loaded." It is prejudicial from the start. Both the sign and the symbol, when correctly used, point, but one points directly or denotatively; the other points indirectly, suggestively, representatively, or connotatively. The word "unicorn" as a sign means a fictional being; as a symbol, along with the lion it suggests the British Empire. Here the sign indicates the fictional; the symbol, the actual. However, the existence or nonexistence of the thing signified, the *designatum*, is not the difference between the linguistic signs and symbols.

To demonstrate this, let us look at another example. As a sign, the word "flag" indicates a piece of cloth of a certain pattern. As a symbol, the word "flag" signifies the country it represents. In this instance both are equally real; but one is indicated by a sign literally, the other by a symbolic representation of it. If I say, "I am going to buy a flag," the sign usage is clear; if I say, "I love my flag," the symbolic usage is generally understood.

A symbol is legitimately used only when there is common under-

standing regarding the nature and reality of that which is symbolized; otherwise, the symbol is vague or misleading. The
expression "Christmas day" as a sign generally signifies December
twenty-five. "Santa Claus" can be a symbol for Christmas if by
custom or convention he represents the general mood and activities
of the secular aspects of Christmas. "Santa Claus" is not properly
used as a symbol for the meaning of Christmas in a historic sense.
The word "crèche" is a proper symbol for the true meaning of
Christmas, the historic fact of the nativity of Christ. Similarly,
the word "God" as a sign indicates the Supreme Being; the words
"light" or "rock" may stand for God symbolically. Neither usage
determines the question whether God is real or fictional.

Trouble comes linguistically when the nature and reality of what
has been commonly symbolized as real is called into question and
disbelieved. Then the literal reality disappears, to be replaced by
fiction. Linguistically, this situation gives rise to the improper
expression "only a symbol," meaning that this no longer is or
never was legitimately a symbol for something real. Thus, when
the supernatural events symbolized by the word "crèche" are not
taken to be historic fact, the crèche is improperly called "only a
symbol." It no longer symbolizes in the accustomed linguistic
sense. Therefore, to call it a symbol in this sense is misleading.
The status of what is symbolized has been changed, and the
word does not now have "only" symbolic meaning, but "different"
symbolic meaning.

The myth, or even the saga, is of similar nature, but according
to custom and convention it is used in the opposite way. A myth
stands for a historic event which is fictitious. A saga stands for a
legendary happening, an event not literally true. Whether or not
these words were differently used before Pindar, for instance, is
only of historic importance. The main dictionary usages now
indicate fictional events. A myth may involve historic reference
with more than human actors or dimensions. What matters is
that "myth" linguistically is properly used only in accordance
with custom and convention, for only thus is communication
reliably effected. For this reason, the expression "only a myth,"
when used to indicate that what is given in communication is not
real but fictional, is a phrase properly used.

II

But is there no other legitimate place for myth? Cannot a myth,
for instance, speaking in literal, historic terms, stand for more
general historic fact that is not fictitious in nature, and yet is not

directly signified by the myth? Cannot the virgin birth of Christ, for instance, instead of being a literal, historic, biological fact, be a dramatic, "metaphysical" myth signifying the literal, historic fact of the primacy of God's initiative in the Incarnation? Or cannot the dramatic death of Jesus on Calvary represent, mythically, beyond any literally ascertainable causation, the total self-giving of God for man? Cannot myth stand for realities suggested by concrete, vivid events of life, historic or fictitious, that are less adequately represented by literal, nonsymbolic language? In such a case, the myth signifies an objective counterpart, a reality beyond itself, although a reality less literally defined. The content of what is signified becomes more general, or at least less concretely indicated. The historic myth can then symbolize, beyond its literal fictional meaning, a metaphysical or theological truth both in[2] and beyond human history. Does not a myth thus used elicit the richness of the imagination and actually convey more of the truth intended than does a nonsymbolic statement? A myth in this sense is the symbolic use of a historic event.

To return to the case of the symbol, can there be a more extended use of symbol that is not improper? For instance, can the sign-word symbolize not a reality beyond itself or other than self but a reality, a depth reality of its own self in which it participates? The symbol then serves to clarify the fuller meaning, nature, or power of the thing, relation, or description which is not obvious in a literal or nonsymbolic use of the word. Thus, says Tillich, the literal meaning of Jesus as a historic figure may fail decisively to suggest the symbolic meaning of his life—the power of being not only to maintain itself in being but to make for harmony of being. Meaning and being can thus be used in the fullest possible way through the symbol of a concrete life. Literally, we know little with full accuracy about this life, but a picture is suggested by it, says Tillich, as to the kind of reality in which that life and ours participate. This is the way in which Tillich uses the word "symbol." In this usage, the life of Jesus is both sign and symbol, but only the symbol participates in the reality of that which is symbolized.

Can myth similarly stand both for the fictitious nature of what is literally signified and also for the richness of experience that cannot be reduced to nonsymbolic, propositional language? This is Bultmann's use of myth. Thus the Cross and the resurrection can be fictitious as historic occurrences of supernatural events—

[2] Cf. Kierkegaard's claim that "the myth represents as outward that which occurred inwardly." *Concept of Dread* (Princeton University Press, 1944), p. 42.

a god dying and being resuscitated in human history literally—but at the same time convey the fullness of such authentic experience as alone affords salvation. The myth, when genuine, then, serves to clarify and direct experience; but when not genuine, Bultmann maintains, it is merely fictitious, referring human historic events and realities to another world which science has shown us to be nonexistent. True myth should be used, but false myths should be destroyed or demythologized.

Is there sound reason why the use of symbol and myth cannot be extended creatively in this way? Language refuses to "stay put." The main requirement of language is integrity of communication. Language requires clarity of usage as well as honesty of intent. Therefore, the following rules obtain: (1) When the natural meaning of the symbolism is intended, as in supernatural activities present in the nativity of Jesus, there is no problem except capacity and depth of understanding on both sides of the communication through symbols. (2) When faith in what is naturally symbolized is gone, with no *new* meaning taking the place of the old, to use the symbol as "only a symbol" is improper use of language. (3) To use the symbol without indicating lack of faith in the nature and reality of what is symbolized is misleading usage, forfeiting integrity of language.

The more difficult case arises when a new content has taken the place of the naturally intended meaning, as in the case of the use of the virgin birth to indicate the miraculous initiative of God in the Incarnation, although not necessarily through a biological miracle. Such usage may be justified, for instance, if the speaker stands within a tradition where these symbols are constantly used. Then merely either to affirm or to deny the signification of the symbol is misleading. Integrity in such a case requires the speaker to clarify beyond all culpable confusion his own use of the symbol, both by declaring what he does not mean to convey and by indicating what he literally does intend. Accepted usage means reliability of communication. Something is offered for knowledge as nearly, completely, and accurately as the speaker can convey the content of his thought.

Tillich and Bultmann have every right to use language creatively, even when they thereby deny and deviate from the historic faith. They claim that they have shed the husks and are maintaining and bringing to light the true grain of the historic affirmations.[3] Difficulty arises when they fail to communicate clearly and definitely what they really mean. Thus, in their use

[3] For detailed discussion of Tillich's position see Chapter 11 and for Bultmann's, see Chapter 10.

of the resurrection or of life eternal they have misled innumerable hearers and readers who have understood them to be affirming the actual rising of Jesus from the dead and literal life after death as the continuation of personal existence within the grace and glory of God. Instead, they have been referring to possibilities for present experience, for resources of reality and healing in this life.

The difficulty has been multiplied by the fact that many readers have mistakenly taken their teaching as a natural but elevated use of symbols, while other readers have been uncertain of what is actually intended, and only a small though increasing number of initiates have accepted these theologies precisely because of their radical difference from the historic doctrines. We find in Tillich's case that he believes it best not to disillusion people by stating clearly what he means, and therefore he advocates the use of symbols with all three groups of people: the precritical, the hesitant, and the initiated.[4]

Now, however, a problem arises in the use of language by Tillich and Bultmann, for that which a few experts have understood for a long time—namely, what these men really mean to communicate —is becoming increasingly clear to more and more people. Their use of symbol and myth to refer not to a separate, uncreate divine realm centering in a personal God who is creator, ruler, judge and fulfiller of earthly and human history, but rather to the conditions, categorical or existential, for human life and authentic existence, is revolutionary, and should have been more carefully communicated in the first place.

To be sure, both Bultmann and Tillich have made some efforts to this effect. In *The Dynamics of Faith*, Tillich has set forth his views of symbols almost in terms of the problem of Clement of Alexandria, as a sophisticated gnosiology, a new gnosticism; and we have Bultmann's famous essay on demythologizing. Tillich of late has been increasingly willing to clarify his use of symbols, as witnessed, for instance, by the second volume of his *Systematic Theology*. The fact is, however, that the Church as a whole has been carried along without knowing where it has been led. Many interpreters have used the writings of these men in the belief that they had intended the historic fact and the historic faith. Now there is increasing confusion among people regarding the use of the theologies of these two great scholars, and many of them find return to classical Christianity impossible after long living with these writings.

[4] Cf. *The Dynamics of Faith* (Harper & Brothers, 1957), pp. 52-53.

III

The question then arises: Have Bultmann and Tillich no right to the use of symbol and myth? If they are convinced of the truth they see, and find their truth centering in the radical reinterpretation of the original Gospel message, are they not delivering the Church from faith in externals of interpretation of cosmology as well as of objective thinking and supernatural terms generally? Are they not, then, midwives of true faith, and should not the delivery be as easy as it is possible to make it? Should it be required of them that they raise the prejudices of their readers, that they paint in bold pictures the outworn shell which they are asking people to surrender for the living kernel of truth? If we assume them correct in their interpretation, have they not a right to their method, which is adapting usage to new truth? Alfred North Whitehead called such strategy the essence of sociological wisdom. If we assume them wrong, however, we may feel that they were underhanded in not being more explicit in their use of symbols and in allowing the general reader as well as numerous interpreters, to read their own meanings into these teachings. We may feel that they are guilty of guile.

The whole question rests on the legitimate use of symbols in communication. Can the usage of these two leading scholars help us to determine the proper place and power of theological language? We can understand their own feeling of allegiance to the historic faith, intellectually and emotionally. We can also enter into their personal need to be accepted by the historic community. We can, besides, identify ourselves with their desire to communicate truth and dispel error as effectively as possible by the use of symbol and myth. These are convenient and potent means. We have no right, therefore, to deprive them of their usage.

In the long run, however, mankind depends on the integrity of linguistic usage, and when the fuller use of symbols by these men is understood, there is bound to be deep disillusionment, widespread confusion, and great hardship in returning to the historic faith or in finding a faith adequate for life. It had been better, far better, I believe, if they had stipulated unmistakably their idiosyncratic usage of symbol and myth.

The proper use of symbol and myth is not easy to define. Suppose, however, that neither the historic doctrines, especially in their literal biblical forms, nor the radically severe rejection by Tillich and Bultmann of classical Christian transcendence is right. What then? What can we say of the proper use of language? Is it possible that symbols and myth in the Bible and in the creeds cannot be used in their usual historic signification? Certainly in innumerable instances this claim seems almost a platitude to modern man. What educated modern man really believes, for instance, in Noah's ark and the flood covering the whole world? Do we have to choose between fundamentalist literalism and Tillich's and Bultmann's denial of the heart of the classical faith?

Suppose, instead, that the symbol stands correctly for a reality more than, other than, "beyond" cosmic existence and human history, and not only a logical presupposition or as an invisible power or as some ground available within cosmic existence and human life, but as an actual, personal Purpose, as the eternal concern of personal Spirit, correctly and centrally indicated by the life, death, and resurrection of Jesus Christ. What attitude shall we then take toward the use of symbol and myth by these men?

If the Christian faith at its classical center is true, as I believe, then to accept the content of these men's faith is obviously disastrous for the Christian community. Without a personal God, without providence as God's guiding activity, without prayer as communion, and without life beyond death, the Christian claim of Christ loses its power and promise. On the other hand, if the biblical myths and such historic faith can no longer be taken literally as reliably intended in that form by the believer, these men have dared to pioneer in their use of symbol and myth. The liberals often dispensed with symbols and myths as irrational and unreal in their signification and reduced them, all too often, to "nothing but myth" and "only a symbol." Can we accept their position? Is truth fully expressible in propositional form or is such usage of language the reduction and eventual destruction of the faith?

If theological language is not thus reducible to propositions, can symbol and myth be used properly without needless confusion, misguidance, and possibly lack of integrity in communication? How can this matter be justly and creatively settled?

IV

There are three ways to arbitrate and adjudicate in these matters: history, experience, and truth in general.

History as man's life on earth is our first judge. To it we address the question whether faith, once it is radically reoriented and transvaluated by Tillich and Bultmann, is the same in basic nature and reality as it was before. Is the new faith at heart what the original faith basically intended? History gives Tillich and Bultmann no right to claim that their new faith was the "original" rather than the "objective" Gospel. They base their assertion on their own conviction that the objective structure of classical Christianity is unreal or false and that therefore it could not have been what gave the early Christians the unity and power which changed the course of history.

The evaluation or appraisal of the truth-claim of the Gospel, however, lies outside the realm and method of history as such and cannot be settled within its jurisdiction. The only claim the court of history can settle is the question whether the original believers basically claimed to believe the objective structure and content of the Christian Gospel, or whether their testimony shows that what really moved them was the power and reality released within their own experience. Boiled down, the question is whether faith in the objectively existing God and in the actually risen Lord, plus faith in life beyond the grave, were indispensable to the original believers or whether in fact these questions were secondary to their faith.

The answer cannot be entirely clear, nor is it easy; but it seems that apart from unself-conscious faith in the God of the Old Testament, the creator, the Lord of history, and apart from faith in the resurrection of Christ and the resurrection from the dead of the believers, the disciples would not have been capable of the faith of the martyrs. Paul summarized this historic fact by saying that if the hope of Christians lay in this life only, they were of all men most miserable. Without this obective faith they felt, indeed, as the Revised Standard Version expresses it, pitiable, and even that they were making God a liar.

Love expressed in a new kind of community and God-centeredness characterized the early Church, as Adolf Harnack vividly explained: the mission and expansion of Christianity could not have come, apart from a driving faith in the supernatural God of the Bible. It was in him they trusted. As far as we can see an answer from history, this answer belies the centrality of the disciples' original faith in what Bultmann calls "authentic existence" and what Tillich calls "the power to maintain and make for harmony of being," rather than the objective faith in the literally living God who created nature and life, and raises the dead. Details of Christ's first coming and coming again could and did vary, but not the fact of his supernatural nature and Lordship—the man whom God anointed and made to be both Christ and Lord.

Then what of experience as judge? What is its answer to the

nature and reality symbolized by Christian terms? When Bultmann claims that we can know only experience, and God as he comes in experience—that we cannot know God objectively without reducing him to a finite, controlled object, one among many—experience becomes both channel and standard of knowledge. But such experience is artificially and fatally cut off from its own history. Apart from knowledge as a social act where sources of experience have been identified, evaluated, sorted, and communicated for countless ages, there can be no rich and deep experience in the present. We bring an objective structure of interpreted experience to the existential continuum to clarify it and to make possible response and appropriation or rejection. The existential nature of all true knowledge is indeed necessary, but the existential interpretation of experience by itself truncates it into impotence. Apart from an objective continuum of social interpretation, the individual experience is thin beyond all imagination and certainly no court at all for deciding about the nature of what is experienced. Even subjective confessional language presupposes such a history of concepts and ideas, the meaning of language within an objectively enduring community. Tillich is aware of the fact and avoids much of the danger of existentialist subjectivism by his use of the logos, or rational structure within the universe, whereas Bultmann tries to skirt the danger by appealing to the New Testament for what God did in Christ. He also aims to avoid it by using objective language like God's "meeting us in Christ," an expression which misleadingly indicates knowledge of an objective reality, the very thing that he passionately rejects. Thus, Bultmann tries to have his cake and eat it too.

The existential language these men use stands for a permanent and intrinsic need of faith and should be appreciated and appropriated. However, the existentialist philosophy is a partial virtue, which when taken as the rejection of objectivist affirmation deals a wounding blow to faith. Such philosophy cannot at all decide concerning the proper use of symbols. It has no basis of common, communicable interpretation. If we assume common human nature, our meeting the same kind of experiences, as Martin Heidegger does, we are already well on the road to objectivist interpretation. Although we cannot draw easy or premature conclusions from this fact, we can see, at least, that experience as such cannot be the court of appeal concerning the proper use of language, whether of symbol or of myth.

The third judge is truth in general, the knowledge of the nature and meaning of what we experience, however hard such truth may be to establish. If there is no such truth, we are left with a completely relativistic, existentialist viewpoint where the subject cannot even be meaningfully discussed. But both Tillich and Bultmann appeal to history and to science as well as to philosophy. They both speak of "modern man" who can no longer believe the classical Christian message at its transcendent center. Whatever be their specific views on science and philosophy, they both affirm that the personal God, the creator and Lord of all earth and history, is a symbol or a myth that educated man cannot accept. They thus affirm a world-view, whether they admit it, as Tillich does, or deny it, as Bultmann does. In doing so, they lean on a faith, a mystique, a naïve ultimate, a credulity far harder to believe: namely, that the long history of creation, with its series of organically related and fulfilling novelties constituting the unity of the universe that we now know, especially at its highest, most complex becoming, has come to be without any transcendent cause, concern, and purpose; or else they leave unexplained, in the order of being, the nature of this process of creation.

To think that there is no creative ground beyond process is to affirm that the most meaningful developments of cosmic process have come from nothing, and completely by chance. Such a denial of the need for explanation is never justified by recourse to minimum hypothesis, for adequate hypothesis is equally important. Explanation must either give adequate account or point beyond itself, by inference to the most likely ground or to mystery. To deny the need for adequate explanation is to undermine the meaning of reasoned knowledge. Such denial may be due to lack of adequate analysis, an innocent ignorance, or it may be due to the subconscious or conscious fleeing from conclusions. Evolution as a theory of explanation, not as a description of development, is a most incredible faith, not worthy of hardheaded thinkers.

No matter how the problem of evil is then approached, this problem cannot nullify the reality of the creator. Perhaps he can also be conceived of as love. If we start with the truth of suffering as seen in the meaning of the Cross, and if we get a view of God incomparably, immeasurably larger, in the reality and in the scope of his working—certainly far beyond our earthly lives—the most adequate faith then remains, and is increasingly to be sought in the nature and reality of God as centrally signified by the Christian symbols and myths. Linguistically it is better, however, to speak not centrally of symbols and myths, but of the Christ-deed or of the revelational event as leading us to the knowledge of faith. As we use these terms, however, symbol fits Christian usage more readily than myth.

On the level of knowledge alone, the question cannot be settled as to the nature and reality of what is symbolized or involved in the true use of religious symbols or myths. But neither a denial of the dimension of transcendence nor the existentialist avoidance of it can satisfy an open, searching, and competent faith. How such transcendence can be pictured and established in the modern world is another matter. "The need for transcendence is one of the most basic needs of man."[5] All philosophizing, claims Karl Jaspers, is directed toward transcendence. To deny the classical Christian transcendence is certainly not the answer. Rather must we understand it in terms of, and in relation to, our best modern language. Faith must remain faith, but faith can be informed.

In the next chapter we shall discuss two main questions concerning knowledge: that of paradox and that of analogy, discontinuity and continuity with human knowledge as two possible main roads for theological language. In the third chapter we shall treat the modern question of linguistic analysis and how classical Christian transcendence can still be accepted by competently informed and honest modern man.

[5] Erich Fromm, *The Art of Loving* (Harper & Brothers, 1956), p. 51.

Chapter 2.

Paradox and Analogy in Theological Language

PARADOX starts with the assumption of the difference between God and man; analogy, with the likeness. Paradox stresses basic discontinuity; analogy, continuity. Paradox is rooted in the problem of not knowing; analogy is grounded in the fact of knowledge. Epistemology also has generally these basic divisions. Epistemological dualism wrestles basically with the problem of error; monism, with the strange fact that we do know. One side is focused on mystery; the other, on meaning. The task of this investigation or analysis is to learn whether we should take one road or the other, or whether, forsooth, we can travel in opposite directions, *par impossible*, and reach the same goal. After all, perhaps truth, like the earth, is not a flat surface but a globe! It could be that what seems flatly contradictory may be the opposite direction of the same circumstance. If there be unity of discourse, may not truth be circular, always leading back to itself? If so, the vital question is the nature and the size of the true circle of truth, and how to find it!

I

Paradoxical language in theology results from the conviction that God is qualitatively distinct from man. He is "wholly other." Søren Kierkegaard spoke of the infinite, qualitative distinction between God and man; Karl Barth, of the complete chasm between eternity and time. Both have introduced, at least in much of their writings and in some stage of their thinking, the contention that the finite is never capable of the infinite. Perhaps Immanuel Kant's Copernican revolution in philosophy, which exchanged the transcendent for the transcendental, or the realm of ultimate reality for principles of validity for experience, underlies the Kierkegaardian-Barthian claim to the unreachable nature for finite experience of *das Unbedingte* (the unconditional) and *das Ding an sich* (the thing itself). Barth, at least, came to see his contention in this light. Kierkegaard and Barth, one one side, have with a vengeance injected this note into modern theology. But it has come with equal vigor from the other side, from Bultmann and Tillich, who are impressed by the claim that the unconditional or the infinite cannot, as such, dwell in human experience or be subject to the human mind.

Within the contention that the finite is not capable of the infinite there are three basic kinds of discontinuities, and three framings of the theological answer to the problem of knowing God within the presuppositions of paradox. The three kinds of barriers between God and man are found in finitude itself, in the dialectical nature of historic thinking, and in original sin.

The claim based on man's finitude, that the finite is not capable of the infinite, is obvious. We can know essentially, the claim runs, only what is on our own level. A grasshopper no doubt can know man as an object in his way or as a roving threat, but it does not know man essentially. Far less can finite man know God essentially. Even to make the claim is to be guilty of unpardonable *hubris* or presumptuous pride. Such assertions are in the nature of the frog who tried to blow himself up to the size of an elephant. No amount of man's puffing of his own nature or of his own knowing can reach the knowledge of God. Such an attempt, this position holds, ends in man's making an idol of God. He makes God a magnified man, the projection of his own dread or striving. He makes God in man's own image. This position stresses that all picturing of God without paradox amounts to nothing other than spinning theories about God out of man's own inner self and trying to catch God in a web of man's own manufacture. Nor can man climb up on the web, for across the gulf separating the infinite God from finite man no one can ever pass to anchor the thread, and no human being is strong enough or can live long enough to travel that infinite distance.

Another version of this objection to nonparadoxical language from the standpoint of finitude as such is to the effect that, whatever truth of God or of God's purpose man may see, God alone can see the reality or purpose as a whole. Man, at best, can see only broken bits of final truth. Jaspers uses the illustration of man being caught in an eddy in a great river of life, and mistaking the eddy for the river. Kierkegaard teases the theologian mercilessly as being nothing so much as comic when he tries to think as God thinks, or to see as God sees. He compares revelation to a prince who tragically and hopelessly loves the peasant maid: reason. For the prince to reveal himself to the maid would be the end of an impossible courtship and the death of the beloved, but for him not to reveal himself is to sin against the very nature of love, and involves the death of love. No wonder, then, that Paul exclaimed that the wisdom of man does not attain even to the foolishness of God, or that Tertullian declared that Jerusalem can learn nothing from Athens.

Paradox, moreover, may be thought of from the point of view of a historic dialectic. All truths in history are in time and develop piecemeal in time; God is in eternity and sees all things at once; he sees *totum simul* or as Martin Luther had it, *Alles auf einmal*. He sees the total puzzle of existence as a finished picture. Man sees only the separate parts and most minor segments. In *Berkeley Square*, man sees only to the next bend in the river of existence, while God from the perfect perspective of heaven sees the whole river of human existence, including all generations from the source of the river to the ocean of eternity. In Hegel's terms, man knows in terms of thesis, antithesis, and synthesis, whereas even the fullest synthesis is only the thesis of another wave of understanding.

Paul Tillich teaches that when the fullness of time, the unique, nonrecurring kairos, Jesus as the Christ, came into history, he was so qualitatively different from the kairic movement of any age that not reason but only daring faith beyond reason can know him. Barth, especially during his Kierkegaardian period, maintained that history is never a predicate of revelation; and Kierkegaard himself understood that the absolute cannot be received by, contained within, or understood by, history. Man is caught not only in finitude as such but within an impenetrable curtain of finite developments that shut out infinite being. Only paradoxical language, thoughts and terms beyond reason and even contrary to man's ordinary thinking, can begin to convey the majestic otherness and fullness of God's reality and purpose. Thus, revelation is paradoxical because of man's dialectical situation in history.

Another reason requiring a paradox for the communication of revelation is the fact that God alone sights along the direction of continuity. The meaning of historic unfolding as well as of creation can be understood only in the light of the end of the process. The meaning of our history, therefore, is antisequential. For the thinker within history, the meaning of history must be essentially paradoxical. Man understands history in line with historic development; God, against it. Man moves forward in his thinking; God, so to speak, backward. Or, to put the same fact in terms of Karl Heim's discussion of paradox in *God Transcendent*: From a one-dimensional perspective, a two-dimensional vision is impossible. In a two-dimensional perspective there is no place for a third. Only the presence of the new reality reveals it. Knowledge is thus grounded not in reason's expectation but in the act of revelation.

Or we can state the same fact in terms of evolution: From the ingredients of any stage of development no new level can be predicted. Genuine novelty cannot be reduced to what existed before its appearance, even by a reasoned investigation after it has come. Thus, its entrance into creation is again literally paradoxical as long as man sights along with history, whereas God from the end of creation sees all things in their organic togetherness and fulfilling relationship. For this reason, evolution cannot be a theory of reality, only of appearance. It is description, not explanation, of development. Evolution is reason's description of the unfolding of what is more than nature and history in, to, and through nature and history. Or, to put the whole matter succinctly, the history of creation is the history of revelation. But such a claim can be made only in line with revelation, and never on the ground of what man actually finds in nature and history as a basis of prediction of where both are going. Thus again, if we listen to this argument, we return to the position that revelation is paradoxical to reason. Continuity is from God down, never from man up, and only God knows and can make known the truth of revelation.

The third reason for paradox in theological language is original sin. Man is by nature sinful and fears God. Therefore, he does not want to see the truth, but to hide from it. Natural man, who was created to behold clearly the eternal power and deity, according to Paul in the Letter to the Romans, has preferred instead to see a lie. Man's reason in religious matters is subject to the total self. The thinking of man is subject to the spirit of man. Man, driven by original sin, does not reason, even if and when he could, but rather he rationalizes. He uses his reason mainly to justify himself. Instead of letting himself be naked before the truth of God he wraps himself in the fig leaves of lies.

Therefore, since theology deals with ultimate truth, it cannot appeal to the wisdom of the natural man. Whatever pleases man naturally, apart from repentance and newness of life, is a theological lie. Theological truth must ever be paradoxical to sinful man. However much man has the capacity to see facts as they are and to see objectively partial truths that do not affect man's relation to God, man always distorts the truth to protect his guilty self and society when these facts of partial truths are interpreted with respect to his standing before God, or in their ultimate meaning and significance. Science, philosophy, and theology are all affected by this fact. Human wisdom is consistency with man the sinner; God's wisdom is consistency with God the judge and savior of sinners, and is therefore contrary to man's wisdom. Thus, the foolishness of God is wiser than the wisdom of man; theological language must be paradoxical in nature.

These are the main arguments for paradox in theological language; they must be taken with full seriousness; how and in what sense God can be known at all will be discussed in our conclusion after we have considered the opposite point of view, the way of analogy.

II

While paradox stresses the difference between God and man, analogy emphasizes the likeness. One glories in mystery; the other, in meaning. The main strength of the doctrine of analogy is obviously the fact that unless there is likeness of some kind, we cannot know God or even discuss him. We cannot talk about something completely unknown, whatever it be.[1] And yet, God to be God most certainly cannot be the same as we are. Therefore, at best some likeness rather than sameness seems to be the only answer. Even Barth, who in his earlier years dismissed analogy of being as the discovery of the Devil, has shown his understanding of the knowledge situation by his weighty discussion of the subject with the Roman Catholic scholar, Erich Przywara.

There are many uses of analogy. For our purposes we shall consider three: the analogy of mind, the analogy of being, and the analogy of Christ. The first kind of analogy is that of mind. Such analogy need not necessarily be based on idealism. Ever since Empedocles, the idealist case has been basically simple: Like can know only like. If mind can know anything beyond itself, what is known must, therefore, in some fashion, be in the nature of mind. The case for idealism was not developed by Empedocles. Anaxagoras, however, began to draw the fuller implications, and in Berkeley the position reached its logical limit. In modern times Borden Parker Bowne, in *Metaphysics*, and Brand Blanshard, in *The Nature of Thought*, are among those who have

---

[1] This is the reason that I cannot accept Carl Michalson's discussion of analogy in *The Hinge of History* (Charles Scribner's Sons, 1959), where he uses it to stress the difference between God and man. Nor can I at this point put the emphasis on Thomas Aquinas' use of the analogy of attribution.

given this viewpoint a strong, critical reworking. If idealism is accepted in principle, all that needs to be said is that God is known as the infinite mind, but that we can know him as mind only by analogy to our finite minds. Man's mind is to finite being what God's mind is to infinite being. Who can frame such a proportion?[2] Knowledge, as Thomas Aquinas knew, is according to the mode of the knower. Only because of likeness in the nature of God and man, however, can we know God at all. We know only because of the likeness of the nature of reality represented by mind.

To return to the illustration of the frog: for the frog to try to think as man is a ridiculous situation. Yet, if the frog can know man at all it is only because it has a brain. Even so, a man can know God only because he has a mind. But the analogy of mind does not have to endorse idealism. All it needs to claim is that in order for there to be any knowledge and communication of divine things the mind must be sufficiently akin to such realities as to perceive and interpret them, however different in themselves they may be in kind or in quality. The question then arises whether such knowledge and communication is veridical and significant. Perhaps it is not entirely foolish for us to wonder to what extent a frog or any animal can significantly know and share knowledge concerning man. Do not animal mothers teach caution of hunters? Can man know God better, comparatively?

But analogy of mind as a general philosophic doctrine when applied to the analysis of theological language cheats adequate theological content. The theological claim accepts the analogy of being which is based on man's similarity to God by the very act of creation. God made man uniquely related to himself. He created man at man's center in his own image. Thus the analogy of being, as Przywara rightly contends in his *Polarity*, is not so much a way from man to God as it is the understanding of creation in the light of God. By revelation, we see creation in general as God's act. Man, however, we see as a special creation endowed by God's grace with the capacity to know his maker. Thus the point is not whether, unaided, man can know God independently because of some general likeness, but rather, whether man cannot know God precisely because God has made him to know his creator. But what if we refuse to accept such a revelation? Then we are no longer in the realm of theological language.

[2] It may help to put the proportion: Man's mind : man : : God's mind : God, instead of man's mind/man=God's mind/God. But, again, who can finally frame the relationship?

Others, however, accept the revelation, contending all the while that man's ability to know God was forfeited by the Fall. Therefore, they deny all legitimate recourse to analogy and choose paradox instead. The reply to such a charge, however, is that either paradox is a way of knowing or it is not. If it is not, we have no knowledge at all to describe and discuss; hence we have no theological language. On the other hand, if it is a way of knowing, then enough likeness is left in man to make communication a worthwhile enterprise.

Suppose, however, that neither the general, philosophic appeal to likeness of nature as the ground of knowledge nor the appeal to general human nature as created in the image of God and therefore as reflecting peculiarly the reality of God, is accepted; what then? There is left the most special case of analogy, namely the analogy from man to God through Christ as the Godman. He is then claimed to be man, but not man in general because he was not oppressed by original sin. He is himself in the biblical phrase "the express image of the invisible God." In this way, man does not know God through reason in general or through human nature in general, but only through human reason and nature re-created in Christ. Thus, man can speak about God as well as know God only through God's fulfilling revelation in Christ. *Analogia mentis* and *analogia entis* have given way to *analogia Christi*.

Let us look more closely at this argument. A rock, a frog, and a man have energy in common. A chemist might say that from the point of view of chemistry there is no essential difference between them. But from the point of view of a loving wife it matters utterly that there is an essential difference between the rock, on the one hand, and the frog and the man, on the other. Both the frog and the man are alive!

To go further, if there is need to carry out an intellectual undertaking requiring human capacity and training, the difference between the rock and the frog, on the one hand, and man on the other, is essential. Mere life is not enough of a difference to matter essentially. Similarly, life is not sufficiently different from creation as a whole to characterize the God we worship. For God to be less than alive is obviously entirely insufficient. We worship the living God. What counts essentially in indicating the nature of God is the kind of life by which we know him. Is not this kind of life the universal love which Jesus lived and taught, for which he died, and by which he was raised to life again? Is not life, raised to its highest capacity in concern and faithfulness, the content that can most adequately indicate the nature of God?

Either this universal love in Christ is open to our nature and knowledge or it is not. If it is, are we not back at least potentially to some such ground for comparison in human experience as such? Without this ground on which to build our knowledge of God, we certainly cannot know him at all. But if God is thus known, does such knowledge give us veridical and significant knowledge of God in all his fullness, or is he now known, after all, in the measure in which he reveals himself to man and according to the nature of the knower? If we overstress meaning we lose the needful place for mystery in our knowledge of God, but if we overemphasize mystery, we lose the reliability of meaning, without which there is no knowledge.

III

It seems, then, that paradox and analogy belong together in some tension necessary for human knowledge and communication. Without the use of analogy, paradox inclines overwhelmingly to our not knowing. Faith's "in spite of" becomes a walking in the dark. God's revelation of himself is kept from becoming knowledge, and the Spirit's witness becomes a substitute for reason's seeing. God appears then only as the dark angel, not as light. Mystery needs to be counterbalanced by meaning, otherwise Christianity becomes a mystery religion instead of a religion of revelation. But if, on the other hand, we let go of paradox, meaning slips easily away from mystery. We slip into flat, earth-bound surface thinking, man-centered and frail. The *mysterion* of the faith disappears. The dimension of the eternal is lost. Revelation becomes equated, however gradually and subtly, with man's reason; and God is brought low within the reach of man. When mystery fades, the life of faith sickens and man becomes wearied with hopelessness.

For both knowledge and communication, therefore, we need the language of paradox and the language of analogy. Such an affirmation springs, we have already seen, not only from the nature of the knowledge of God but also from the nature of the man who is finite, lives within the waves of history, and is blinded by original sin. The answers to the arguments for analogy, given by those who believe in paradox, are: (1) that even though finite man cannot know God, God can make himself known to man through faith's paradoxical thinking; (2) that even though the waves of historic antitheses blind man to eternal truth, Christ, the eternal Lord of history and meaning for history, has himself come to us, albeit by means of God's incognito; (3) that even though sinful man cannot dare or bear God's truth he can be forgiven, and as a new creature, or as a spiritual man, can see within God's grace the revelation as truth, which to the natural man is foolishness or offensive. Therefore, paradox is itself a way of knowing, with no need of analogy.

The fuller answer, based on our analysis, seems to be that man the finite and the sinful needs to live within a dialectic of paradox and analogy. Paradox comes first because of the incomparable priority of God's being and initiative of communication; but analogy maintains the secondary stubborn reality of God's bridging the difference between the uncreate and creation by the very act of creation. For truth to be real and moving, man needs to live in the drama of this dialectic. Only a dynamic synthesis can achieve a dramatic situation for the creative background of theological communication.

Theological language is also up against a problem that can best be discussed after our analysis of paradox and analogy. This problem goes as follows: What right do we have to affirm any transcendent reality? The claim is made that either we use our words referring to the transcendent realm *univocally*, that is, in their ordinary sense, or else we use them *equivocally*, in some different sense, but in either case the words carry no linguistic freight save their this-worldly content; for if the words are used univocally, nothing but this world is indicated, but if the words are used equivocally, all that is added is a dimension of mystery. At best, all we have done is either to refer a reality in this world to another, duplicating "essences" needlessly while Occam's razor is still fatally sharp, or we have purported to indicate a different reality "beyond" this world, while giving no content to that other world. All that is not known in terms of the words we use is their sign of nescience or of our ignorance. The aspect of mystery indicated by words used equivocally gives no meaning. The way of ignorance may be the way of affirmation, but it affirms nothing. It leads to no new understanding. Therefore, the argument runs, theological language in the sense of classical Christianity with its faith in a God who created the world and in all that is entailed in the doctrines of providence, incarnation, and resurrection, finds no linguistic justification. Either we speak univocally and are stuck with this world of history and experience or we speak equivocally and talk sheer mystery without meaning.

Nor is there any escape from this dilemma in either paradox or analogy. Both paradox and analogy depend linguistically upon words from human history, and all such words designate only their sign content and their symbolic content from our world of ordinary experience. Thus we have no words, it is claimed, that can legitimately be extended by symbols beyond this world. To say that the flag stands for the country is meaningful because in ordinary usage we know what the country is. To say that Santa Claus stands for the secular side of Christmas also accords with ordinary and meaningful use of language. To speak of God at all, however, we must find content for the concept within our experience. We must use such terms as "living" and "personal," or "father," "guide," and "judge." When we do, we immediately find ourselves confronted with the linguistic dilemma of the univocal or with the equivocal use of terms.

This problem of the question of the meaningfulness of any transcendent realm is the subject for our next chapter. It is, I believe, the most critical issue for modern theology. Unless this attack be honestly joined and fairly overcome, we have no earned right to theological language. Even though religion is too widespread and immemorial, yes, too indigenous to the very life of man, for theological language not to be used, nevertheless its critical use must be bought with labor and competence in the market of truth. Up to this point, the conclusion we have reached is that somehow paradox and analogy as the two roads to truth within the circle of reality are both necessary if human beings are to know and to communicate effectively the full Gospel of mystery and meaning. Is there, however, a fuller synthesis beyond these two approaches where we can know as we are known? Can we find an overarching faith for our times, the cry of a thousand trained lips?

Tillich has struggled with this problem throughout his life. For many years, he called all theological language, in its description of God, symbolic, except "Being itself." For him, God was, symbolically, personal, living, and love, but literally, God was only Being itself. Now, in the second volume of Systematic Theology, Tillich writes that all theological terms are symbolic except the statement that they are symbolic. The symbols referring to God even have to be "broken," i.e., they must indicate that the finite is trying to communicate beyond speech concerning the infinite. W. M. Urban of Yale University finally convinced Tillich that to call all theological language symbolic is to land in Ernst Cassirer's pansymbolism where, if all language is symbolic, symbol itself loses its significance. Consequently, Tillich now says that at one point theological language must be both symbolic and nonsymbolic, and that point is, again, Being itself.

Such an interpretation of theological language, however, fails to differentiate it from language in general. All *theological* language can be symbolic without landing us in a pansymbolism of language as a whole, since all language need not operate on the logic of theological expression. Is it meaningful language, however, to speak of the synthesis of paradox and analogy? Or must all language of the finite world with reference to God remain a continuing dialectic of paradox and analogy? May there not be some reality underlying the use of theological language that will reach more firmly into a theological usage where paradox and analogy are not central channels but flow out from the main stream?[3]

[3] For my main theological method see Chapter 12.

Chapter 3

Linguistic Analysis and Transcendence

NUMEROUS contemporary philosophers are centrally interested in the problem of language. Many theologians who are in touch with their times are rapidly catching this interest. Perhaps at no time in human history has the nature of linguistic meaningfulness been more scrutinized than now. On the other hand, as Ronald Gregor Smith contends, "the crucial problem for human life and thought is the problem of transcendence."[1] But even to raise this question is to invite theology, which is the science of the transcendent. A central interest of modern philosophy and increasingly of theology thus meet in the topic of this chapter: linguistic analysis in its bearing on transcendence.

Language is the door to man's life as man. Paul Tillich has pointed out that "man is free, in so far as he has language. With his language, he has universals which liberate him from bondage to the concrete situation to which even the highest animals are subjected."[2] Thomas Edmund Jessop has told us that "man emerged when an animal spoke."[3] An American psychiatrist, Clemens E. Benda in his profound work, *Der Mensch im Zeitalter der Lieblosigkeit,* has made clear how language is the chief means of human socialization, how consciousness as conditioned by speech is originally strange to self (". . . *das Bewusstsein als sprachbedingt ursprünglich ichfremd ist*").[4] If man's freedom and social nature in the human sense are both dependent on speech, the profound nature of the topic begins to become apparent. Ernst Cassirer in his famous *Essay on Man* may have ridden the subject of the symbolic nature of speech almost to death, but

---

[1] *The New Man* (Harper & Brothers, 1956), p. 55.
[2] *Systematic Theology* (The University of Chicago Press, 1957), Vol. II, p. 31.
[3] "The Scientific Account of Man," *The Christian Understanding of Man,* (Harper & Brothers, 1938), p. 10.
[4] P. 141. Trans. by N. F. S. F.

he could hardly exaggerate the climactic nature of modern man's concern with the nature and meaning of speech.

I

Our discussion will center around three topics: (1) the rise and history of linguistic analysis; (2) the problem of transcendence in the modern world; (3) the Christian answer to linguistic analysis with regard to transcendence and theological language.

Linguistic analysis in the modern sense has a long history. Perhaps the string is best knotted at Ernst Mach's discussion of the logic of physics and the consequent rise of the Vienna circle of logical positivists, represented by philosophers like Rudolf Carnap. This position spread to England after the First World War, particularly through the influence of the Cambridge philosopher, Ludwig Wittgenstein, and was popularized by men like A. J. Ayer in his *Language, Truth and Logic.*

The gist of the logical positivist position was that there are two kinds of logic: analytical and empirical. The former deals only with propositional meaning; the latter deals only with scientifically verifiable meaning which is methodologically confined to sense data. Necessity belongs exclusively in the realm of analytical logic; the empirical realm at best is limited to probability. The proper work of philosophy is to analyze language according to the nature of these two areas of investigation: the internal relations of propositional meaning and the relevant relations of language to empirically verifiable data. Such an understanding of the task of philosophy leads to its severe limitation of function. Metaphysics as the knowledge of ultimate reality, and ethics as a normative science of conduct, for instance, were completely eliminated from philosophy.

Perhaps it may be suggested that the reason for this radical shrinkage of the philosophical field was due to Immanuel Kant's monumental criticsm of metaphysics, to his Copernican revolution away from the realm of the transcendent to the transcendental, or from the region of ultimate reality to principles of validity which were no more than the logical presuppositions of experience in general. Then, too, the specialization of modern science had pre-empted the more limited areas of interpretation, whereas the growth of modern knowledge was so staggering that a philosopher's attempt at synoptic vision seemed sheer presumption.

The shrinkage of philosophy gave philosophers both a sense of relief and a distinctive reason for existence. Philosophers now saw their proper task to be linguistic analysis in the manner specified. They made virtue of necessity, heralding the redistricting of field as the critical revolution in the history of philosophy. In whatever proportion the ground for this messianism was divided —on the negative side, between guilt feelings occasioned by the abandonment of philosophy's urgent tasks and insecurity concerning the worth of the work within the new scope; and on the positive side, joy in the cleanness and clarity of the limited field and the newness of the concentrated approach—logical positivism became a vital, missionary philosophy.

During recent years, however, linguistic analysts have themselves claimed that logical positivism is "dead as a doornail." The movement has, indeed, enlarged the means and area of verification, and has turned to the study of the proper usage of language. "Ordinary usage" has become an important category for analysis. As far as the question of transcendence goes, however, the main attitude and approach of logical positivism's basic limitation of legitimate meaning to propositional analysis and empirical data have persisted. "Ordinary usage" has grown to include common sense and such practical extension of method in the sciences as cannot be reduced to public verifiability in terms of immediate sense data.

Linguistic analysts have recognized, beyond the need for extension of method in the sciences, the fact that man cannot live within the confines of its approach, but that life must go on, be accepted, and be meaningfully communicated on a wider basis. Such growth in no way changes the basic contention of the position as to the meaning and scope of reliable knowledge. "Functional analysis" is primarily a change of name in order to get rid of the odium and impossible restrictions associated with logical positivism. There are a few minor indications of radical shifts in attitude and position, where knowledge of genuine transcendence is accepted. If such changes become general, the importance of linguistic analysis will remain, while the logical restrictions of the philosophical field—restrictions due in fact, whether or not consciously realized, to religious attitudes and metaphysical assumptions—will disappear.

With regard to the question of transcendence, linguistic analysis has conducted a consistent attack on the meaningfulness of theological language, for the following main reasons:

1. The necessity entailed in analytical logic and the probabilitics of empirical logic are realms different in kind. They may not be confused. To mix the two categories is to indulge in meaning-

less language. Theology presupposes God as necessary being. The concept of necessary being is an illegitimate mixing of logical realms and, therefore, linguistically meaningless. To prove God's nonexistence, as some have tried to do by this very argument, is, of course, equally meaningless. On this level the problem of God is not the problem of proof but the problem of meaning.

2. On the level of the empirical, only that is meaningful which can be scientifically proved. Verification must be on the level of publicly ascertainable truth, which is, in fact, in terms of sense data in a controllably strict manner. But the existence of God, if granted meaning, cannot be thus verified. No vision or experience will do, nor will history. All such attempts can be reduced to psychological states or to content of experience in this world which is projected on another.

3. Then, too, a sovereign God of love cannot be responsible for a world containing evil. Even the argument of the "compossible," those things which are possible together—to the effect that if genuine freedom is to develop there must be some opportunity for man to learn from choices and for God to control those choices ultimately by following bad choices with painful consequences— some analysts dismiss with the observation that a God who has to depend on evil means is smaller than a God who can effect the same result without such evil means.

4. It is further claimed that no argument holds water unless it can be falsified, i.e., unless something concrete is also denied by the positive assertion. John Wisdom developed his famous illustration of a garden, the care of which bespoke the presence of a gardener; but when all possible measures were taken, such as electric fences, for instance, to find him, and he could not be thus caught, then the negative evidence canceled the positive. Antony Flew went further, using the parable to assert that an invisible gardener is equal to no gardener. Similarly, God's work cannot be falsified, some insisted; for, although the good in the world is used to prove the existence of God, so also, is the bad, the proof being in terms of God's holiness or his correctional work. Thus the arguments for God cannot be meaningfully falsified.

5. God is all-inclusive, and we have no analogy for the whole. The "all" is unique. Thus we see organisms and purposeful processes on a finite scale, but no indications of purposeful process in the world can be an argument for God, for the whole is by definition unique and beyond comparative language. Moreover, how can a finite being deal with the whole? If man con-

siders himself outside, there is no longer any whole; but from within he is dealing only with finite comparables, and cannot get perspective on the whole.

Thus run the main lines of attack, by analysts, on theological language.

II

Transcendence is obviously in a critical state in the modern world. Not only analysts but existentialists like Martin Heidegger and Karl Jaspers wrestle with the question. Carl G. Jung has told us that modern man turned to psychology when he lost his faith. Charles Coulston Gillespie[5] has documented the extent to which this question haunted the scientists who formulated much of our modern world-view. Modern man hungers for the meaning that transcendence can give, but he does not know how to find it.

By transcendence we mean whatever goes beyond the world of ordinary experience. The nature and manner of what goes beyond are not the formal question of transcendence. If there is transcendence, these matters are, of course, of decisive importance. A main argument against all knowledge of transcendence, which we examined in the preceding chapter, is the linguistic dilemma of the univocal or the equivocal posed by the consideration of the nature of language itself, dealing unavoidably according to this dilemma with the world of ordinary experience only. We saw the nature of this dilemma to be:

Either language is univocal or it is equivocal. Univocal language deals with words in their ordinary sense. If words are thus used, we have said nothing concerning another world. If, on the other hand, we use language equivocally, or in another than the ordinary sense, we have said nothing in terms of any known meaning about another world. This dilemma is claimed to be both inescapable and exhaustive. Therefore, the conclusion runs, there can be no knowledge of transcendence.

Analogy is no escape, for even the analogy of proportionality— which claims that God is personal in proportion to his being, as man is personal in proportion to his being—ultimately is reducible to the dilemma of our using either univocal or equivocal language. The part of analogy that is drawn from ordinary experience never leaves this world, and the part that claims difference has no concrete content, only mystery or the appeal of ignorance. Thus added to linguistic meaninglessness and to the charge of

[5] *Genesis and Geology.*

lack of verifiability of theological language is this general charge
of the emptiness of theological assertions.

To that we may add the reports of psychology. Some psychol-
ogists insist that theology is a science, dealing with man's attempt
to give meaning to the unknown. The unknown makes man
anxious, and therefore it needs to be discovered. Man also is
threatened by the negative things he knows: failures, dangers, and
death. In his despair he manufactures religions to protect him
from these threats and to give him comfort. Religions are illusions due to the process of dream-fulfillment, especially as they
project some fanciful realm beyond the experience we know.
They are imaginary compensations for the ills of this life. They
cannot be created consciously and deliberately, but are the slow
growth of man's collective and racial adjustment to his actual
world. The same line of approach can be taken by all the be-
havioral sciences, such as sociology and anthropology. Thus, transcendence as a whole may be dismissed.

We have now mentioned some definite objections to theological
language on the part of modern man. Most of the objections,
however, are not stylized like that of linguistic analysis. Some are
vaguely agnostic. Who is man, to try to know ultimates? One
world at a time! Some are anticlerical and antichurch. Some are
opposed to theologies of narrow limits and of low moral visions.
Much of man's objection to theological language is ambivalent.
It is a building up with one hand and a tearing down with the
other. Even great theologians have reared edifices of theological
thought only to affirm at the end that ultimately we are left with
nescience. Much of the thought on the subject is hopelessly confused and wistful.

Many modern thinkers, hankering for religious help, yield to
theologies of authority where no understanding is sought, while
others give way to esoteric cults. Some seek for substitutes within
experience, in the analysis of experience, or in the presuppositions
for experience. We have, for instance, the attempt to establish
"horizontal transcendence," which is in effect the picking out of
strands of higher experience in history to challenge and to direct
the lower and the general. Obviously, such a procedure is illegitimate with reference to transcendence. Much of modern existentialism is of this nature, as is the attempt to make science
or certain philosophies into ultimates for life, in order to substitute
them for classical transcendence. The word "transcendence" is
now altered to indicate a functional substitute which will give
continuity with the past. Certainly, linguistic analysis itself has

become religion for many, the way to, and of, the only reliable truth available to man. It has sometimes become a missionary religion attempting to replace both past philosophies and past theologies.

To this question of transcendence and of the charges of linguistic analysis in particular, what has theology to answer? Can it give an open, positive answer, without defensiveness, witnessing instead to its own security in the life of the truth?

III

Here we have the charges by linguistic analysis, namely, the general problems of the meaninglessness or impossibility of theological transcendence. What answer can we give? First of all, the theologian must be genuinely open to any and all serious criticism and not merely make a polite bow in its direction. Real security dares to face facts.

Let is then consider the charge that there are two kinds of knowledge and that theology is neither purely analytical nor merely empirical. Theology is neither one nor the other. Therefore, the ontological argument—in the definitional sense that perfection involves existence by the very analysis of meaning, and therefore that God, who is by definition perfect, must necessarily exist—will not do as a serious argument for God. There is no analytical or deductive way to the knowledge of God. For all who are intellectually informed, the precritical identification of mind with reality came to a definite end with Kant. Nor is any empirical argument able to produce, for knowledge of God, the kind of measurable, controllable knowledge that we have established, at least comparatively well, in the sciences. If such demands are made of knowledge by the analysis of meaning, theological knowledge is impossible, for theological language has become meaningless.

The further question, however, is whether these two categories exhaust the areas of meaningful language in the sense of the kind of knowledge that directs experience, or whether, in fact, the two areas can be kept apart. The matter of transcendence as such must wait until these two questions are answered.

No one lives by analytical knowledge. That is obvious. The only way analytical knowledge is known at all is as it relates itself to, or is part of, the knowledge or the experience of the knower. In other words, the two realms are known only together, and then the one is abstracted from the other. This fact is primary. But neither does anyone live by discrete particulars established by science. These are known only as they are abstracted from total experience. To live is to make a stream of responses with regard to other people, the world of nature, and the whole world of thought as it confronts each life. Some of these responses are deliberately the performance of logical analysis and of scientific experiment.

When life as a whole is normal, this stream of responses takes some shape. It becomes a configuration. It becomes organized in some way. This evaluative, or interpretive organization as a whole is neither analytical nor reducible to an empirical science. Analysis and experiment can clarify this total but can never be exchanged for it. As a way of living or as an attitude we take toward life as a whole, this configuration is the general presupposition of our lives. It is a way of neither analytical knowledge nor scientific knowledge. It is subject to a presupposition or presuppositions of wholeness which cannot be logically established by either method.

The content of this total response is then arational or meaningless in the strict sense of linguistic analysis, and yet it is inescapable. It is the totality of this evaluative response that directs and shapes life. It is in the positive sense a way of faith, a total, evaluative response to the world in general. In this sense, all persons live by faith and must live by faith. If religion is, by standard definition, man's evaluative response to reality, then everyone is religious or lives by faith, and such living is not optional. It is situational. We all have presuppositions for living which we cannot prove.

In this living, moreover, the two categories are constantly mixed. Even when the logician carries on analysis and the scientist, verification, he does so from within a total context of life within which these activities are included. The processes of analysis and verification are constantly taking place informally as part of living and thinking, and even formal analysis and verification root in this more foundational process of living as a whole. Living can be better because analysis and verification are well done, but analysis and verification have no meaning for life at all except as they improve the total, evaluative response to, and of, experience as a whole, which is life itself. Even when isolated from the living total for the sake of methodological abstraction, analysis and verification are still related to the general experiential continuum of living.

When these methodological activities clarify knowledge and provide a more dependable basis for life, they are of genuine importance. To call the result of these critical activities knowledge of a special kind is right. This knowledge is valid in a different sense from general experience that has not been critically examined. But the meaning of these processes is not isolation from life, which is possible only as pathological blockage or as methodological contrivance. The meaning is in the evaluative response that directs life, for only with the knower is there any usage of linguistic tools.

To limit language to the segments of life that can be thus abstracted momentarily from it, is linguistic suicide. As far as both meaning and verification go, the question boils down to whether or not living language is meaningless. Is actual usage meaningful? Is life's communication itself meaningful? If there is no relation between knowledge and living, then all language is meaningless, indeed impossible. Logical positivism is dead, analysts now claim. Dead, too, should be the body of death that still persists in functional analysis. The author's *Faith and Reason* has made full room for the truth in analysis, while avoiding its body of death.

Or, put in another way, the question runs thus: Is all faith for living, arbitrary and unconnected with knowledge? If there is no connection with life and no connection between the two realms, there can be no knowledge, for such a complete division is impossible except in theory. Such logical necessity if known by life cannot be known necessarily, for it is now connected with the empirical, and hence it is by definition meaningless!

Theology should grant unhesitatingly the fact that theological knowledge is neither analytical nor empirical truth in the sense of logical necessity or of strict, scientific verifiability. These tools deal with validity. Theology must take these into full account but not be reducible to them. Rather, it is the confession and communication of faith as the total response of experience. This total will be communicated in any case, and the whole history of the human race and the nature of experience itself testify unmistakably to the meaningfulness of such communication. Life cannot be limited to the formal exercise of logic or pursuit of science by the experts. Nor can language.

Before we deal with theological transcendence as such, a prior question, therefore, is whether the kinds of truth represented by analysis and science, strict or extended, exhaust the realm of accessible knowledge. If knowledge is now to be given a restricted definition, the way science has been, the question concerns the nature of the realm of meaningful truth that can be communicated. It seems wiser, however, in the light of the history of analysis itself not to strangle the word "knowledge," but to leave it flexible for proper usage and tests, according to the nature of the different fields of knowledge.

Men do in fact interpret experience by their very living; their lives become contexts of evaluative responses; some presuppositions not verifiable by logic or science shape their lives. Throughout the ages men have made basic interpretations, called religions, that have outlasted all other forms of human, large-scale organizations, such as nations. Are these completely arbitrary, merely relative, and devoid of ascertainable truth? Men have found in their deepest wisdom that mutual concern gives satisfaction in family relations as selfishness does not.

If such an insight is put up against the demand of controllable proof, analytically or empirically, there is neither sense nor reason to it. That an open society is better than a dictatorship likewise is a complicated, conditional assertion that can never be proved but that may be both meaningful and significant. That health and life are better than illness and death is a general assertion that people find meaningful, but it is conditional to the point that it cannot be proved. That education is worthwhile and should be carried on with competence and integrity is a meaningful and even important statement to faith, but beyond proof of both logic and science. That freedom is part of the fulfilled life is beyond both kinds of knowledge and yet it is in accordance with man's total evaluative response.[6]

All of these statements combine the registered, evaluative responses that approximate universal statements. As a matter of fact, the more predictable the findings of science, the more they intend universals that can be reversed and applied back to particulars without need of immediate verification. Thus, practically speaking, the more knowledge of anything we have, the more the two kinds of logic come together; and the quest for meaningful and trustworthy knowledge is a maximum of coming together of logical consistency and coverage with empirical data. The distinction between the two realms is, therefore, basically a methodological contrivance.

Before we deal with theological language in terms of transcendence, we should treat the proposal that theological language is impossible because theology deals with the whole, and the whole cannot be known since all knowledge is analogical or based

---

[6] Logical analysis as a meaningful human activity is itself beyond the kind of proof demanded by the analysts themselves.

on comparison. The reply can be brief. If there is no direct knowledge anywhere there is no knowledge. Knowledge grows from comparison but roots in direct awareness. Growth in knowledge is aided by comparing one item with the other. From the thorough knowledge of one oak there can be meaningful discussion of the nature of the oak in general. The wholeness or generality in any case is known through sampling.

For instance, an ocean can be tested for general salinity without testing the ocean as a whole; yet, statements are made about the ocean as a whole rather than about the single spot where the test was made. The rest is inference, not proof. Similarly, there is only one inclusive realm of gravitation, and statements are made concerning it from various samplings. Our knowledge of the sun did not come first from comparing its nature and operation with other suns equally well known. Albert Einstein worked on formulae for the whole universe without access to comparable, detailed formulae for comparative universes. To say that science can have a unit of discourse, a universal framework, but that theology cannot, is to beg the question. To maintain that physics knows in one way and theology in another is an accepted assumption. The argument itself is obviously contrived and manufactured, but it is an assertion of faith provable neither analytically nor scientifically.

The interpreter, to be sure, is either inside or outside gravitation, or considers himself either inside or outside the whole, but actually this observation has only the value of the subjective conditionedness of all knowledge. The interpreter can still generalize concerning the nature and operation of gravitation or the whole without claiming an abstract, absolute knowledge. No finite being can know infinitely, or as the inclusive reality; but such a fact does not preclude meaningful knowledge of the totality to which he responds in a meaningful and even significant manner. In claiming to speak meaningfully about God, the theologian never claims to know as God knows. Just as the analyst can know necessity, while himself being finite and part of the empirical world, so the theologian can know the absolute but not absolutely, for he is far more known than knowing.

For that matter, knowledge can be from finite samples of process to the totality as process. If there is sameness of kind there is no reason that size would debar valid observation and comparison. The natural assumption is that there is likeness of nature between the whole and its parts. But both kinds of knowledge are approximate, and neither needs to be total.

What then, finally, of the general question of transcendence? If there is meaningful, general truth, not reducible to the two kinds of valid knowledge in the narrow sense, can we know anything more generally beyond our ordinary experience? Are we not still caught within the univocal or equivocal dilemma of all knowledge? From the point of view of knowledge it is obvious that unless what is known comes to and through experience, it cannot be known. In experience, the content of knowledge is of this world. For this reason the Christian faith has antedated the modern emphasis by linguistic analysis and existentialism that valid knowledge exists in terms of accessible experience. It centers its knowledge in Incarnation, which means in a kind of life, a kind of love, seen and become effective in this world. Such a basis in Incarnation does not by itself solve the problem of transcendence or the dilemma of the univocal or equivocal nature of knowledge. No matter how a kind of life may illumine and guide experience, the question of transcendence as such is obviously still unanswered, at least in the classical and proper sense of the word "transcendence."

Transcendence roots in the claim that God is creator. The fact of transcendence becomes clear in the light of the history of creation. The facts of science, as far as the history of "evolution" goes, constitute a series of fulfillment where emergent novelties are seen not only to be organically related to the previous process but fulfillingly related. That such a series has come to be without cause and without purpose is a faith-judgment not only incredible but preposterous. If that can be believed, whatever be the verbalization which hides the emptiness, reason itself loses its meaning. An organic universe that has come to be through a series of organic fulfillments bespeaks a cause at least as real and as purposive as the most inclusive and integral "evolvement" of that process. And since process is not completed, is perhaps far from its peak, the cause most probable is indescribably more potent and purposeful than the small and incomplete process we now see. The most likely faith is in the creator.

Merely to look away from the question is to accept in effect such a mystique without examination of the issues. Since any handling of the question of the new and the process as a whole involves difficulties, and since the process is not without resistances and brokenness, the fact of God as creator cannot be established by any proof. But that there is a ground, both eloquently meaningful and immeasurably mysterious, is a faith far more near adequate organization of what we know than the denial or neglect of such a ground. Thus, since we have to live by faith-judgments anyway, God as creator, or classical transcendence, is a better choice than other alternatives.

Proof we cannot have, by the nature of the situation; choice we must make. Our most credible faith, mysterious and staggering as it is, is God the creator. The main fact of process, furthermore, is that it moves; it points ahead. And this process has been accelerated incredibly, as far as meaning goes, within the most recent moments of cosmic time. If each new level relates to previous levels and goes beyond them fulfillingly—for instance, life was a basic novelty, then self-conscious, then interpretative, and just recently concerned with world problems and universal forms of evaluative responses to reality—we can expect further fulfillment. The evidence is not yet in.

Such incoming of meaningful life has leaped into being with a rapturous sound. Not life as such, but the best life, seems to be the key that finally fits cosmic process. Not the past by itself which cannot account for the surge of the process, nor the mere, tiny now of lightning-quick cosmic development, but the unimaginable future beyond the now of time and the here of earthly space, as indicated by the direction of development up to now, has the best credentials for pointing us to the meaning of existence.

From among the three—the past, the present, and the future—we must choose as far as the context of life goes. Or we must choose between the lowest beginning, the present average attainment, and the highest pointing of process.[7] All three present choices of faith. Realism favors the choice of high hope in line with the upshooting of cosmic meaning, with the pointing of process in life, and in the highest kind of life. Our weary, confused, and guilty selves may demur, but the universal Concern, the ever faithful God, seen in the kind of life Jesus lived and taught, offers the most credible faith in line with the highest plane of cosmic process. The implications of such an organization of experience and knowledge stagger all imagination and transcend all knowledge. Nevertheless, a serious accounting for total meaning in terms of the total process offers no alternative faith that is not even more incredible.

Besides, there is the transcendence of true human potentiality. Man needs such love lived with genuineness and interpreted with integrity. The more one practices co-operative concern, open com-

---

[7] Cf. the close and fuller arguments of Ferré, *Faith and Reason* (Harper & Brothers, 1946), chap. iv. A careful analysis of the same theme is Teilhard de Chardin's *The Phenomenon of Man* (Harper & Brothers, 1959).

munity, and truth in freedom, the more is life fulfilled rather than frustrated. This is true for society as a whole. The persons, moreover, who live for this end speak to the depths of people as people, men like Socrates, Jesus, St. Francis, Gandhi, and Schweitzer. A behavior pattern of this kind is, to be sure, so exceptional as now to seem entirely idealistic, but the fact is that the more it is lived the more the true interests of life are promoted.

Such statements cannot be proved by analysis nor crammed into exact scientific experiment, but they represent the heart of human wisdom at the depth of its need. Faith lived in line with such wisdom is surely more real and significant that the kind of skepticism which, in practice, assumes no ground or goal for the process, or the kind of timid faith that is frozen fast where process is now passing through to its fuller unfolding. From a near view, the process of fulfillment seems slow because of man's stubborn freedom, his determined sinning, and his little faith, but in the scale of cosmic movement the changes are indescribably, breathtakingly rapid! Human history appears with cometlike speed. Faith is a quality of life that can never be reduced to the quality and feel of reason; but the fulfillment of reason best occurs when it is in line with the truest and highest faith.

What, however, of the charge by psychology that such faith is wishful thinking? Is it not compensation for the bitter disappointments of life and the threat of death? In line with the main objective pointing of cosmic process—the God of love as creator, guide, and fulfiller of life—psychology should come to a different conclusion. Fearful and faithless man fears God, who threatens his individual and collective selfishness. Therefore, he flees and hides from God. Sinful man seeks to kill God, to bury him. But no matter how much he pulls down the shades to keep out the light, there are cracks at the window. It is the sinner who rationalizes, who makes false gods, who seeks substitute ultimates. More than we know, science when abused by being perverted into a world-view or made to debar all other roads to truth is largely the attempt to shut out God.

At least this much can be safely said: Linguistic analysis in its absorbing concern with theological statements should be subjected to the test of fire to determine its reasons for branding theological statements as meaningless at the very time modern knowledge has rendered God in terms of an allegedly scientific view of the world as mechanism without meaning. What fighting of God is this? Psychology, too, can become a substitute for genuine faith, internalizing even the objective problems. Now the world of thought is beginning to pass "beyond psychology."[8]

We must listen well and long and thankfully to the criticisms of linguistic analysis. Strong faith can never bypass validity. Somehow, minimum hypothesis and adequate explanation must continue together for living truth. Nor can that truth ever be settled by mortal man. Dynamic, alert, open, and critical must be man's faith. No other faith can be held without defensiveness. We thus learn from linguistic analysis without accepting its metaphysics or the method that is contrived to guard it. Truth lies deeper and is fuller. The truth lies in the fullest faith best tested in the service of man's deepest need. Faith is man's most valid and adequate evaluative response to life's meaning and direction.

Where lies a faith that will neither try to lean on logic but rightfully use it, nor build on science but heed its facts, that will, however, first of all know and accept its own nature? Such a faith will recognize the genuineness of the statement by Augustine: "They only understand it who compare that voice received from without with the truth within."[9] There is no easy or safe way to verifiable knowledge or to dependable faith, but there is no full life without bold walking in the direction of both.

[8] Cf. Otto Rank, *Beyond Psychology* (Dover, 1959), and Ira Progoff, *The Death and Rebirth of Psychology* (Julian Press, 1956).

[9] *Confessions*, X, vi, 10.

II

FAITH AND FREEDOM

God and Freedom

FAITH and freedom are the two most important aspects of man's fundamental need: love. Where love reigns, faith and freedom follow. When love dies, faith and freedom die also. Love, however, is almost impossible to assess from without. The reality or absence of love can best be seen in terms of faith and freedom in the case of persons and of civilizations. The New Testament relates these realities in different ways. In one sense, love is the first fruit of faith: We love because God first loved us; only by trusting that love can we ever find our fruition of love. But in another and deeper sense, love is the greatest of all spiritual gifts and, beyond gifts, the only way to fulfillment of life. In this sense faith follows the finding of love, and is, indeed, as Emil Brunner explains, the affirmation of love, while freedom, as the title of this section suggests, follows faith.

I

Our first task is to understand our basic terms, faith and freedom, with particular reference to the former. Faith is primarily a quality of life, a dynamic state of being. Faith is somehow a response of life. We must depend here upon the general, ordinary use of language. Faith is the opposite of fear. Faith frees the self. Fear binds the self. People of genuine faith are in the deepest sense free, while people oppressed by fear lack freedom. What, more particularly, do these general affirmations mean?

Faith is an evaluative response to reality. It is hard to know whether what is outside self or what is inside self comes first, or whether they are, in fact, so closely interrelated that they cannot be taken apart by analysis. To do so, nevertheless, is the task we have undertaken. Conscious of how inseparable these two aspects of faith are, we shall try our best so to analyze their relationship that they are not left apart. Technically speaking, we are dealing with the relation of *fides quae* to *fides qua*, what we believe with

43

how we believe, with the relation of *notitia* to *assensus*, the content of faith with our response to it.

It is difficult rightly to relate what is outside the believer to what is inside. When what is believed is generally taken for granted or at least held naturally by a community, the priority of the content of faith seems obvious. Then the objective side dominates. When, however, many differing faiths are compared along with the intensity or naturalness with which they are all held, the subjective aspect becomes the more prominent. Those firmly within a given state of faith have little patience with those who stress difference in content, the strength of the subjective side, and the almost relative nature of what is called the objective part of faith. One thing is certain: faith has both sides. For myself, the vision of what is actually given for faith, the objective side, is so overpowering that I have to make myself face the fact that I find communicating what I see, convincingly and contagiously, difficult beyond belief; others, like Søren Kierkegaard, have been almost equally impressed by the subjective side of faith.

One side of faith is acknowledgment; the other is affirmation. We acknowledge what is outside us; we affirm that which is within. No acknowledgment, however, is mere reception; no affirmation is without reference to the outside world. Even existentialism refuses to be reduced to mere subjectivism. On the other hand, extreme objectivism cannot do without subjective appropriation; in the most objective field, physical science, we are increasingly aware of an element of construction: Ernst Cassirer has observed that

the scientist cannot attain his end without strict obedience to the facts of nature. But this obedience is not passive submission. The work of all the great natural scientists—of Galileo and Newton, of Maxwell and Helmholtz, of Planck and Einstein—was not mere fact collecting; it was theoretical, and that means constructive work. This spontaneity and productivity is the very center of all human activity.[1]

We have to acknowledge because knowledge itself is a social act, depending upon ages of accumulative work. Language itself is necessary to knowledge, and language depends upon a process coeval with man as a human being. In other words, what is outside comes to us already largely interpreted by the history of the race. The interpretation may not be either necessary or right, as witness, for instance, the change and difference in all fields of knowledge; but no one can start to think without any previous interpretation.

[1] *An Essay on Man* (Yale University Press, 1944), p. 278.

All new insight depends upon depth of background. Whether the acknowledgment is conscious or not, faith in what is outside us begins, on one side of its nature, with this act of knowledge.

Since faith on the content side is evaluative response, acknowledgment must involve selection. Not all experience is equally valid, good, or trustworthy. Evaluation means choice and preferential arrangement of what is experienced. What is given on the outside is not merely produced by the self; it is received, but it is received differently by different responders. This is the mystery of faith. Some contents of faith are selected by some; other contents, by others. Certain realities given for experience are trusted by some and feared by others. Usually both the selection and the response involve ambiguities. They are seldom clear cut. Therefore, at this point acknowledgment and affirmation come together. Why should there be such difference, beyond difference in background, in the interpretation of what is outside us, and in the evaluative response? How does affirmation affect acknowledgment?

The secret of the relation between affirmation and acknowledgment is freedom. We are free *from* the truth. We are free from the truth by the power of acceptance or rejection. Neither act is fully pure but is mixed with our own finitude both of seeing and of willing. Freedom from the truth also resides in our power to distort what we see in line with what we want to see. But neither is such distortion whole cloth. Acknowledgment presides over affirmation, demanding recognition, and if rejected by the conscious mind, takes vengeance in the subconscious. Truth can be distorted, but the distortion is registered in the self.

Freedom from the truth also comes through the power to select from what we see. Affirmation chooses to acknowledge certain data more than others. We choose context from what we acknowledge, and assume the right as well as the need to organize our experience around our preference. Such organization and interpretation of experience is both acknowledgment and affirmation. Truth cannot be forced. No one and no content can compel us, because of our freedom from the truth.

We are also free from the truth by the power of acceptance or rejection in terms of our seeking it or of our fleeing from it, our trusting what we find or our fearing it. Not all freedom from the truth is indirect through distortion or subtlety of selection and organization. We are free to face reality or to hide from it. In short, we are free to have faith or to have dread. Perhaps man's fundamental choice is his attitude toward acknowledgment; his affirmation or rejection of reality; his opening up or closing in on himself. Whether we take Martin Heidegger's positive choice of defiance or Rudolf Bultmann's passive acceptance, the choice of faith, what matters is the quality of affirmation, the intensity of affirmation, and the direction of affirmation. No state of being, no stance for response, no act of affirmation or rejection is without admixture, but the quality of life is determined by the relation we accept between affirmation and rejection.

We can also be free *in* the truth. Such freedom leaves no subconscious frustration and feeling of guilt. It precludes the sense of meaninglessness. Such freedom is the fullest possible relation between acknowlegment and affirmation, integrity and trust. And we can be free not only from and in the truth, but *for* the truth. Truth is always a construction, a combination of acknowledgment and affirmation, and therefore is creative. Truth is both had and made. This is why there is an adequacy and validity of personal truth within the unending ocean of truth, far beyond all social control or conventional tests. Truth requires faith and freedom. Besides, there is the freedom for the truth that comes from discovery and invention. The genuinely new is seen in the mode of knowledge and art, of direct receiving and indirect presentation. Truth requires both prose and poetry for its fullest expression. The new truth craves new language, while language itself facilitates freedom by liberating man from the concrete.

There are three stages of faith in its freedom: believing, believing in, and believing that. Believing is straight affirmation of what we acknowledge, the way we acknowledge it. It is confrontation, encounter, acceptance, and if we may coin a word, "faithing." Its opposite is rejection and fear. This stage of faithing is Martin Buber's I-thou relationship. Here belongs Karl Jaspers' insistence that whatever transcendence man can know must be known through *Existenz*. Here also fits Kierkegaard's exceedingly subtle analysis of existence-communication as opposed to objectification. Believing *in* is one step in the direction of abstraction. It can be a stage of alienation from primary confrontation and acceptance of reality, a weakening of affirmation in its acknowledgment. But it can also be the fuller acceptance of the nature of the affirmation, a trusting of the understanding involved in the affirmation.

Believing *that*, the third stage, Buber calls the greatest disaster of faith, its death by abstraction. Believing *that* involves something "coming between" affirmation and acknowledgment. It can nonetheless be faith's fullest fruition; the understanding of the content involves its fullest implications. By freedom, the stages can either weaken faith by abstraction or fill trust full by under-

standing. For instance, I believe God, I believe *in* God, I believe
that God, can be a progressive weakening of faith or, oppositely,
its crescendo. I believe God, I believe *in* God the savior of men, I
believe *that* God will save his whole creation.

II

Our first task was to consider in general the nature of faith and
freedom; our second, is to take up the relation of God to faith. We
shall consider God as the ground of faith, God as the goal of faith,
and God as the glory of faith.

God is the ground of faith. Neither God nor faith is optional.
Man must relate himself to God through faith. God is, as Martin
Luther claimed, that on which the heart depends, on which it
wholly relies. God is the ultimate context of our lives, the center
of our evaluative response, whatever governs life. The Second
Epistle of Peter affirms that whatever influence gets the better of
a man becomes his master. Finite man cannot be self-sufficient in
knowledge or in life. He comes from, and is dependent upon, the
reality in which he finds himself. God is whatever is most important and most real, whatever has the highest value and the strongest power for life. Faith is our response to God. Luther said that
as we believe God so have we him. The choosing of context is inescapable; it is part of man's situation in living. The choice is faith.
Man is incapable of total fear. Faith may be fear-laden or hope-
filled, but every man has faith. To live is to believe.

Paul Tillich in *Theology and Culture* distinguishes between the
ontological and teleological way to God. The former knows God
as the presupposition of life, the unconditional ground of meaning and power. The latter seeks from concrete existence to gather
evidence for God, or to interpret God in terms of experience.
Tillich chooses the ontological way. The truth is, however, that
both ways are necessary. God as the presupposition of life is
immediately available and logically inescapable. Every man has
faith. To live, we repeat, is to believe. But the nature of God
is more than formal meaning, more than the unconditional element presupposed by experience. Concretely for each person
God is what is put first in life. This is the God of affirmation.
But the God of reality, the God acknowledgeable beyond mere
affirmation, is whatever has the right to be put first. Our ultimate
is the true God only insofar as we interpret knowledge rightly
or construe aright the truest indications of knowledge.

Thus God is not only the ground but also the goal of faith. Man,
in the first sense, would not seek God, as Pascal knew, unless he

had already found God. We seek God, and afterward we know, as the hymn writer claims, that it was God who first sought us. Or, to think with Abraham Heschel: "to have faith means to justify God's faith in man."[2] But these affirmations refer to the objective, ontological side of faith, with God as its ground. The other side of faith is the quest. The comparison of Augustine's "voice from without" with "the truth within" is the life's hardest as well as most important task. It involves the correct joining of acknowledgment and affirmation. It means the making of a finally right evaluative response.

This is the goal of life. God is thus not only the ground but the goal of faith. Made by him and for him, our restless hearts seek him. This statement is true by definition and by experience. God is the ultimate ground on which our lives depend and by which they are grasped, but we have to discover the nature of that dependence and that grasp. The need for such discovery is life's constant task, giving it good reason for restlessness. This quest of faith for God involves man in what Kierkegaard called "the dizziness of freedom."

Whatever fulfills life is its ground and goal. Whatever frustrates life alienates it from the ground and goal. If life offers both, only a fulfillment large and deep enough to give meaning to frustration can be God. As Gardner Murphy has eloquently shown, frustration augments tension, and tension is the condition for creativity.[3]

The ground of faith and the goal of faith must together justify the way of faith. If no context for life and thought can join together the ground of faith (God as the presupposition for life and thought) and the goal of faith (God as the fulfillment of life and thought) in such a way as to give appropriate meaning to the relation between both, we are left with no God rightly to worship. Then acknowledgment and affirmation fail to come together, and we are left with confusion and fear, with Jean Paul Sartre's empty freedom, with Heidegger's defiance, but never with the faith that sets free through fulfillment.

The Christian faith claims, far beyond our proving or explaining here, that God is holy, faithful love. Reality, in such a view, can be trusted. Right acknowledgment and right affirmation come together in trust. Such trust is the glory of faith, for it sets man free. It sets man free with respect to the objective side of experience: God can be trusted. It sets man free with reference to the subjective side of experience: man can be free from himself. Man,

[2] *Man is Not Alone* (Farrar, Straus and Young, 1951), p. 174.
[3] Cf. *Personality* (Harper & Brothers, 1947), p. 305.

in accepting God, can thereby know himself to be accepted. Such trust sets man free for others and toward nature.

Acceptance of reality and self, of life's ultimate and intimate center, gives man freedom to accept all else. Man is caught in no choice between inner- and other-directedness; rather, he finds God-directedness. Such God-directedness gives freedom within and without, with respect to self. What this freedom is, and how it is to be had, we shall discuss in the next chapter. Even now we know enough, through our experience of the way the fever of life shuts the self in on itself and how fear poisons, weakens, and binds the self, to be convinced that its opposite, faith, when really attained, can set the self free in the fullest and best way possible.

This, then, is the glory of faith. God can set free the self that has futilely struggled with its own chains. Fear suffers, or as the Bible says, has torments. Joy and peace come through believing. Such analysis we know to be right. To lose fear and find faith, especially in God as the ground and goal of life, is, existentially speaking, life's hardest lesson. Most people miss the glory of faith. Fear-filled eyes acknowledge as reality the dark spots or the drab gray of the average life. The life of fear keeps pulling weeds anxiously without permitting time for the enjoyment of life's flowers. Few find the faith that lifts life and gives it glory. Such faith roots in God as the ground of life; puts ultimates unequivocally first in life; and in the goal of life, trusts most fully the best we have seen in life. No facts can force such a choice. To be sure, certain experiences and insights can facilitate such a faith, but such soaring faith, the glory of man, can finally be nothing but a free act. Therefore, we turn from God and faith to God and freedom.

III

God is the ground not only of faith but also of freedom. Within a world of many wills there must be some ultimate unity of willing, if freedom of fulfillment is to be open for all. The condition of such freedom for all is an ultimate order, generally available, where persons are fulfilled by willing together some common good. God is the ground of such freedom. His will is for the highest good of all. He has so ordered and so controls the world that there is a lure for harmony of being within the self and among selves, both as a direct possibility of intrinsic human need and of resources in superhuman reality for meeting that need, and also as an indirect possibility of learning through the nature of experience in terms of the consequences of choice.

Just as the realm of faith of some kind is inescapable, even so
man cannot elude freedom. Sartre is right. Freedom is a necessity.
Choose we must. Freedom is the birthright and the responsible
heritage of every life. Each person is unique and is created to
choose. Man becomes increasingly what he chooses. No one can
ever choose for anyone else the ultimate meanings and qualities of
relationship.

God is the ground of freedom both as the condition for freedom, without which the many wills would conflict and frustrate
each other, and also as the giver of life where choice is the core of
its inner nature.

But God is also the goal of freedom. Just as in the case of faith
its presuppositional nature gives it no concrete content but only
the necessity of choosing context, even so God as the ground of
freedom gives it only the general conditions for the freedom of
all and the inner necessity of the freedom of each. God as the goal
of freedom provides the content in experience for the fulfillment
of freedom, personally and socially. Freedom as self-determination
is given to each and all; there is no choice whether or not to have
it. The primary choice is how to use it, whether to affirm it or to
try to flee from it; the lesser choices involve the ways in which
we implement our primary choice. Freedom as goal involves the
actual discovery of the nature of our freedom and how it can be
fulfilled.

God as the goal of freedom is the destiny of man. The more man
asserts his freedom the more he becomes a real self. The way he
asserts that freedom determines his nature as a self. The assertion
releases and creates the self. The content of that assertion makes
the kind of self we become. Nicolas Berdyaev is surely correct in
designating man spirit and in claiming that the essence of spirit is
freedom. The more man becomes spirit, the freer he becomes, and
the freer he becomes, the more he is spirit. Tillich knows that
"freedom without destiny is mere contingency and destiny without
freedom is mere necessity."[4]

Aldous Huxley began by extolling freedom; now, in later life,
he sees that the freedom he advocated was false, a mere cover for
self-assertion. R. G. Owen has written that Marxist Communism
understands that "real freedom has to do with the knowledge of,
and conformity to, the true end of life, but it misunderstands the
nature of man's true end. The point, however, that libertarianism
misses altogether, is that real freedom resides, not in endless, un-
restricted and capricious choices, but in choosing the true end and

[4] *Systematic Theology*, Vol. II, p. 130.

in committing oneself to it."[5] Certainly such a claim is the immemorial heritage of Christian freedom: to this fact the history of theology bears eloquent witness.

God as the goal of freedom is beyond law. To be bound is not to be free. As long as the law is over man or against him, he is not free. Full liberty is not within the law but beyond the law. The stage of obeying the law, as law, is over. This is the jubilant cry of Paul. This is the triumphant shout of Martin Luther. This is the preposterous claim of John Wesley. Law lies dead where freedom reigns. But such a claim has nothing to do with lack of right relation. Freedom never violates the true nature and function of law. God as the goal and glory of faith is the God of love, and love fulfills the law. It overflows the law. It drowns law's claim to priority by the fullness of righteousness and in the end leaves law a dead structure, powerless over the man of liberty who walks according to "the law of the Spirit." Where Christ is, there is liberty. Fear needs the law; full freedom encompasses the law but never lives by it. Freedom lives the law not as duty, i.e., as law, but as love, as the new-found joy of right relations, spontaneous in its motivation.

God as the goal of liberty is the God of co-operative community within the creative resources for common fulfillment. It takes freedom to learn to trust such love. Freedom lives in the love learned by faith. Freedom to learn is given by God, the ground of freedom. The conditions for learning, the school of freedom, are given by God, the ground of freedom. Learning such freedom through experience is, however, made possible by God the goal of freedom. He abets its attainment. This is the case where the meaning and function of frustration, of evil, can be included in the process between God the ground of faith and God the goal of faith, whose means and media are the responsible choices of freedom.

The freedom of choice can be used to find the freedom of life. Freedom of life is the fulfillment of the freedom of choice. It is the state where neither fear nor duty oppresses choosing; the choice is authentically free in motivation as well as in exercise. Such choice is autonomous, not as self-limited liberty, but as God-fulfilled freedom, good for all and available to all. Brunner and Tillich rightly name such freedom theonomous. In this sense God is not only the ground but the goal of freedom. He is the beginning and the end of liberty. The process in-between belongs to our limited, learning selves. The process of life in human time is pedagogical. Man's full liberty comes in the joining of acknowledg-

[5] *Body and Soul* (Westminster Press, 1956), pp. 211-212.

ment and affirmation, the two basic aspects of faith in the free service and the full friendship of God.

God as the ground and goal of freedom is peculiarly the giver of freedom. God is love. The nature of love is to fulfill other persons. Persons, to be real, can be fulfilled only in freedom. Therefore, God as love gives freedom as the condition for learning and living love. In giving love, he gives himself; in giving freedom, he makes possible our true acceptance of his greatest gift. Therefore, love is not only a spiritual gift, but "the more excellent way" of Paul's hymn to love. God is Spirit and the nature of Spirit is freedom. God made us spirits. The foundation of our lives is liberty. The more we accept ourselves the more free we are. True self-acceptance is the receiving freely and fully of reality: God the ground and goal of freedom.

God is personal. To be personal is to confront other persons. Genuine confrontation is a meeting of free persons. It may be encounter or it may be communion. Community is unity within togetherness. Love is the total gift of God, the experience of oneness ultimately and intimately within the richness of creative diversity. Spirit makes us free within, in our internal relations. Personal being is authenticated by our receiving freedom toward what is outside us, in our external relations. Rightly to receive God is to be set free by the Spirit both in our personal and in our social relations. Such freedom comes from trusting God as love. Faith and freedom come together in God, and go out insolubly from God universally and unconditionally. What the conditions for such freedom are, and what such outgo of faith and freedom involves for individuals and societies, we are to examine in the next two chapters.

Our age can accept or deny the effective living of faith and freedom, but it cannot do so except in relation to God, for God is the ground and goal of both faith and freedom. The problem is to walk wisely all the way from ground to goal, from the necessary conditions of faith and freedom to their fruition.

Chapter 5

The Individual: His Faith and Freedom

MODERN man's attitude toward himself is ambiguous: he worries neurotically over himself, wondering who he is, while fearing to be himself and fleeing from himself. Self is in the saddle but with no horse to ride, for faith is gone. Existentialism is modern man's insistence that he must ride his own horse where he will. It is the cry for freedom without faith. With self as goal, modern man has nowhere to ride. He sits in the saddle of self on a phantom steed of freedom, for faith is the carrier of freedom in directions beyond self.

This chapter is a presentation of man's personal freedom within the presupposition of the Christian faith. It deals with three basic levels of freedom: the physical, the moral, and the spiritual. The aim is to interpret facts aright within their proper context.

I

Physical freedom is fundamental in nature. There are many interpretations of freedom which are, in fact, what William James called "soft determinism." They exclude freedom from the natural order of cause and effect. They relegate freedom to some attitudinal realm of the spirit. But if freedom roots in faith in God the creator, there can be no place from which freedom is basically excluded. This assertion is poignantly true in the case of the physical realm. The individual must have the capacity to relate himself in freedom to every major aspect of life.

There are limits to the freedom of the individual in the world of fact. There is the limit of time. Man is born, lives, and dies within a severely circumscribed bit of time and, while living, he has time for only an infinitesimal segment of affairs. He is not free to do or to participate in more. Man is likewise limited in space. In physical fact he can be in only one place at any given time, less than a pinprick in the illimitable universes. Man also is bound by the physical equipment of his body and by what seems to be semiphysical dispositional drives. In Gordon Allport's vocabulary these drives become autonomous.

Man is bound by a vast order of cause and effect outside himself, over most of which he has no control at all, and by involuntary functions within himself which seem nearly to usurp mastery over him. A Boston physician once offered money to anyone who could demonstrate scientifically that by thought or by willing he could change the functioning of his kidneys. Man is also limited by the acts of others in the physical realm. He can be literally confined in prison or shot to physical death.

If these are some of the limits of physical freedom, what, then, is the nature of this freedom, and what measure of freedom does an individual possess? Man's freedom in nature cannot be isolated from nature. Man is physically a part of it. There is a positive relation between the field theory in physics and its application by Kurt Lewin to psychology. In the old physics, reality consisted of minute particles that at least in theory could be isolated and located. They affected each other externally and mechanically. In the new physics, there are no isolated particles but fields of magnetic forces where the smallest units are limit-points, altogether a part of the whole field and internally related to it. Nor is the relation between whole and part mechanically external, but even as the whole exerts determinative influence on the parts, the parts act back and influence the whole. A seemingly inert and passive table actually hits back at the hand that touches it. Thus even on this physical level, determinism and freedom are correlative terms. Every part plays its role, but within the conditions of the whole and in relation to it; such freedom and determinism characterize all that we know.

In the organic realm, the unit is more markedly defined and distinct from its environment even though it is subject to the same situation. In this realm, however, the meaning and measure of freedom are intensified. The part played by the organism is more complex and original. The unit of exerted influence is more pronounced. In an animal, complexity and originality depend on the animal's degree of development. A monkey can employ tools to change its environment even beyond its field of immediate perception, and animals can be conditioned to an artificial world of values by learning to enjoy substitute rewards. Even a cat may, I believe, respond to the stimulus of the food bowl when out of sight of it, or may sit waiting for a person to come to open a door, weighing motivations, not mechanically as on a scale, but organically within complex drives. An element of hesitation in the cat indicates more of originating influence than does the hesitation of a flow of water waiting for the easiest path to take. In no case is there decision without motivation, all the way from the more causally controlled event to the more organically conditioned act. The whole plays its full part of influence while each event or agent exerts its own proper degree of influence.

The same is true a fortiori in the case of human psychology. No act is free in the sense that it is apart from the conditioning power of the whole of its environment both from without and from within. External stimuli and internal associations of past experience basically penetrate, form, and color every act. No decision is free of the influence of the dominant field. But neither is any decision reducible to such external and internal influences as though there were no unit striking back. The more complex the unit, the more defined and originative is its influence. The freedom of man in the physical realm is along the same line as that of the physical and the organic realms as understood by field theory.

Man, however, adds a new dimension. Man's consciousness and self-consciousness define him as a unit of originating response of peculiar complexity and power.[1] The table, an inorganic event, hits back at the hand that touches it. An animal, a complex organic event, modifies the world it meets. For example, it builds a home. A man not only reacts but responds. He meets the world uniquely in terms of self-conscious reflective evaluation. He thinks. By means of his ability to abstract and to create an alternate world to the one he finds, man receives a new level of freedom. For this reason there is real truth contained in Thomas Aquinas' assertion: *totius libertatis radix est in ratione constituta*.[2] Freedom is not basically of the mind but of the total person; without the ability to think, man would not be uniquely free. David Miller, in *Modern Science and Human Freedom*, has well said that freedom proceeds through planning by means of symbolic projection of possibilities into the future and involves a continuity of physical, psychological, and ethical factors.

But there is also discontinuity, uniqueness. Uniqueness means definitive distinctiveness, an isolable *kainos* that is neither some quantitative *neos* nor some unrelated wholly other. There is continuity between the freedom of the table, the animal, and man, but there is also qualitative discontinuity. For the purposes of discussion, such a distinction is all important. Sir Charles Sher-

[1] Kurt Lewin and Gardner Murphy have been especially perceptive in their application of the field theory in physics to psychology.
[2] *De Veritate*, XXIV, 2.

rington, in his famous Gifford Lectures, declares that from the point of view of chemistry to make "life" a distinction between a person and a corpse, for instance, "is at root to treat them both artificially."[3] When a person dies, he writes, "chemistry not knowing the word 'life', says the proteins are [merely] irreversibly altered."[4] But to the widow, life or not-life in her husband is a "root" difference, and in the lecture hall whether or not Sherrington is alive makes the crucial difference. There is no denial of the continuity of the whole field of chemistry, including man, alive or not; but what is to chemistry simply a matter of the irreversible alteration of proteins is for man a matter of life or death.

Similarly, man's freedom is both continuous and discontinuous, but its uniqueness is all-important when man is understood on his own level, not to mention his fullest relation to God. The measure of man's freedom varies, then, with his capacities and the development of those capacities. Obviously, the limits of physical freedom overwhelm man in terms of his finiteness. But as a part of the field, man is able to affect the field uniquely. By purposing he can initiate new changes of causations in the physical world, reversing, altering, or redirecting through his body the flow of energy. Self-determination is not apart from the field, but in response to it, and is in turn part of it.

There are also new ranges of understanding of extrasensory perception and kinokinesis. Invisible energy can affect the visible without direct contact in the body. The function of consciousness itself is determination of personal existence. There are also, the Christian knows, resources in the spiritual realm which enhance the power of man in and over the physical world. The measure of freedom thus varies with each person; but within the conditions of the field and of the person, man has a genuine measure of freedom in the physical world, especially through consciousness, self-consciousness, and the deeper reaches and relations of man as spirit.

II

Moral freedom is the ability to know the right and to do it. Right morality is a matter of conduct in relation to law or to life, or in some way to both. In a world of many moral agents (if right is to have any dependable meaning for the community), there must be some objective reference centrally common to all. Historically and analytically, law and life are the main references for morality. Self-fulfillment can be a standard in a world of many

[3] *Man On His Nature* (Cambridge University Press, 1953), p. 78.
[4] *Ibid.*, p. 87.

moral agents only if the fulfillment is of such a nature that its realization does not frustrate the moral situation or the moral life for others. If this requirement is carried through, we are back to some objective order of relations, *law*, or to some subjective order of relations, *life*, or to a synthesis of both.

The limits of moral freedom are within and without, and in the relation between the two points. Human beings do not see and know the total order of relations, either objectively or subjectively. Therefore, they act ignorantly and unwisely. Nor do they have the power or the will constantly to live up to the fullest they know. Moral failure is part of the human lot. Either the external requirement is too hard or the inner equipment too slight, or both; or else such failure itself has purpose within the moral order.

The Old Testament, on the whole, makes law, in the wide sense of the term, the standard of morality. God has revealed his way and man must walk in it. Gerhard Von Rad writes in *Moses* that "the basis for all life of men in community is law."[5] The fulfilling of such law was the highest obligation, ideal, and joy of the dedicated Jew. Von Rad also writes that "in the whole of the Old Testament we do not find one single word which suggests that the Law is a burden, or that turns life into weariness."[6] Such understanding of God's objective rule and of man's fulfillment through obedience to it represents the highest morality based on law. The Jews further believed that it was possible to keep the law. Therefore, they could have moral freedom within the law and fulfillment of life by means of law.

The Christian position is that moral freedom is a matter of conduct in relation to life itself. Law is a matter of right relations, and right relations among men is love. Love therefore fulfills the law. The Jews in their two chief commandments approached and almost arrived at this position. Love means inclusive acceptance and outgoing concern. In full Christian love all men are accepted and have the same care for each other. Law then formulates the conditions for concern. These conditions depend on the nature of man and the world in which he lives. Law formulated as rules of conduct is necessary, but that does not touch the inner relation of persons. The fuller understanding and keeping of law as right relations among persons requires love. When love is realized, the conditions for right relations among persons are included, but they are relegated to an external means of involvement, and as such are no longer normative to human conduct. It is at this point that

[5] Unpublished manuscript.
[6] *Ibid.*

the objective and subjective aspects of morality are synthesized. Law is fulfilled in the service of love.

Faith is the affirmation of love. Faith presupposes that God can be trusted. By faith we justify God's faith in us. Such faith releases our lives for freedom. Those who love are free from themselves in proportion to the depth of their love for others. God's love alone is fully mature and therefore fully free.

Growth belongs to the life of man. As we trust God, our capacity to love grows. Paul writes that Abraham grew strong in faith as he gave glory to God, fully convinced that God was able to perform what he had promised. Erich Fromm tells us that mature love never springs from the needs of others but instead, that it needs others precisely because of its own outgoing nature. It is free. Faith and freedom come together in the person who knows true love.

But the ability to love is blocked by sin. Being self-centered, we fear that we will be hurt by loving, and therefore we shut love from us. We want to be loved, but we know deep down that if we accept love we shall have to love; therefore, we fear being loved. Lovelessness is due to fear of loving. We can love, as finite creatures, only by first being loved. Love depends on acceptance, even of ourselves. God is the source of love because he is love. Therefore, the biblical witness is true that we love because he first loved us.

With sin blocking love, and self fearing love, we are bound by existential anxiety. We are imprisoned in self. And the prisoner is ill. We cannot will freedom. We are free to want it, but as we try to grasp it neither heavyhearted defiance nor lighthearted acceptance of freedom secures it for us. We fear and fail. We fail and fear. And there is no health in us commensurate with our desire. Our hopes disappoint and our expectations frustrate. We talk freedom—and act bound. We shout freedom—and crawl slaves to self, to others, and to circumstance. Our confession neither carries nor communicates conviction. Our claims, high or low, hurt and hinder us. We have freedom to choose, but not to be free by choosing.

Not until we own up to our plight can we be helped; not until we see ourselves within the total field of freedom and relate ourselves rightly to it. Not until we will be free within the will of God for the total good! Then, freedom to choose becomes freedom of life within our restoration to reality. We repent of our false fight for freedom and accept our native right to freedom. We then pine to be forgiven and to be made free within the full field of freedom.

Forgiveness frees the self by removing the block of sin, the fear of self. Forgiveness frees the self by relating it rightly to God's will for the common good. Forgiveness frees the self by making it authentic before God. The twisted conscience hears again the voice of God, as the image of God becomes clarified at the depths of life. The tortured spirit of man is released from the guilt that makes him want to hide from self and others as well as from God. Forgiveness comes by faith in God's love beyond our moral attainment. Forgiveness is therefore the gateway to fullness of life; it is, as Jakob Boehme says, "the open gate of grace."

The forgiven man becomes opened to the creative powers of faith. He is made free to love. He lives a new creature. Peace begins to flood life and faith, to give man the creative satisfaction of zestful freedom. Faith finds freedom through forgiveness.

The nature of moral freedom is freedom of life as fulfillment by means of freedom of choice as inescapable responsibility. Faith finds that freedom, as trust in God, leads to repentance, forgiveness and re-creation. These words may seem old-fashioned for modern man, but they are nevertheless prerequisite for life and truth. The Old Testament is right: the way of the law at its highest leads into the way of faith. Through Abraham's faith comes the promise of blessing to all peoples. The highest revelation of the Old Testament is a wondrous way of faith far beyond our ordinary understanding or achievement. But its own fulfillment comes through the Gospel of the love of God, where faith as law reaches its fulfillment within the freedom of love.

Thus, moral freedom is within the total field of righteousness. The law is the way of right relations among all people. Community is based on law. It cannot be done away. We are free to choose or to reject it. But right relations among people are beyond law as law; they are a matter of full acceptance and creative concern. Law is fulfilled by love. Such love engenders creative individuality and enriching difference within the total fulfillment of the common good.

III

In the Christian view, the meaning of both physical and moral freedom is to be found in spiritual freedom. Man is spirit by creation, but vague, inchoate spirit, a spirit largely brooding over the void and confusion of the physical drives and moral problems. The purpose of both drives and problems is to learn freedom by freedom. The very nature of spirit is freedom, freedom of choice and freedom of life. We are born free to become free.

Since man is spirit by creation, he can become free through self-fiulfillment only when he is rightly related and developed as spirit. God is the personal Spirit who is holy love. Man is created to become free spirit by learning to live holy love. Only such a mature spirit can make man truly free. Man can become free from self only by becoming an authentic self. Man can become free from others only by accepting them, identifying himself with them, and being concerned for them. But such freedom is no physical choice, not even a moral choice. Such freedom does not come by fear or by duty. It comes only on the spiritual level when man learns to receive, to be, and to live love.

Freedom on the spiritual level comes from participation in the life of God, the eternal Spirit. Freedom for man comes through God's infinite resources for freedom. But the limits of that freedom are frightful. To gain such freedom is life's fullest and final task and is therefore man's hardest and longest struggle. God never gives freedom on the spiritual level for some simple asking. Man must suffer for it. The freedom of Jesus to have and to give his peace on the way to the Cross was paid for by the Cross. Life begins with suffering, and suffering continues throughout life. He who never knows suffering is not human. The greater the scope for freedom, the higher the cost. No life wins the prize of peace without the price of suffering. In every realm of life there is pain: physical, moral, and spiritual. The mind enters into all these sufferings. No spiritual freedom comes without the free and full acceptance of suffering, and the right, redemptive use of it. Søren Kierkegaard identified the stages in man's spiritual growth as the aesthetic, pleasure; the ethical, struggle; and the religious, suffering.[7]

The limits of spiritual freedom reach into the depths of anguish because of man's need for freedom from God. Man longs to remain an infant in every sphere of life. He dreads being weaned. But God nonsentimentally withdraws the breast from the crying child. God seems cruel as he lets even Jesus cry his bitter cry of being forsaken. God leaves the child alone in unfriendly hands; and dread, rebellion, fear, suspicion, hatred, enter the child's life. Like the eagle, God "stirs up the nest" and hurls the eaglet down the precipice. Such insecurity, such being let alone, such fright,

---

[7] Naturally these descriptive phrases are no summaries of Kierkegaard's rich, complicated analysis. For a full discussion see Concluding Unscientific Thinking, Appendix, pp. 244-266, especially p. 261; or Walter Lowrie's Introduction to Stages on Life's Way, especially p. 10. Different translators render the Danish variously, but for our purposes the only point is the fact that the religious (and highest) stage is characterized by suffering.

such suffering, are man's lot because he has to find freedom from God.

The more developed the animal, the longer the period for raising the young. A human child requires years of rearing. But who can number the years required for moral and then spiritual rearing? This life seems but the beginning, and those who die may still cry: "My God, why hast thou forsaken me." Spiritual rearing is lifelong and few know in this life effective fostering; with fuller understanding and commitment, suffering often increases. Full of the Holy Spirit, Jesus goes to be tempted by the Devil. He was free not to escape the suffering of temptation but to meet it by divine power. We do not know whether man in this life can go beyond such a state. In any case, all golden prescriptions for peace of mind and ease of life are sleeping pills that soothe for the moment but cannot ensure the surcease of sorrow. No psychological tricks or false faiths can substitue for the God who hides himself in order for us to learn to become free by the choices of freedom.

Freedom comes in large measure by suffering as we learn to be free from God, free from others, and free from self in order to be free in, by, and with God, with and for others, and as a true self. We are free to say "no" to God, and we do. We do so, not for the most part directly, but in our interpretation of him by denying or distorting his presence, or by disguising his nature or changing his will. When by freedom from God, which is the gift of God's humility for our learning, we say "no" to him, we get out of relationship to the reality for which we are made. Maladjustment, guilt, and suffering ensue. We say "no" to others, and suffer through trying to use them or because of being rebuffed by them. Social by nature, we thus suffer by denying our nature. Social by God's demand, we deny God, and guilt brings us anguish. We refuse self by denying God and shutting out others. The perverted selves that we become starve, are driven, and suffer.

Or, we may suffer even when we say "yes" to God. He may hide himself from us or demand the seemingly impossible; and we suffer. Our conscience separates itself from God's image in us, and divided we suffer. Our spirits, not yet enlightened or tempered, burn with a false fever, or become exhausted; we suffer. When we accept others, to live for them, they may fail to understand us, causing us to suffer. Or, understanding us all too well, they feel our love a judgment upon them, thus rejecting us, and we suffer. Or, as we accept ourselves, the Holy Spirit may lead us into the wilderness of temptation, and we suffer. We find ourselves and, by so doing, find that we have to deny or be denied what seems nature itself, physical, mental, social or spiritual, and we suffer.

Life is learning to become free by suffering. There is no other way. Sooner or later, freedom, when we get it, comes through the choice of suffering. Sinner and saint alike suffer: the one hopelessly and without remedy, the other in hope and healing. Nor is there escape in this life or beyond, for God controls the consequences of our choices and makes us meet them. The saint, however, does suffer with hope and with help. If any way of life could be free of suffering, selfishness would always choose it. The lot of the saint, indeed, seems harder than that of the sinner. It certainly is no attraction to self-seeking. Therefore, only goodness can lead to repentance and to freedom. The frustration of fear is only to lead man to consider the good he once knew. Even then, man is free to follow either way.

Suffering with God for others, as a genuine self, nevertheless finds hope beyond suffering. The joy is set before those who choose the Cross. The suffering is for a moment and brings an exceedingly worthwhile reward: faith's final freedom in love. God has a sabbath prepared for his people. Life on earth is a school for love; perhaps it is only the kindergarten before we learn to read the divine communication directly. Learning continues beyond man's physical death. Heaven is no empty symbol to be despised by modern man. Heaven is man's home. It is the fulfillment of life beyond God's school of suffering. Heaven is love's final freedom when faith rests in God.

And love's suffering has help on its way. In the struggle there is a companion who knows the depths of the Cross. Often, the loneliness of the Gethsemane struggle is life's bitterest cup. Yet man is not alone even in that loneliness. He is not Godforsaken. Even when God hides from us, faith that has once found God suffers on in the agony of its aloneness, knowing that even then it can commit its spirit into stronger hands. And often after the fiercest struggle, God sends ministering angels. The life of faith, too, has its long hours of trusting joy and its shorter moments of transfiguration. To exaggerate suffering, even as pedagogy, is to dim the reality of the Gospel. For faith, suffering is real and must be accepted, but suffering is not all of life nor life's deepest meaning and experience.

What, however, is the measure of faith's freedom in this life? Who can tell? Let the heart of each one answer from his own experience. Let each one look as far as he can at human history. Jesus gave the formula: "according to your faith." According to your faith, your *lived* faith, you will have freedom. Freedom from

God is our inescapable stewardship. God never becomes guilty of "momism." We can choose through faith in God, as best we know him, to find freedom of life. The kind of freedom we reach depends in some measure on the kind of faith we have. Faith in God as love can give us trust's assurance, even at times the Bible's "full assurance of faith" and the "joy and peace in believing." False faiths deceive and mock; but even wrong faiths yield some fruit, for all faiths are mixtures of truth and falsehood, tangled up with a finite and sinful self.

We are born, in any case, into a sinful situation and accept before we know it a self-centered drive which is partly nature, partly social heritage, and partly situational, as frail man trembles in an overpowering world that is not only precarious but threatening to the depth self in terror-striking dimensions. Some spirits are damaged in the bringing up. Faith's fullest acceptance seems not to redo what family and society have hurt. In such cases, suffering hunts hard on suffering. Who can tell what others alone can know? Who can share the pain of the unbidden suffering? Who can rationalize the human story of Job? Who can give the equation of Jesus' peace and pain? We hurt ourselves, others and God, because often we suffer, not knowing why.

Freedom is therefore to face life at its center. Freedom is to put aching lives into the hands of God to be used in his service, and at times to feel the touch of his hand and see the smile of his approval. Freedom is to reach out to others for companionship, seeking their good, even when the self within cries for approval and recognition. Freedom is to find creative interest in the normal activities of life, even when suffering would blanket the mind and suffocate the spirit. Freedom is to accept oneself, suffering and all, and to go on living, even when one's picture of oneself is smashed and one's confidence in doing genuine good seems broken. Freedom is to have faith in God, others, and self when doubts assail and life seems to declare the doubts to be justified.

No man can speak for humanity. Life is too complicated and the response to life too varied for generalizations. Our next task will be to consider the possibilities of the social freedoms that can be attained, to use and to enjoy. For these we must live with wisdom and effectiveness. But to believe that external conditions for freedom will give persons true freedom is to court disaster through superficiality. There can be no social freedoms until persons win victory in their own lives. Such victories are of faith, life's positive, evaluative response to reality. Such freedom is most deeply the gift of God. Man is spirit and must learn by freedom that only where the Spirit of the Lord is can liberty be found.

Full freedom is a gift that must be both received and learned. Freedom can be given only to freedom, and no self can become free except it learn of what true freedom consists. No lessons cost more or last longer. Life is for these lessons. Life is for learning love. Love alone is fully free both to choose and to live. Faith affirms, and finds, that there can be growth in freedom as there is maturation of love. To teach this kind of freedom is well nigh impossible. Those who try must communicate the truth that the Christian Gospel of freedom has a Cross at its center, a Companion in suffering, but also faith's hoping and faith's finding.

Chapter 6

Society and Freedom

LIFE oscillates between analysis and action. Thinking is for living. The two should be kept together, but one cannot be reduced to the other. The Buddha recommended action as opposed to speculation. He advised pulling out the arrow in the wounded man, rather than discussing the situation. After Martin Luther King, Jr., a Negro emancipation leader, was stabbed, however, all night the doctors worried the paper knife out of him. The thrust was right next to the main artery of the heart, and one pull would have finished the earthly life of so great a man as King. Action waited on analysis.

An elderly man found a driver pinned under an overturned car. Carefully he was weighing how to remove him without harming him when four college youths jumped out of their car and ran to lift the overturned vehicle. The older man cautioned them, but to no avail, for as they lifted, their feet sank and slipped under them in the swampy soil. Down came the car on the victim! This was action without analysis. Both analysis and action are needed. In life, they belong together.

This chapter concerns analysis of our social freedoms and how faith can help secure them. Correct analysis aids action. Trouble from analysis comes mostly when it takes the place of action or when the analysis is wrong. We shall consider three different forms of social freedom: those connected with our physical, with our mental, and with our social life.

I

Man's physical freedom is not a lower kind of freedom. As human beings, one indispensable element of earthly life is physical. Too often spiritual or moral freedom is pictured as separate from physical freedom, whereas it ought to be included in any genuine human freedom. The Christian faith as incarnational honors the physical realm and works to fulfill it. In this first area, we have selected three basic social freedoms: freedom from want, freedom from war, and freedom to travel. All of these will be treated as both actual and symbolic needs, i.e., what we select for mention is only a small part of physical freedom, pointing to the larger total need of man as a physical being.

During the Second World War, Franklin D. Roosevelt promised that the Atlantic Alliance would work to secure for the world freedom from want. For a long time before this declaration, the Communist nations had defined freedom in terms of economic security and opportunity. Many experts in the underdeveloped lands of the world have argued that political or other freedoms can have little meaning as long as people are starving. Freedom from want is a basic freedom. Negatively, this freedom can be expressed as the security on the part of all co-operative citizens not to be without needful sustenance for living: the freedom not to have to starve. The means to realize much freedom would be responsible promises by society, through whatever agencies, to provide sustenance for all. But food is more than bread and meat. Food is physical sustenance for people who are not only animals but sensitive social beings. Therefore provision for food alone does not meet the need for freedom from want. Such promises can provide security against the threat of starvation and are that far good, but they leave man, the human being, frustrated, for living depends on purpose. Man eats to fulfill a purpose; he does not fulfill a purpose to eat. This truth is often forgotten, minimized, or ignored.

Freedom from want is therefore organically connected with freedom to work. The right to work is intrinsic to creation. Society is under divine order so to organize its economic life as to provide to the maximum of its wisdom and resources the opportunity for all for creative work. With automation in a new dimension at our doorsteps, such a demand is difficult to fulfill. The old economic talk of a labor pool was irresponsible of human purpose. The new threat merely to replace men with machines is equally a revolt against God and man. It is not enough to produce as never before, perhaps soon in terms of atomic and solar energy or by the utilizing of our oceans, if such production be at the expense of inclusive human participation. Whatever the future holds, to promise men bread without work is to ruin them where they live most deeply, as useful human beings carrying on a meaningful existence. Since obviously we cannot get back to before the machine, as Gandhi advocated, in order to meet man's basic need both to work and to eat, we must find ways of providing creative uses for leisure that shall call for ever new kinds of meaningful work. Naturally, people must be fed while they are unable to find work, but feeding them cannot fill their need for work.

Such economic freedom to provide both fulfillment of purpose and the feeding of the body requires fullness of faith. When faith in God as concerned with the common good and the whole man becomes real, society will become so organized as to center its attention on the needs of the whole man and of all men, finding ways for them not only to have food but to feed on the bread of purpose. The Welfare State is here to stay. We will not go back on the Social Security Act of 1935. But the larger task is effectively to improve the state's concern with physical freedom and to organize and marshal all property to this end. This task is a world-wide demand, summoning for constructive co-operation both halves of the world to surpass the past in re-examining both the purpose for living and the production and distribution of goods to all peoples of a new age of world-wide freedom from want. We must have a whole new level of creative work to utilize God's creation and to release man's spirit.

A second vital freedom in the physical realm is freedom from war. As long as society can command some bodies to kill other bodies, to spend years in training for destruction, or put people in camps, or prisons, or even kill them if they refuse military service, man is a slave in the realm of his body. Besides, the major portion of physical resources levied for the common good is wasted for economically useless purposes and even for making the means of destruction. Then, too, millions have lost their lifetime earnings and physical property in war, or they have been uprooted from their native lands, becoming homeless and purposeless in refugee camps, or bewildered and frustrated in lands not of their free choosing.

A minimum physical freedom is absence of such physical threats. War is an irrational hang-over of barbarism. Man must face the fact that now he will either conquer war or be destroyed by it. War among nations in terms of man's full destructive powers is no longer an option. Man now chooses basically war *or* life, but not war *and* life. Man's faith, the very basis of his freedom, has of late become nearly buried by his outright defiance of God in the practice of war. Man's abuse of his physical community has reacted as a paralysis or as a thick curtain both in his relation to God and to his fellow man. Crime and all other abuses of the body, such as alcoholism, are due in greater proportion than we know to man's deep fear of war. The dread of war oppresses the depth-consciousness, particularly of our young people.

To destroy war, however, and set man physically free in this respect, man must learn to live as a civilized being, using a minimum of physical force under judicial processes. He must learn to depend on nothing but police force, and that not as a constant threat but only in the solution of exceptional situations. In other words, society must become organized with a maximum view to social security and creative fulfillment. Such organization centers in the co-operative society. Wealth should be produced at the maximum, shared at the maximum, and enjoyed at the maximum. Thus freedom from want can help cure the overagainstness and the personal and organized greed which indirectly promote war.

The surest antidote to the inner and outer conflict which eventuate in crime and war is faith in God as the ground and goal of community. Immaturity, insecurity, sin, divided responsibility and faulty organization, where a limited loyalty is made more important than loyalty to the whole, conspire to produce war. Only faith, lived, following as well as engendering confession, can provide the kind of directive and motivation that can now wisely and constructively outlive war and secure social freedom. When society persists in preparing for, and engaging in, war it denies a physical freedom in God which alone is the bedrock and ample foundation for social freedom.

A third freedom in the physical realm is the freedom to travel. When man is chained to one spot he is not free, whatever the nature of the chain may be. No flight of the imagination can take the place of flight in the air. When the government of a nation withhholds a passport from any sane and law-abiding citizen it makes man's final loyalty the nation, and robs man of his humanity. Man has a right of access to every land. When a country denies access to any sane and responsible individual of another nation who is physically able to travel, such a country shuts out God's access to its border in some of his children.

But such negative considerations are not enough. Each man should increasingly be given the positive opportunity to travel. The countries and the world should make possible the larger circles of education in human life that travel may provide. As resources in an economy of abundance become ever more ample, as means of travel grow ever better, and as time for creative leisure becomes more and more of a usable commodity, needing wise spending, freedom to travel generally ought to become at least as common as a creative vacation is now for an increasing number of people. Without forcing people to travel, which also would be a form of robbing them of their physical freedom, every chance ought to be provided, and people given the strongest possible incentive for it. Freedom for travel can be a vital, positive extension in the physical realm of the freedom from want and the freedom from war. It is a symbol, and more, of the fuller physical freedom.

The problem with advocating physical freedom is that where it has been given it has often become the substitute for faith. The strongest argument against the Welfare State is that where it has been best developed, religion has also withered and nearly died. Consider the case of Sweden where outstanding social progress seems almost to have destroyed religious interest. Can it be that religion is, after all, the opiate of the people, a vent for deep dissatisfactions? Does religion die when man possesses the physical land? Is Karl Marx right after all? Or is such disaffection due to false religion, the religion of fear, of invidious comparison? Is religion a psychological aid to the aggression of the strong? Is Paul Tillich right, in the *Theology of Culture*, that religion as a separate activity is due to man's refusal to accept himself and his culture at its own dimension of depth? True religion, we believe, is acceptance of reality, and reality is the ultimate dimension of life. False religion, however, dies with man's fulfillment, but reality is rooted and grounded in personal relations among men and within the Father of men. Such religion eventuates in worship and gratitude, when things are right, and in concern and outgoing aid, when things are wrong. Such faith is the precondition of the full experience and exercise of freedom, even in the physical realm.

II

Man's mental freedom is his God-given, inalienable right. Man needs physical freedom, to be sure, but without mind, man is not man. No amount of physical freedom from want, for instance, can ever take the place of man's freedom of mind. Both kinds of freedom are intrinsic elements in the full human life. Negatively man should be free from mental duress. All brainwashing and "social engineering"—the manipulation of the many by the few—are illicit manipulations of human beings and are sin against humanity. Such practices treat human beings as objects or, at the highest, as animals. The avoidance of social engineering is, nevertheless, not easy. In a day of mass communications, a few have power over what people know, feel, and even do. Negatively, man has the right at least to the assumption that each human being needs to be and to become himself. All external interference with the processes that go into the decision of self-being is false manipulation of persons as objects.

Positively, each individual and each group ought to be encouraged to be itself. Nonconformity ought to be a social goal, as long as such nonconformity is constructive and creative. Diversity of expression is the glory of God's creation and the indication of genuineness of being and of productive security. Such freedom to be oneself comes from faith, for man's authentic self is neither primarily other-directed nor inner-directed but God-directed. The lonely crowd and the lonely self both need fulfillment of their basic aloneness in the eternal Companion whose compassion and creative richness never fail. Most people suffer because they have never been properly introduced to God.

Freedom of mind comes with the freedom to be oneself, not only to seek but to find oneself. Freedom of mind needs also freedom of thought. The general set of society, of course, determines to a large extent freedom of thought, but what is especially important is the way the pattern of education, both informally and formally, either opens or closes thought. Authoritarian institutions breed external acceptance of faith or the acceptance of faith as an obligation to the institution. Free thought in such a situation becomes dangerous, sometimes in terms of penalties actually imposed on nonconformity, often in terms of the inner pain that results when the indivdual tries to think for himself.

Our Roman Catholic friends are deeply disturbed by their failure to produce scholars commensurate with their numbers. The reason for the failure is surely lack of freedom of thought. Before a sweeping generalization is made at this point, however, it must be remembered that Nazism did produce, and now Communism is producing, first-rate scholarship and educational results. Can this fact be due to the creative novelty resulting from the overthrow of traditional faiths, and the stimulus provided by the challenge of the radically new, or are they within their collective concerns less afraid of truth than a traditionalistic institution like the Roman Catholic church?

Perhaps, indeed, the most important element in creative freedom of thought is not the manner of organization but rather the kind of truth that is furthered by any society. Perhaps supreme weakness comes from either the kind of authoritarian faith that knows all the answers and controls them in every realm and the kind of liberal faith that never can come to definite conclusions with regard to dependable truth. The most successful schools are the ones that come from a religious background that is still operative in general but that is freely seeking truth in particular. A fundamentalist turned constructively liberal generally has both the drive and the courage to be open, both to seek and to find truth. Freedom of thought lies, it seems, within a broad framework of faith that lacks a general fund of specific answers. Freedom needs a dependable context of faith without a completed content of answers. Social freedom in the realm of thought comes from a faith in God as truth and concern which makes important both the acceptance of such objective reality and the dedicated search rightly to interpret it and to embody in one's life the proper answers.

Freedom of thought in one sense cannot be controlled. This is the reason the closed societies fear the men of faith who individualize truth. But freedom of speech can be better controlled and is therefore often the crucial test for the freedom of thought. Speech is a privilege and a responsibility and ought not to be abused, but, short of speech that leads to physical interference with other people, free speech in its proper place and manner should not be prohibited. Naturally, freedom of speech involves the freedom from speech in certain places. A Christian, no matter how sincere, has no right, unbidden, to enter a synagogue to preach Christ. God has allowed man proper privacy, even real freedom from speech, and man must respect both. Freedom of speech, then, means the right to public address in proper places. Hyde Park in London, open to all, is a symbol of free speech. Every city and town, every village and county, should have a public platform for all responsible speech, no matter how unpopular, nonconformist, and exceptional.

But such opportunity is only the negative side of free speech. Everywhere, free speech should be encouraged by providing for the requisite conditions and atmosphere. Free speech should be extolled as a social virtue. Society should develop the art of creative conversation in all media of communication. Conformity is the product of the herd, the mass mind. Conformity is not democratic but demonic. Individuation and individualization of truth come only from a highly developed society that can keep position and person apart and that can weigh new ideas dispassionately while being firmly committed to the possibility of knowing significant truth. The knowing of truth depends, more than we realize, on the doing of truth, and the doing of the truth depends on people's being the truth. Only free souls can think free thoughts. Only people who think freely dare to speak freely and to listen freely.

Freedom of speech is a fruit of freedom of life. Social strength is known by its fruit: vigorous, creative speech, free in the giving and in the receiving, within the community of commitment for the common good. Such a community of freedom is the community of integrity, for only the truth can make us free. The deepest truth of life, however, comes through faith in God, the eternal guardian of integrity and love. The fullest freedom of mind comes from faith in God, the ultimate context of man's truest thinking. Social freedom needs the fullest possible right faith to undergird it, for faith determines life. No society has ever grown strong by living the minimum hypothesis, but by living the maximum right faith. Minimum hypothesis has its function on one side of the method of establishing knowledge. Alfred North Whitehead rightly advised us to seek simplicity and to distrust it! Maximum faith is the only road to freedom of life that can cherish the liberated and quickening mind.

III

Physical freedom is part and parcel of human freedom, as is mental freedom. Social freedom is less personal in nature although it involves, of course, individuals. We are now concerned with social patterns, organizations, laws, sanctions, and attitudes. If the distinction is made between objective and subjective society in terms respectively of civilization and of culture, we are fully concerned with both. If the subjective side is called good, and the objective, right, we are after the fullest possible synthesis of both. With this standard of dynamic synthesis in mind, the three social freedoms we are selecting as of primary importance for us now are freedom from racial discrimination, freedom from nationalism, and freedom from religious intolerance. Humanity has a God-given right to be free from racial, national, and religious bias.

When God made the world, he beautified it with difference in color. He enriched the world with the creation of race. Whatever be the anthropological development of racial differentiation, back of nature and history stands their God. Immature, fearful, and invidious man dreads what is different. He fears the unknown and the unlike. Difference both attracts and repels. Such ambivalence of feeling is registered in the unconscious and becomes there a reservoir of irrational fear and hate. When the sex drive becomes involved in this, across lines of both race and sex, and when economic and social frustrations are added, a depth chasm results that mere rational or moral exhortation cannot bridge.

Therefore, wherever there is distinction of color to any considerable extent, there is irrational fear and hatred, at least in society in general. The sharper the color contrast, the deeper the chasm in some proportion to the numbers and social background of the races involved. The case of modern Britain's acute race problem wherever colored population pours in, after that country's long years of pride over racial tolerance, is most instructive. Maturity of civilization, history of relations, and class contacts also play important roles.

Freedom from racial discrimination is therefore a rationally unsolvable problem. It cannot be cured either by education or by legislation alone. But proper laws giving equal opportunities and public access to all races can at least provide a legal framework for solution. Where such laws are lacking or where contrary legislation exists, the race problem is, of course, inflamed. Law has an integral, irreplaceable function in social relations and is a prerequisite for freedom from racial discrimination.

But the deeper freedom, by far, depends on social acceptance on the part of all races. Such acceptance, we have said, goes contrary to the ordinary patterns and attitudes of social relations that are generated by ordinary human nature. Idealistic preaching and teaching will not do the job, nor will enforced indoctrination. Fears and hatreds lie too deep to be cured by any power of social motivation except love. Love at its fullest meaning involves the universal acceptance of man as man, within his stature as a common child of God. Faith is the affirmation of love, of love in truth and deed, in personal relations as well as in word.

God as the creator of all races for the enrichment of humanity waits on our acceptance of his Spirit below and above our conscious problems. Well does Nicolai von Hartmann say that consciousness separates; spirit unites. Man's deepest togetherness is within the ocean of his common humanity, the Source and Sustainer of which is God the Father of our spirits. Thus, freedom from racial bias, whether through the law for the common good or through the love of the common good, depends ultimately on faith. Freedom roots in faith. Only when the fruit of the Spirit is lived love, implemented concern, love in attitude and action, in just law and common acceptance, can the fruit of faith be freedom in racial fulfillment.

Freedom from nationalism in the modern world is not easy. Nationalism is rampant in some parts of society and of the world, and where it is not, all too often no adequate loyalty has taken its place. We human beings find our at-homeness in the world in terms of the familiar. Person, family, and local habitat become dear to us but also hem us in. When loyalty to nation surpasses these, therefore, a real victory has been won. Until recently there has been no concrete, larger loyalty to lure us beyond nationalism.

There is, however, no way to freedom from nationalism that does not lie through nationalism. This stage as a larger loyalty is a stage necessary for us to pass through. When this is successfully surpassed, loyalty and affection for the nation can remain deep and enriching just as loyalty to family and locality can remain when nationalism is fruitfully attained.

In the modern world where nationalism does not reign, national loyalty has all too often been repudiated in the depth-affection of people. Modern man now needs decisively to grow into a citizen of the world for whom every local loyalty only enriches and intensifies his dedication to mankind. On the other hand, no country has the right to assume the place of God. To consider that national safety or good is man's final duty is to revolt against God. The nation which assumes that it has full and final right over people's lives blasphemes against God. The state cannot substitute for God. The state is itself under God's judgment. It rules rightfully only as long as it represents the will of God for the common good.

Our generation has witnessed the nations growing obsolete even as the largest political units of law and order under God. "One world" is now our only sane choice. The form of law and of rule of this one world has to be worked out with effective patience and unbelievable urgency. Regional, representative government, preserving regional autonomy in appropriate areas and activities of human concern, might create the world-wide authority to police the world defensively and to provide the economic and political framework for the marshaling and utilizing of world-wide resources for the common good. The steps to such world-wide order must surely be taken in faith in terms of realistic negotiation, increasing disarmament of nations, and a stepped-up vesting of effective authority and force in supernational authority.

The task of educating people and peoples for such citizenry of the world is staggering not only informationally but emotionally. For it we need a world-wide frame of faith, of thought, and of duties, born of and engendering in turn a universal faith. As full freedom from racial bias comes only from faith lived in the love of God, who accepts all for creative fulfillment without invidious discrimination, so freedom from nationalism comes at its fullest only from the religion large enough and good enough to serve all men, a religion strong enough for one world. We need a world-wide discourse for communication, a world-wide ethos for effective law, and a world-wide faith for the spontaneous motivation of the inclusive and creative good.

If we are to find this freedom *in* and *by religion,* man's central evaluative response to reality, we must find freedom *from religions.* Religions are man's response to what he considers and lets reign as ultimate. Religions, therefore, are mostly man's work, and reflect man's state of being. There is no help in religions. Some are better than others, but all religions are touched by human frailty and sin. Religion, beyond all religions, is man's positive response to God's revelation of himself as ultimate concern and his universal will for the creative fulfillment of the world. Unless God is creatively and fulfillingly for the whole world as well as for all and for each, he is too small for human need. He is then only a manufactured product of man's partial loyalties and of his larger fears and overagainstness.

Only the God of universal truth and concern is large enough to be real. What he is beyond that, man cannot know. We know as men, finite and within history. Further than that we can only trust God's faithfulness beyond our knowing as a small child trusts his mother beyond his understanding. Christ is God's declaration within human frailty of his universal love for all beyond human discriminations, and his faithfulness beyond human time and life. Fulfillment waits on God's future for us far beyond our every expectation. The history of human growth basically has been the history of the growth of man's understanding of God. Freedom *in* religion comes only from freedom *from* the religions of the world. Symbols and contents of religion both tell how to be transformed within the free faith in God's universal faithfulness.

Concretely, such freedom means that no religious affiliation— except possibly with some demonic groups openly defying the common good in terms of demonstrable social destruction, like the Ku Klux Klan—should debar anyone from any public opportunities, politically and socially; no creedal confession should shut out anyone from the normal processes of public life. Jews the world over should have every chance at public participation and should be fully accepted socially on all public occasions. Roman Catholics have only recently been given their freedom in Sweden; Protestants still wait for their freedom in Spain and Colombia. Obviously, public responsibility that is held by believers of any faith which is grounded in Reality beyond nation involves and invites double loyalties. There is no escape from faith; nor in faith is there escape from the choosing of priorities and the arrangement of loyalties. If faith is no more real and large than the nation, that faith is not large enough for the nations. Therefore all competent men of faith must from now on have the problems of divided or subordinate loyalties until mankind becomes effectively one world.

This negative problem, however, can be solved if religions yield to Religion, if all churches give way to the true Church of universal humanity. This Religion will include such local loyalties as are implicit in the common good. Man needs to find Religion for one world which offers the foundation for faith in the God who works ever to promote all that is constructively and indigenously human. What such faith will involve institutionally, ritually, and socially must be discovered within the creative, flexible will of God for cooperative humanity. Such faith waits on the future, but as it becomes more widely and effectively accepted, it will fulfill, not destroy, the highest in all religions. It cannot be far from Christ's stress on complete integrity and universal concern. Only such faith will kindle and keep aflame the holy light of universal and full freedom.

Thus our section on Faith and Freedom comes to its close. Freedom is essential to satisfactory living. It is indispensable to human life. Faith, again, is inescapable. Life, as lived, cannot be proved. We choose our way of living, and choice is faith. Faith determines life. When life is depressing or fails us, faith very likely is at fault. Only faith in God, the ground of freedom, can fulfill life, both personally and socially.

Freedom itself is not enough. Freedom is for fulfillment of life. Freedom of choice is for freedom of life. When faith is in God who cares for all and who shares of his life and love that all may live for the common good, freedom of choice is fulfilled by freedom of life. The fruits of such freedom are not only personal fulfillment but also the social freedoms apart from which no true and lasting satisfaction can be attained.

Fortunate are those who in a world of confusion and despair find the fountains of freedom in the world of faith. To find such freedom through faith and to help find such faith for freedom offers life's hardest task and richest investment. Those alone are truly free who, living, praying and working, have found such faith.

CONTEMPORARY THEOLOGY
AND THE FUTURE OF FAITH

Chapter 7

Can Classical Christianity Be Defended?

THE Christian faith centers in Christ. Christ is God come to earth in a human being. The God who came is love. He is best known through the Cross and the resurrection as suffering and victorious love. To all who believe Him, who repent and are forgiven, God gives eternal life, both here and beyond death.

Those who know such eternal life form a community of Christ, of free and full love, creative and redemptive. Such is forever the heart of the Christian faith.

Classical Christianity is flanked on both sides by false views of the Christian faith. Let us think of the classical Christian faith as the central castle in which true Christians live with deep satisfaction, a stronghold that they are bound to defend, and a home in which is the kind of life that is best for all people. It is the true home even of those who are not within it. It is beset from without by enemies anxious to raze it because they falsely feel themselves threatened by it.

Of the false positions two are on the right and two are on the left of the castle. On the extreme right are the fundamentalists. They are the ones who are stirred into great rage because the true defenders of the castle in this day of modern warfare are no longer using the crossbow.

They are more given to crying "heretic, heretic" at the true defenders and to shooting them in the back with their bows and arrows than they are to defending the castle itself with modern weapons and against the real enemies.

This is to say that the fundamentalists want to identify true Christianity with a literalism of the Bible which is impossible for any honest and educated man of our day. We cannot believe in a world made 6,000 years ago, in a flat earth with corners, or in a sun that goes around the earth.

Nor can we believe that things in the Bible inconsistent with the love of God in Christ are true or Christian. Neither is he blessed or right who dasheth the little ones of his enemies against a stone or who attributes the tortures of an eternal hell to the sovereign God of love.

Next to the fundamentalists on the right side of the castle of classical Christianity stand the neo-Calvinists. They believe in the castle, but they do not believe it needs defense from, or communication with, the people who are attacking it. They cry: "Our castle is beautiful. Let us worship in it. It cannot be taken. Let us praise it and enjoy it."

To interpret this part of the parable is to say that the neo-Calvinists, such as Karl Barth, do not believe in relating the Christian message to the world either in terms of defense or of intercommunication. They insist on the principle of unconditional surrender on the part of the enemies. While they are right that the castle is its own best recommendation and defense, they do not see that the enemy outside is made up of those who belong inside and who can be reached by concerned communication.

The Christian faith can win those outside when it is willing to show on every needed level that it is saving truth and that it can truly help and satisfy the very ones who are attacking. The Christian faith should remain stoutly itself and at the same time reach out to influence educational, social, and civic behavior.

Farthest on the left stand the demythologizers. They believe that the castle of classical Christianity has no place in modern life. It can no longer be defended because it is no necessary part of the Christian faith. Therefore, they have gone out on the field in front of the castle crying that the flag and the uniforms are what makes Christianity Christian. Out on the field they fight both the defenders of the castle (those who believe in an evangelical supernaturalism centered in Christ) and those who are arrayed against the Christian faith as a whole.

Within this body of warriors stand great thinkers like Rudolf Bultmann in Europe and Paul Tillich in the United States, who have become convinced that the objective structure of classical Christianity, a God beyond this world and an eternal life beyond this world, can no longer be believed in by men stringently trained in science.

They believe, however, that the original faith of the early Christians was in the Cross and the resurrection as the power to overcome all the enemies of human existence *in this life* by the power of reality, the power for life and for love that are being contained within the very ground of being. They keep, therefore, the symbols of faith and discard the castle with which classical

Christianity identified these symbols. They give up the structure of faith while believing that they have kept the faith itself.

Next to the castle on the left stand the liberals. They are busy with plans to put new conveniences in the castle, to modernize it. They want new plumbing, central heating, and some even want air conditioning. Then they want to invite the enemy to inspect the castle to see for themselves if the castle is not the best place in which to live.

Interpreted, this part of the parable means that the liberals want to be accepted by those who use general methods of truth. They do not want to think of the Christian faith as different in kind from other truth. They want instead to show that it is the forefront of all truth concerning life's meaning.

Christ becomes the great example and helper for men. He shows man what true humanity can be like. He contains as much of God as man can; and by accepting the God whose will and way we see in him, all men can find their way to heaven and home.

Man is good because the God whom we see in Christ made him, and man's reason is a reliable tool for knowledge of salvation as well as for knowledge of how to navigate the seas. What man needs is to become serious and concerned with regard to the will of God. Then the God who is love will give him a new social order and will grant him at last either peace after life or life after death.

What then shall I say of this parable? I believe all positions to contain genuine truths, but all positions, too, need to come home to the castle. They need to move into the center. Fundamentalists are right in defending classical Christianity in supernatural, evangelical terms. God in Christ as creator, redeemer, and consummator is our only hope. Christ is our Gospel, the God who came to earth as universal holy love and who waits and woos to save us now.

The fundamentalists, however, need to listen to the demythologizers. The extreme right needs to listen to the extreme left. The Bible needs to be radically rethought in terms of Christ and the best knowledge we have. Whatever in the Bible can be shaken by legitimate science is of earthly knowledge. The heart of the Christian faith, God in Christ as holy love, cannot be shaken.

Those on the extreme left, contrariwise, ought to recapture the vision of the evangelical faith. My book *Faith and Reason* shows that the structure of the classical Christian faith alone can satisfy the fullest and most stringent demands for knowledge.

If the extremes come together in Christ, we shall keep the heart of both the fundamentalist and the demythologizing drives: the drive for a full, saving faith and the drive for integrity of knowledge within faith.

Similarly, the neo-Calvinists ought to learn from the liberals, even though the liberals revolted originally against them. Any neo-Calvinist movement that has not passed through the liberal concern for knowledge and for social responsibility finds itself in a brittle position. It is an isolationist position that denies the Christian faith at its heart.

At the same time, the liberal position has lost the Christian heart, God's own unique presence in Christ as Savior. It has surrendered the claim for a special revelation that is obnoxious to man, who is dominantly sinful and in need of redemption. The sinner will not and cannot see the Christian revelation unless he repents and is born again. When he does so, his eyes are cleansed by faith.

Let the neo-Calvinist learn that the Christian faith, though distinctive, can and must be related to education and social responsibility, even though in an unexpected and revolutionary way. God's love comes also as light, albeit as the "subversive fulfillment" of the expectations of the natural man.

Let the liberal, too, return to the center of God's holy presence in Christ. When he does, he will find that his concern for the relevance of truth and for social responsibility is helped, not hindered, by Christ, the truth. He will have to reinterpret human nature as sinful in the stronger light of God's revelation in Christ, and the whole question of community and communication will be revolutionized.

Those who return to the center will not, I believe, quickly leave the castle. Christ is the answer, not the easy answer of repristination, but the creatively demanding answer of constantly discovering how rich and deep and satisfying is the universal love of God, issuing always in open and concerned community. Christ is the creative, revolutionary answer to man's need for life and truth.

Chapter 8

Contemporary Theology in the Light of One Hundred Years

CHRISTIAN theology deals with the eternal reality of God and the eternal relativity of man. The theologian confesses that in Christ the Eternal has come, but within the limitations of human time. Gustaf Wingren, the Swedish theologian, has written that theology moves between the poles of hermeneutics and anthropology: the steady truth of the Bible and the changing way men in history must necessarily interpret and apply its truth.[1]

Søren Kierkegaard calls the attempt to look forward in the light of the past "repetition." It is, he says, repeating the past forward.

Hope [he writes] is a new garment, starched and stiff and glittering, but it has never yet been worn, and hence one does not know whether it will fit or how it may become one. Memory is an old garment, and quite useless, however beautiful, for it has been outgrown. But repetition is an imperishable garment, fitting intimately and tenderly. . . . Hope is a beautiful maiden who slips through your fingers; memory is a handsome old dowager, never quite serving the purpose of the moment; repetition is a beloved wife, of whom one never tires.[2]

In this spirit of repetition we have chosen to look at the present in the light of the past for the sake of the future. Mere memory is death in the past; the future, too, tempts us to escape from reality. Full health and vigor is evidenced by learning from the past in the present in order the better to live in the future.

I

The last hundred years of theological thinking inherited two main lines of theological pursuit: classical Christianity and anti-

[1] *Theology in Conflict* (Muhlenberg Press, 1958).
[2] *Philosophical Fragments*, Introduction, p. xxi. I cite the passage from this book rather than from *Repetition* because of David Swenson's beauty of translation.

supernaturalism. In some real sense the two streams may be called respectively the theology of authority and the theology of autonomy. The two rivers, however, are far from being fully visible and distinct. There are places where the main beds lie fairly open to clear view, but often they are all but hidden. Especially difficult is the task of determining exactly from what stream certain underground branches come and whether in the lower reaches between them at times the waters do not in fact flow together.

Classical Christianity affirms a living God who ultimately is creator, controller, and completer of human history as well as of the conditions necessary for it. Its God is supernatural. He sent his only Son in the fulness of time to die for the world's sin and to give eternal life by his conquest of death through the resurrection of his Son from the dead. Man is a fallen creature who can find salvation and eternal life, now and after death, only by believing in Christ and by appropriating his work on man's behalf. Faith in such a God rests either in the authority of the Church, a supernatural institution, or in the authority of the Bible, the deposit of a supernatural revelation. New England Calvinism lived within the assumed authority of the biblical revelation. A hundred years ago classical Christianity was in a larger measure precritical in the sense of not having faced modern man's problems: the natural sciences, the historical consciousness, and the social sciences. For most churches, classical Christianity was also their naturally assumed faith.

The antisupernatural stream, at least in the Hebrew-Christian understanding of "supernatural," may be thought of as making a new methodological beginning with Descartes.[3] Actually it runs back through Scotus Erigena to Plotinus, and before them who knows how long and far back into historic thought. Part of this river is pantheistic, part of it agnostic, and part of it merely thisworldly. The stream goes back in a special way to Descartes, however, because of his sharp break with external authority as the road to truth and because of his substituting for it a subjective method and standard. Spinoza's "God or nature" was a natural step from there, as was British empiricism. Hume then carried out the logic of both the mood and the method when he attacked the

[3] Actually, Descartes made God central ontologically, as in his use of the ontological argument, and operationally, as in God's mediation between thought and substance. Both the operation and man's certainty of the world depended on God. But methodologically Alfred North Whitehead is justified in attributing to Descartes the basic origin in the Western world of "the subjectivistic bias," and William Temple has reason for calling his method "the Cartesian *faux pas*."

teleological and the cosmological proofs for God and showed that from within a world of finite causes, considered as effect, we cannot arrive at an infinite cause, but only at a finite cause that is subject to continual regression. Furthermore, this finite cause cannot, from the facts of experience, be shown to be wise and good. Kant thereafter claimed to kill reason to make room for faith, but his major achievement was actually to undermine all intellectual faith in the transcendent, as he called the supernatural, and to reduce religious knowledge to a dependence upon a this-worldly morality. The religious thinker then faced the dilemma: if knowledge is univocal we do not go beyond this world; if it is equivocal, we can know nothing beyond this world. The ontological argument (Kant showed) is merely verbal or definitional and without all power of proof unless the equation of thought and being is presupposed.

As a result, positivisms began to flourish with theological agnosticism as a natural accompaniment. We need recall only such thinkers as Comte, Mill, and Spencer in the fields of general knowledge. Of far more influence, however, were foundational leaders of learning like Darwin, Marx, and Freud. Darwin was himself both an expression and a formulator of the evolutionary theory that had already become, generally and mysteriously, a wave of thought, sometimes rather carefully expressed, as in Chambers and Spencer. Explanation from below became current in biological, sociological, political, and psychological thought.

Evolutionary ideas fitted best theologically, of course, with divine immanence and with belief in religious progress. Hegel, Schleiermacher, and Feuerbach, with their several kinds of pantheism, were part of the stream and added to its dimensions. The growing power of physical science, without need of the hypothesis of God, as Laplace pointed out, the new interest in history and the development of stringent historical methods, plus the birth of the psychological and the social sciences, combined to focus man's attention on this world. Overwhelmingly, the nontheological intellectual leadership veered sharply away from all suggestions of supernaturalism as an active alternative for man's understanding of himself and of his world.

II

Into such a world theological liberalism was born. This movement was an attempt to conserve the distinctive truth of the Christian Gospel in the light of man's catapulting knowledge and of his growing absorption with the problems of this world. Liberalism was an attempt at an honest and effective synthesis of classical Christianity and modern knowledge. Classical Christianity, in ecclesiastical or biblical terms, became increasingly isolated and defensive. Incidentally, out of this situation and mood fundamentalism was born as a biblical authoritarian reaction to liberalism. Liberalism was the attempt to give Christian content to the stream of man's general nonauthoritative knowledge and to do so by means of a nonauthoritative method based on reason, experience, and history. Liberalism sought the reality, or at least the values, of the Christian faith, but wanted these established by, and related to, man's general knowledge.

Liberalism is a complex response to God and the world and cannot be defined in any simple terms. The Unitarians revolted against Calvinism's harsh view of God and its low view of man. The more conservative William Ellery Channing was almost classically Christian, revolting mainly against tritheism and a docetic, mythologized Christology, whereas the more radical Theodore Parker carried the liberal method and message to a fuller conclusion. John Murray could not square the teaching of a God of sovereign love with eternal hell, and he carried his faith in the sovereign God of love to its reasonable conclusion by proclaiming love's ultimate victory over man even beyond death, thus breaking with an external biblicism. Albrecht Ritschl and his followers threw away metaphysics, anchoring theology in the historical Christ and in the Christ of faith, discoverable by man's judgments of value. Others like Walter Rauschenbusch and Washington Gladden applied to man's social conditions the promises of the Gospel, but by means of a method of reason and experience that had been enlightened and touched by the compassion of Christ. American theologians like William Newton Clark and William Adams Brown, and British theologians like John Baillie, William Temple, and Herbert Farmer took various streams of Christian tradition and general thinking and wove noble tapestries of Christian syntheses.

Of particular importance for their present perseverance as perhaps the strongest existing liberal group are the personalists who, generally speaking, combine German idealism with Christian perspectives. Borden Parker Bowne, owing much to Rudolf Lotze, was a towering liberal figure and his book, *The Immanence of God*, was once required reading in many theological seminaries. Followed by the Kantian, Albert Knudson, and the Hegelian, Edgar S. Brightman, Bowne still lives in highly competent advocates of personalistic liberalism.

A careful study of liberalism's method and standard of authority will reveal how deeply it became enmeshed in general theories of knowledge. Such a study can compare on this point James Martineau's *The Seat of Authority in Religion* with Auguste Sabatier's *Religions of Authority* and with John Oman's *The Vision of Authority*. Even P. T. Forsyth's *The Principle of Authority* shows the persistent power of the liberal synthesis, the combination of Christian content with various degrees of dependence on the methods and attitudes of man's general knowledge.[4]

No one who is sensitive to man's despair in the face of the evils and the brevity of life can fail to honor the liberal thinkers for their concerned faith and work in trying to keep the Christian Gospel and man's best knowledge together. Nor can liberalism be dismissed as a unit of faith or of thought. Sometimes the synthesis was mostly Christian including only from man's general knowledge some sensitive adjustments as to the age of the earth or the patent nonscientific character of the Bible. Sometimes the method of general knowledge carried the liberal thinkers way out into the stream of humanistic optimism. Accommodationism went far enough at times to place man's hope in science, education, or ameliorative legislation. It cannot be said that liberalism was merely a way from man to God, from reason to revelation, from general experience to religious experience, but it can be said with weight that the fact that liberalism sought to justify and secure faith's claims by means of the methods of general knowledge tended to drag it continually by a heavy burden toward the human side of the God-man relation.

Christian content, however, can be adequately accounted for and made available by no lesser means than a thoroughly Christian method. For the Christian faith to be self-consistently strong in thought and motivation it needs as central both a Christian method and a Christian content. As it was, the Christian faith was often advocated for its social effectiveness. Liberal Christian apologetics, in fact, usually assumed as right and determinative the general standards of human thought and hope. Thus an inner dry rot set in, to the point where, when the cold winds of despair and disillusion followed our two irrational conflagrations of this century, liberalism itself generally collapsed. The inner inconsistency of liberalism could not be detected so long as it was itself carried along on man's human confidence and general cultural achievement. With the collapse of cultural optimism the liberal synthesis

---

[4] A fascinating discussion of this question is found in Robert Clyde Johnson, *Authority in Protestant Theology* (Westminster Press, 1959), chap. iii.

between Christian reality or values and general methods of knowledge was shattered. Its inner inconsistency was laid bare. Its repudiation was merely a matter of time.

III

The smash was sudden and dramatic. Karl Barth, a young Swiss preacher, resurrected "the terrible Dane" in the second edition of his *Epistle to the Romans*. The risen Kierkegaard pounced upon the liberal inconsistency between message and method, and pulverized liberal theology with his grinding fury. Once again classical Christian authority was majestically enunciated. The Christian faith is not the word of man but the word of God. Its method is not from man to God. Its mood is not the high hopes of human dignity and achievement, but human despair in the woes of utter crisis.

The synthesis between Christian reality or values and man's general knowledge was riven lengthwise and crosswise. Armed with Kierkegaard's dictum that there is an infinite, qualitative distinction between time and eternity, Barth demolished every base in human knowledge, experience, history, or conscience. At no point, not even in the historic Jesus, could there be sure knowledge of God or sure hope of salvation. Knowledge demolishes Jesus Christ; from history we learn nothing; there is nothing of God in nature, history, or man. Christian preaching centers in the Bible as God's living speech to man, particularly in the Christ who condemns and does to death completely the old man before he accepts man by sheer grace and faith. Nothing in humanity or history, which at best is proximate, can ever one whit secure or add to the absolute revelation in Christ. God himself is his own method and message.

Nearly one hundred years before, Kierkegaard had spotted the inconsistency between content and method in liberalism and had driven home with terrible vehemence many of the truths which now underline linguistic analysis (verification philosophy) and existentialism. Forsyth felt the problem and saw it in part, but he never could cut loose completely from his liberal involvements. Barth has changed in many respects and at many times both in method and in content, but on the main point of keeping Christian content and method together he has never wavered. Neither has Emil Brunner, who has given more room to man and creation in his theology. Other theologians of first rank, like Gustaf Aulén and Anders Nygren, have maintained an equal consistency at this point.

The problem of all of them, however, is the problem of arbitrariness of standard and the need for full relevance of their theology to our actual world. The Swedish theologians just named have stated specifically that our time is one for diastasis and not for synthesis, but it is also obvious that they are increasingly aware of the missing dimension in their thought. Brunner has made several attempts at a relevant outreach, particularly in *Christianity and Civilization*, his Gifford Lectures dealing with natural theology. He has not violated, however, his basic unity of method and content, but neither has he obtained the desired contextual control or relevance for relating the Gospel. Barth also repents of his complete absorption in *Diastase* rather than *Analogie*, as he puts it in *Die Menschlichkeit Gottes*, but neither has he solved his problem.

We are left with the situation that the smashing of the liberal synthesis was needed, that the reunion of method and content within an existential, Christocentric, biblical theology was good as far as it went, but that the need which liberalism tried to meet, namely to relate effectively man's general knowledge to Christian realities and values, has not been met at all by the theologians of sharp transcendence. The breaking of the liberal synthesis by means of external authority, with whatever room for existential response, met a powerful need and found an overwhelming theological response. But the theology of transcendence was no full answer to our theological problem.

IV

The liberal synthesis was shattered with equal vigor from the opposite direction. The return to the authority of the transcendent on the right was accompanied by a return to autonomy on the left. This autonomy was not, to be sure, that of humanism, epistemologically or ontologically, but rather that of antisupernaturalism. It was even called theonomy. Supernatural revelation based on external attestation, however, was definitely rejected. The autonomy was, in fact, an unashamed revival of the stream of immanence based on man's best knowledge and analysis of the world he actually knows. Classical Christian supernaturalism was dismissed as primitive superstition which had long since ceased to be a live option for educated man. A God before and beyond the world was dismissed both as extraneous to it (supranaturalism) and as a being beside other beings, merely one of many and therefore finite. A personal God was accused of being localized and limited.

Since there was, thus, no being or realm beyond our world of knowledge, all talk of creation, providence, incarnation, atonement and resurrection, whether of Jesus or of life after death in general, became futile in every literal or direct sense of reliable intention. Consequently, they became myths or symbols. These were held to be part of the objective superstructure of the precritical world within which the Gospel was manifested, not the original reality and power of the Gospel. The kerygma itself was the power of reality, called God, to resist nonbeing and to make for harmony of being; or the kerygma was the faith that through the passive acceptance of the Kingdom of God men could be set free from the anxiety of life.

The man in Christ, especially Bultmann's man in Christ, became the one who shared with Christ in his own repeatable experience the power of the Cross and the resurrection, namely, to die to self and to rise into the freedom of the resurrection power. The past contained in the present was understood to be open to the decisive victory of God for an open future. The Gospel rightly interpreted ensured no fancied life beyond death by some wished-for personal God beyond this world, but was the actual power of God, of the very ground of being or of the stream of reality, now to set men free in this life from the powers of sin, law, and death. Supernaturalism, in short, according to this view, belonged to a precritical world. Its rejection did not forfeit the true Gospel, but became a help to the true and full proclamation of the kerygma.

The men who shattered liberalism from the left were Paul Tillich and Rudolf Bultmann. They were less prophetic, to be sure, than Barth in his dramatic smashing of the liberal synthesis, but they were equally convinced, competent scholars, and persistent prophets in their mounting attack on liberalism. They started out with Barth in his revolt against liberalism, and have continued their sharp antiliberal attack. They also reject, of course, the content as well as the method of the new biblical authoritarianism, except as they present its truths in terms of symbols. In this realm of myths and symbols there is strong common ground, most of which is aggressively antiliberal. That is the reason why this school of autonomy is often mistaken for its opposite, so-called neo-orthodoxy.

Tillich rejects supernaturalism on both philosophic and scientific grounds. His ontology precludes taking literally the framework of classical Christianity.[5] Nor can he get there by means of the

---

[5] In my home, before a gathering of philosophers, Tillich recently characterized his thought by the following interesting analysis: "My spiritual father is Schleiermacher; my intellectual father is Schelling; my grandfather on both sides is Boehme."

existential aspect of his method. He rejects liberalism for the mixture of method and content that it actually is.

Bultmann also rejects supernaturalism as unscientific. While rejecting all philosophy or *Weltanschauung* as the importation of Stoicism, he nevertheless assumes as generally consistent with the New Testament teaching the existentialist analysis of Martin Heidegger. From these two bases, science and Heidegger's philosophy, Bultmann throws out both supernaturalism and liberalism. Barth's star is beginning to wane perceptibly while the star of Tillich's and Bultmann's antisupernaturalism has been rising rapidly, until now a cloud suddenly seems to be sweeping over that star as well.

This cloud has been created by the confusion concerning the relation between myth or symbol and reality, in the position of autonomy. The supernatural nature of the Christian faith is, in fact, indelible. It is intrinsic and cannot be shed. It centers in the personal God, the personal Spirit who is agape, who came in the fullness of time in Jesus Christ and who, in being and beauty, transcends eternally every created order. For a time, Tillich and Bultmann were interpreted as merely modernizing the faith in terms of the demythologizing of outworn world-views. Then many began to question the relation between myth, symbol, and reality in their systems. Finally, it is becoming more and more obvious that *ontologically* the whole Christian interpretation and offer of salvation are not only radically altered and shrunk, but in fact surrendered.

As Barth has done the Christian cause great service, however, by pressing the claim for message and method to go together, even so Tillich and Bultmann have put Christian thinkers deeply in their debt by rejecting the inner inconsistency of liberalism. They have also rendered a service by decrying the arbitrariness and irrelevance of Barth's biblical authority inasmuch as this is informed by total transcendence and worked out in terms of the sheer ontological discontinuity of God and man, without some mediating category for the purpose and semi-independence of creation.

V

Where, then, shall we go in theology? The two main streams now are Barthian transcendence, which lacks adequate incorporation of the order of creation, offering unity of content and approach, but at the same time being guilty of arbitrariness and irrelevance; and antisupernaturalism, which, for modernity, scuttles classical Christianity in its own essential dimensions as the full

Gospel of salvation in and beyond this life. Two minor movements persist as well. Fundamentalism is the modern, partly defensive and partly aggressive response of precritical, classical Christianity. It creates a permanent gulf between the believer and the thinker, and offers no real way out. Its adherents now respond ambivalently between a bitter attack on nonfundamentalists and a new openness to the problems posed for educated man. The other minor theological movement of our time is the continuation of the liberal movement; but besides being out of fashion (which is no criterion of truth!), liberalism suffers from internal bleeding and from weakening due to inconsistency between its content of faith and its method.

This summary is obviously no place wherein to launch a new theological movement! It can be said, however, that whatever the new approach may be, if it is to stand the tests of time and truth, it must center in the Incarnation. Incarnation is neither a movement of transcendence nor a school of immanence. In Christ, the Event-meaning who is agape, we find the God of the Bible, the personal Spirit who is the faithful creator, ruler, and savior of the world. With utmost care I have tried to show in *Christ and the Christian* how Incarnation when interpreted in Scriptural terms becomes the key to both knowledge and life. He who cannot be contained nor explained by this world, but who best fulfills and illumines the meaning of life, mysteriously and imeasurably transcends the world we know; while as the central meaning of life and existence he is also least arbitrary and most relevant. He who once came to us in the fullness of time comes to us now not primarily as explanation but as salvation. Indeed he explains only as he saves. Not description but prescripition is the way to the knowledge of God and of man, of history and of nature.

Those who advocate transcendence are right in that God is God and not man. We need to pull out all the stops for this theme. Nevertheless, God has become man in order to become relevant for us. The truth we see is for experience. It is existential, calling for decision beyond explanation. Therefore, those who refuse as revelatory the arbitrary and the irrelevant are also right in their concern. Those liberals who sought for a meaningful relation of the Gospel to the world of experience were surely right in their deepest commitment as far as it went, but truth was permitted to degenerate into meanings continuous with the world we know.

The advocates of transcendence knew that the Gospel could not thus be scaled down to man's scope, therefore they denounced and renounced meaning for the sake of God's revelation through events and encounter. In this they were mainly right. Christ is God's own incoming, the mighty Christ-deed of God. He never can be reduced to meaning, but nevertheless from him all full meaning stems. This life is also the light of men. The Christ who is best communicated in the Bible by the verbs of God's activity, by story and event, also gives rise to the biblically needed propositional truth: "God is love."

Without in any way trying to develop or even suggest how the Incarnation of God as agape answers the internal requirements of the Christian faith and also the demands made upon it externally by man's best thinking, and without relating this central fact to other channels which help authenticate, secondarily and confirmingly, the supreme authority of the Christian faith—the Bible, the Church, and Christian experience—we end this analysis by the confession that beyond the historic problems of the theology of the last one hundred years lies the eternal truth of the Christian Gospel: "God was in Christ reconciling the world unto himself."

Chapter 9

The Rise and Role of Neo-Orthodoxy

IN THE previous chapter we considered briefly the theology of transcendence. We stated there that it arose as a pent-up reaction against liberalism. In general, this theology of transcendence grew in America into a school called neo-orthodoxy. This confessional stance started almost as a rumor within the first decade of Karl Barth's climactic switch from liberalism to Kierkegaardian theology. A few Americans—Edwin Lewis and Douglas Horton, for instance —wrote articles about, or translated the writing of, the theological powerhouse of Basel. A few alert spirits of every category of theological readers set their sails toward Switzerland. Some literally made the voyage there to thrill to the thunder of Barth's theological orations. Others hoisted both mainsails and jibs to catch from afar the mighty wind of his prophetic denunciations. A few turned their skiffs into the gusts. Still others scudded complacently with the breeze. But the majority tacked back and forth.

The one source of the new wind of doctrine soon turned into several. As a whole, these followed the main direction. Some, however, did branch off on definite tangents. Emil Brunner, who started with Barth, and whose writings were soaked in antiliberalism, began to take exception to Barth's complete denial of God's presence in man's history and nature. Brunner believed that man has at least a point of contact in his answerability to God. The content of the image of God may be universally lost, but not its form. Following that break, Brunner carried on a rich conversation with Barth. While maintaining the same general direction, he more and more tried to find relevance for the Gospel on the level of creation. He enriched contemporary theology incalculably. Others like Gustaf Aulén and Anders Nygren shared Barth's rejection of liberalism, refusing on the whole all precritical metaphysics, but making at least formal use of philosophy to establish the categorical legitimacy of the Christian faith. In America, the Niebuhr brothers at Union Theological Seminary and Yale Divinity School caught part of the drive, which justifies placing them within the neo-orthodox approach in its widest sense. Because of his particular relevance to the American scene, I shall devote one short section of this analysis to Reinhold Niebuhr. Most of my treatment, however, must concern an elaboration of the positions of Kierkegaard and Barth, for they are the prime movers of the movement, and a fuller appraisal of this theological position than I have given before.

I

Søren Kierkegaard abominated Hegel's intellectualistic evolutionary panlogicism that in fact centered in human history and culture. For reason, therefore, he substituted the absurd; evolution of ideas he replaced with decisions for eternal destiny. Born long before his time, Kierkegaard became the precursor and effective founder of the contemporary neo-orthodox movement.

Kierkegaard lived in Denmark, just over one hundred years ago. In fact, the centennial of his death was observed in 1955. Writers on Kierkegaard often attribute great importance to his strange bachelor life. He was the son of a moody, melancholy Dane who, with vivid imagination, took him for fascinating imaginary walks right in his own living room. The father's belief that he had committed the unpardonable sin weighed down the young Søren. Speculation also keeps soaring on the relation between the attractive and lovely girl, Regina Olsen, whom he jilted during their engagement in spite of his own seemingly undying love for her, and the writings which appear to be strongly shaped by this tragic experience. There are innumerable angles to his strange life which affect his literary production, especially his bitter relation to the established Church. For our purposes, however, it is enough to say that the main meaning of his theological thinking is in no way dependent upon the conditions and the circumstances of its discovery.

To Hegel's conviction that modernity must go beyond Christianity, Kierkegaard countered that to become a Christian was man's hardest and his lifelong task. Instead of the highest objectivity being the way to truth, Søren Kierkegaard held passionate concern for one's own eternal salvation to be the door. Faith is incapable of becoming knowledge; faith is risk, choice; it is precisely *not* seeing. Truth is subjectivity. Instead of the need to eliminate feelings for clear seeing, as in Hegel's system, truth comes through suffering. Man is real in proportion to his suffering. Only participation and involvement in such self-knowledge as comes from one's irreversible and irrevocable decision in time for eternity can make a man religiously real. Faith is inwardness. In one's own present tense of life lies buried all one's past, but accessible to change. The present movement contains all of life. To arrive at purity of life one must "repeat the past forward," beyond both memory and hope. As we have written, hope is a beautiful maiden beyond reach; memory is a useless old dowager; repetition is a lovely wife of whom one never tires.

God, for Kierkegaard, was in no way continuous with this life. For him there was rather an infinite qualitative distinction between time and eternity. Kierkegaard's was an uncompromising supernaturalism, as radically different from this world generally as Buddhism's nirvana. Only at one point had the supernatural broken through—in God's becoming man for our sake in Jesus Christ. But this Incarnation was no general truth to give us speculative ideas about God or to illumine our world of experience. Christ was no Socratic occasion who revealed a universal truth, equally valid apart from its bringer. Christ was, rather, a Christian moment wherein the message and the messenger were indistinguishable. Christ's becoming man, instead of being man's great joy, best hope and longest light, was offensive, absurd, and to be dreaded.

There are universals of science and philosophy, but none in religion. A theological system is impossible and indeed comic; it is pretentious to the point of blasphemy. Nor can anything add to or help prove God's own incoming. God is absolute. Christ is absolute. Not the Lord Jesus of human reason, but the hidden Christ, the absolute open only to contemporary faith, became the basis of Christianity. Nothing in history, nothing in man, nothing in social effectiveness, nothing in man's reason, as for instance metaphysics, and nothing in man's experience, even ethics, can help one whit to establish the fact, reality, or value of the Incarnation. All are proximate; and proximate testimony can never establish or add to absolute truth. As a matter of fact, reflection helps thin out and weaken faith. Faith lives on paradox, on the absurd, in the realm of maximum spiritual passion.

Nor is there any help in community. Religion is a matter of the individual. The crowd is untruth. As Kierkegaard points out, no soldier by himself spits in Jesus' face. The individual stands directly responsible before God who demands all. Not even ethical rules, directives, or analyses are of any avail when one stands before God. Religion has *no* universals, not even for conduct. There must instead be a suspension of teleological ethics. In the light of ethical rules, Abraham would be a murderer in intent of his own son, Isaac. Obeying God, he becomes instead the father of faith. Sin consequently is no matter of human wrong doing, subject to psychological understanding or social assessment. It is not a matter of quantitative more or less. It is qualitatively distinct from ethics, a standing before the absolute God *in guilt*. Guilt is the characteristic relation of man to God. The Christian must surrender all. He must become a "knight of infinite resignation"; but even the pagan can follow him in so doing. Beyond this surrender, the Christian must become a "knight of faith" who unwaveringly expects the right answer from God.

Kierkegaard's writings are divided into indirect, pseudonymous material and direct works written under his own signature. He believed that men must be surprised, "wounded from behind," by the judgment and Gospel of God, since otherwise all men's barriers will already be up against them. His religious writings, however, are open, devotional, inviting the clear understanding of the glad news of the Christian Gospel. Through some of these, like *Christian Discourses* and *Purity of Heart*, radiates the reality as well as the sound exposition of the God of love.

In one way, Kierkegaard makes the initial, basic break with the scientific and philosophic mentality based on man's reason and general experience from within this world. He is through and through a radical supernaturalist—here David Swenson is right—in his presuppositions and analysis of Christianity. His method centers in the existential acceptance of the Christ who is absurd to our ordinary standards of truth and conduct. He thus lifted the method of the Christian theologian to supernatural revelation, revealing God's stark transcendence and man's sin in the light of Christ. Unfortunately, he failed to find as integral to the faith the apostolic doctrine of the Church and God's secondary presence and revelation within the realms of nature and history. Thus he gave to neo-orthodoxy, from the beginning, both its strength and its weakness.

II

Barth it was, however, who founded the modern movement called neo-orthodoxy. To be sure, Barth himself disowns the word. He will have none of it. To a Continental European, a neo-orthodox is a stuffy Lutheran theologian of years gone by, primarily associated with Erlangen, who tried to revive the Lutheran orthodoxy of classical times. Between these and Barth there is a chasm. Besides, Barth can no longer be called Barthian, as we shall see. He is far too great a man for that. And yet, for impetus and leading, neo-orthodoxy goes back to Barth, and Barth still holds on to its main characteristics, in actual fact if not in profession.

Barth, born 1886, started as a Ritschlian liberal, greatly influenced by the great Wilhelm Herrmann. As a precritical theologian he was at first concerned with moral categories and their realization through the power of religion. No eschatology for him. His task was to overcome the relative and the historical. Redemption is for creation and works its power in history. Barth knows liberalism, for he was a liberal.

But he broke radically with liberalism. In 1919, in the first edition of *The Epistle to the Romans,* he was still a liberal. By the publication of the famous second edition in 1921, he had made one of history's most drastic and dramatic turnabouts. He himself designates as life-shaking his face-to-face encounter in 1920 with his great teacher, Adolf Harnack, who challenged him to say something also on the theme of the humanity of God. His answer was a shouting, tumultuous, triumphant "No!"[1] Right then was born Barth's hypercritical theology of crisis. With fairness, Paul Althaus has called it the theology of the unknown God. Barth was then no theologian constructing a system. He was the prophetic preacher hurling Kierkegaard thunderbolts at lightning-struck church people. He gave voice to the bitter despair of human beings, disemboweled of all hope after world catastrophe. He cried the wind of suffering humanity, nauseated by liberal, this-worldly optimism.

Back to the Bible meant for him back to man's sickness unto death, his need to cry utter woe in the absolute crisis before God. Man is a mess and a mass of sinfulness. He cannot in any way know God. Not through reason, not through experience, not through good works, not through mystic immediacy, not through theology, not through history, not even through the historical Jesus. There is no God to be known in nature, in man, in conscience. Kierkegaard's infinite qualitative distinction between man and God gapes with abysmal depths. Its priority of assertion is unviolated. The dualism betwen time and eternity is in effect made into a philosophic structure, complete, unmitigated, unbridgeable. God has made himself known in one place, and in one place only—in the revelation in Christ, and that not in history but tangent to it. God never enters history; he only touches it to

[1] By the way, once Edgar S. Brightman was challenged by Vida Scudder to distinguish the positions of Barth and Brunner in two words. His reply was, "Brunner—yes; Barth—no!"

bring judgment upon it and salvation out of it, in particular by the death and resurrection of Jesus Christ. History is no place for redemption; history is no predicate of revelation at all in any sense of means. History is judged by God. Over against it stands eternity.

The Christian faith is through and through eschatological. Barth scorns liberalism's weak appendix on eschatology. No Christian social ethics, no Christian education are valid; there is only soul tension under the impossible weight of eternity. But even the experience of utter crisis before God gives no knowledge of God and no assurance of salvation. Nor does man's recognition of his own worthlessness or his acceptance of God's promises ensure salvation. God's election, and God's election alone, counts; and no one ever knows whether he is elected to salvation or to damnation.

This hypercritical period underlies neo-orthodoxy and what is characteristically meant by "Barthian." Barth himself changed. He is no longer, as he himself asserts, either neo-orthodox or Barthian in the fullest sense. In 1925, he became a professor; and prophetic denunciation, whatever be true of the pulpit, does not wear well in the classroom. Then in 1927, Barth published his *Christian Dogmatics*, later to become *Church Dogmatics*, and dogmatics requires at least a minimum of positive construction. Besides, he himself, as early as this, saw that his radical dualism was due not to biblical thought but to Kantian analysis. Therefore a new, more constructive, less tense period started in Barth's theology that may best be called the Theology of the Word. He took another long step forward when in 1931 he stated in his book on Anselm, *Fides Quaerens Intellectum*, that even a Christian philosophy is possible provided it has its focus on Christ and is carried on by eyes of faith.

On the side of the social application of the Gospel, Barth's fight with Hitler and his exile from his post at Bonn, Germany, begged no support by theological construction. Social ethics never! Only faith acting out the resurrection! But later, in *Christengemeinde and Bürgergemeinde*, he saw God's work in the social order as a dim or suggestive analogy of his work in the Church. Thus he stepped forward once again toward a more complete theology. Then in the forties, with the publication of the first part of the third volume of *Church Dogmatics*, Barth definitely broke away from the blasphemous double predestination which attributes to God what is life's worst conceivable act, and proclaimed instead, with the power of Christian vision and concern, the only final outcome that is consistent with the sovereign God of love who has elected all unconditionally and irresistibly in Jesus Christ. Man's freedom was not now lost in Barth's theology; man never had any. But salvaged at least in his theology was the majestic character and freedom of God, the God of the Cross, the God of universal love.

More changes were to follow, the greatest of which can now be seen only as beginning. In 1956, Barth wrote his startling booklet, *The Humanity of God*, in which he repudiates the extreme one-sidedness of his theology of crisis. It was called forth by the needs of the times, he admits, and it ministered to those needs. But Barth saw then only half the moon. He sings a new song lately: "Now is the time for the fuller Gospel!" One expects the fifth volume of *Church Dogmatics* to supply the lack in his theology of God's presence and work in nature and man. In any case, this volume will be yeast thrown into baked loaves. His preliminary sketch of the lack and the task, in *Die Menschlichkeit Gottes*, gives no serious indication at all that Barth has seen the organic, pedagogical work of God indirectly through his purposed passivity, or his general working, in nature and history.

Be that as it may, it was Barth who thrust Kierkegaard athwart the sickening optimism of liberal cultural progressivism[2] and almost singlehanded threw the stream of Christian thought into a new channel of Christ-centered method, mood, and content. All hail the name of Barth for reinstating the unity of Christian method and content. All hail the name of Barth for his world-shaking vigor. Whatever fate his great system (more than two million words when finished) may meet, Barth himself will surely be placed among the great prophets of God and among the forefront of Christian leaders in history.

III

Reinhold Niebuhr is usually classed as neo-orthodox. As a matter of fact, most Americans make the two terms synonymous. But he has spewed the term out of his own mouth. There is also a considerable question as to the nature and measure of transcendence in his thought. Some class him with Barth in the school of classical Christian supernaturalism. Others place him within the existentialist-neo-naturalist stream. He owes much of his inspiration to Kierkegaard. He definitely has become an antiliberal in the dominant stress of his confession. But when all is said, Niebuhr is hard

[2] A critic claims that here I am being unfair to liberalism as a whole, but I am now mentioning only its weaknesses.

to group because he has related himself positively to both the Barth-Brunner axis and the Tillich-Bultmann focus. My own judgment is that he has learned immensely from Tillich, but even more from Kierkegaard. Ontologically, he stands nearer in feel to Tillich than to Barth, but he has learned most from Kierkegaard with respect to the latter's mood and method of analyzing experience. The fundamental question with regard to Niebuhr, however, is not his metaphysics or his method, for he has never worked out, to my knowledge, a definite position, in structure and detail, in either field. Niebuhr is the social prophet. He is the great spirit who inspires others. He is the exciting lecturer and teacher who fires others to imitate him or to try to hold his position. It is in the combination of theology and Christian social ethics that his influence has counted the most. His hold on his followers is usually personal beyond his own sort of general identification with the prevailing winds of doctrines. Niebuhr is no initiator of new analysis. He is the prophet, the applier, the popularizer, and the inspirer.

Niebuhr as a theological social reformer inherited the great Rauschenbusch mantle. In his first church in Detroit, Reinhold Niebuhr's whole being ached with compassion for the workers. He was captivated by the Marxian social analysis of the plight of society by the means for its redemption. Without forfeiting Walter Rauschenbusch's personal faith in, and concern for, individual salvation, Niebuhr's main interest became social-political reform. His first book, *Leaves From the Notebook of a Tamed Cynic*, vibrates with human compassion and cogent criticism of capitalist society and bourgeois church life. He was also caught by another prevailing wind among intellectuals: pacifism. He even became president of the Fellowship of Reconciliation. True to then current ideas among advanced thinkers he could advocate pacifism among nations while at least condoning violence as the workers' method of changing society. Niebuhr has always been sensitive to vanguard movements of shifting mood and thought and has therefore consistently identified himself with some intellectual frontier, generally adapting his thinking because of it in a living, amorphous way.

His method of applying his theology has usually been opportunistic. For this reason he cannot be systematically classified among theologians, for in fact he does not operate from theological analysis as a primary base. His theology has in large part resulted from borrowing, but it has become vibrantly a whole position. That is the reason why, when he writes, he takes his huge paintbrush and throws on masses of colorful ideas, which communicate for the most part neither analytically nor intellectualistically-synoptically but from the whole man in his concern to other men in their concerns. Theologically he has used myth and dialectic in a way that precludes nonparadoxical exposition of systematic theology. His main allegiance has been to biblical theology in general and to the whole history of Christian experience in its total impact on faith. Niebuhr, however, has always been sympathetic to all genuine attempts to understand the Christian faith and to communicate it, within the limits of human capacity and God's special grace.

The reason that I have placed him among the neo-orthodox is that his main stress has been on the sinfulness of man (even more than on the topic under which David Wesley Soper introduces him, "the insufficiency of man") and on the ambiguity of history. Not that Niebuhr is strongly concerned with any realm of transcendence fundamentally beyond history. His focus is on God's relation to man in history, *not* basically on God's action beyond man's sinfulness in human history.[3] With regard to the first, he has consistently stressed the persistence of sin even in the life of the redeemed. He has opposed the Wesleyan doctrine of sanctification as perfectionism. For him, this doctrine is basically self-deception and hypocrisy.

Similarly, he has opposed all hopes for basic historic progress as collective perfectionism and group sham. More than any man in America, and possibly in the world, Reinhold Niebuhr contributed to the collapse of pacifism in the churches and thus to the fact that the churches were generally behind the government when America entered the Second World War. He punctured the liberal positions of radical pacifism as personal perfectionism and of gradual improvement as utopianism. To be sure, he was one of the earliest thinkers in America to work with Nygren's distinction of agape and eros, but he limited the use of Christian love to personal and church relations. Politics was almost solely a matter of justice and a matter of the balance of power. Christian realism became identified with power politics.

Niebuhr's general disparagment of man, his preaching on the pretensions of reason, his main stress on biblical theology as a faith-judgment, his use of myth, paradox, and dialectic, swept out most liberal theology or cowed it almost completely. In spite of all the liberalism left in Niebuhr—and there is much, including his

[3] As a matter of fact, Niebuhr's position on what actually is beyond the world of experience, the scene of history and its analytical presuppositions, is ambiguous.

central view of Christ, all learned claims to the contrary notwithstanding—and in spite of his present definitely mellowing and more constructive estimates of man's possibilities and of God's grace in human life and history, Reinhold Niebuhr stands in the very forefront of neo-orthodox influence. More than any other contemporary American theologian, he must carry the responsibility, in my opinion, for having undermined Christian opposition to war.[4] Along with this, stand his decidedly positive contributions to religious and social thought and action. The man Niebuhr, however, is far greater than the mottled neo-orthodox theology of which he has long been made one of the world's chief spokesmen.

If neo-orthodoxy is to be summarized in a paragraph, the following aspects should be included: (1) It rejects the philosophic buttressing of the Christian faith. It repudiates Christian apologetics. (2) It dismisses revelation in rational terms, especially in propositional form. Instead, it speaks of revelation through events or encounter. (3) It declares the basic sinfulness of man. Man is fallen. He is both blinded by original sin and made impotent for unambiguous good. (4) It refuses to accept the improvability of human nature and of progress in human history. A high Christian confession of sanctification from its point of view is sheer moralism, perfectionism, and utopianism, the expression and report of human pride. (5) It usually connects in some way with one form or another of existentialism.

The emphasis or proportion may vary, but several of these aspects are always present in any theology that may properly be called neo-orthodox. Our own differentiation is that neo-orthodoxy started with Kierkegaard and Barth in the main line of classical Christianity, which assumed supernaturalism. Therefore, we have cleaved to this distinction, except for the fact that Reinhold Niebuhr, who will not fit completely into either category, is placed here because his main influence has gone into the furthering of a vague neo-orthodoxy where the lines of Christian superstructure

---

[4] The reason for my opinion that Niebuhr's influence in one respect has been negative is that he forfeited the power and perspective of the Christian Gospel in its bearing on social problems by baptizing secular social science into "Christian realism." We were left with worldly "power politics." Such an acclimatizing of the Gospel was welcome to an age of teachers and ministers who were becoming increasingly less sure of the truth-claim of the Christian Gospel and were equally anxious to be accepted by the sophisticated. But we are now perishing for lack of Christian analysis, impact, and power. We no longer dare hide the real issues. We need to return to the full perspective and power of the Christian faith in its radical judgment of the ways of the world, its call to repentence, and its guidance into a new creative age.

have been decidedly blurred, and most disciples have simply assumed that some form of classical Christianity, merely rethought in modern terms, was presupposed.

Can we now evaluate this movement, at its heart, in the light of a steadier and fuller Gospel? For the most part it is correct to say that we should accept the affirmations and deny the denials of this theological position. Certainly we must be thankful for its stress on the primacy of faith. *Objectively*, this means God-centeredness. It involves decisive emphasis on Christ; it includes placing the Bible once more in an authoritative position. Worship returns. God himself meets us in the sacraments. God is the Lord of history, of all humanity. Christ is the Lord of his Church. *Subjectively*, new emphasis is put on the whole man as believer. Faith is understood as decision before God. Once again, too, the power of sin is understood to darken counsel.

Freedom is conceived of as less intellectual and metaphysical and is understood instead as man's basic choice, either of God or of evil forces. The natural sinfulness of man is wrestled with both in the sinner and in the saint, both in the world and in the Church. Revelation is grasped as encounter. Instead of making meaning or propositional truth central to theological knowledge, reason is grasped as subject to the striving self, and God promulgates his revelation through people and events. The permanent, or at least the persistent, ambiguity of life, personal and social, becomes vividly comprehended. What has happened is actually that the split between method and content of the Christian faith has been healed (as we saw in Chapter 7) and the Christian faith speaks again with forthright unity and confidence.

What is dangerous, weakening, and even evil in the stress of the neo-orthodox position, on the other hand, is its failure to find God active on the level of creation. Revelation becomes arbitrary; and man's faith, capricious. It becomes mystery without assignable meaning. Reason, experience, and social effectiveness are not given their secondary place as vital signs and fruits of the Spirit. Therefore, the organic unity in God between redemption and creation is forfeited. Therefore, too, the Gospel loses its directing power for judgment, repentance, and growth in grace. The Christian faith is not allowed its proper place with Christ the light at the center of history. Neither is a proper context available for constructive theology or for communication with the world at large.

Besides, although actually and undeniably man is a sinner, at the heart of his being he is nevertheless from God by creation, under God by providence, and for God by destiny. Man is not primarily a sinner in the sight of God. He is a sinner who is basically a prodigal son. He belongs at home, if only he will come to himself, to his true self. Finally, neo-orthodoxy has taken the nerve out of social action by substituting man's place before God in the locus of justification for his place before God in moral and social responsibility. Man *is* saved by sheer grace. He is accepted out of God's pure love. He can never earn or force his salvation. But he can and ought to improve, to grow in grace; and history is improvable within limits.

Therefore, we are bid to be leaven. God reigns in a different way in the world from his rule in the Church, but he still reigns among all men in some sense and in some way. Consequently, our social task is to be faithful and to change things for the better within the limits of history's improvability. History can be neither heaven nor hell. It is neither all good nor all bad. It is made as the medium and the means of our growth through responsible choices, preparatorily before conversion and consummatingly afterwards. Our total lives count even in the realm of our responsible action and giving. And finally, all of history is God's medium for our total pedagogy here and beyond death.

Neo-orthodoxy has sold man short and has belittled his efforts under God to achieve a more than tolerable environment. We must therefore deny, carefully and with the right stress, the basic denials of neo-orthodoxy. God is constructively active on the level of creation as well as in the realm of redemption. What is needed is Christian theology with the best of the positive neo-orthodox stress, but with a more ample appreciation of God's general work on the level of creation. We need a postneo-orthodox theology.

Chapter 10

The Meaning and Power of
Neonaturalism and Existentialism

IN THE previous chapter we considered neo-orthodoxy. In an earlier chapter we called this school the theology of authority. In contrast to this school of transcendence on the right we then described in brief the theology of autonomy on the left. Our task now is to elaborate this position more fully, especially with regard to its two leading representatives, Rudolf Bultmann and Paul Tillich. The title of this chapter should be explained. Bultmann is an existentialist outright, but Tillich is one only halfway. Indeed, Tillich claims that the fundamental intellectual problem of our day is the proper synthesis of the existential and the rational approaches. He combines the existential judgment with the logos, or with the meaningfulness of experience as a whole. Because of these two aspects of Tillich's theology, I could not call this chapter simply existentialism. On the other hand, the positions of both of these men are so deeply interpenetrated with existentialist thinking that the term could not be left out of the title.

Then again, from the point of view of classical Christian transcendence, possibly now misnamed supernaturalism, Bultmann and Tillich both are complete naturalists. The transcendence they accept is never that of the personal God who is literally the creator, controller, and completer of the world. In the light of what naturalism has come to mean on the American scene, however—objectivistic scientism which rejects as unreal whatever cannot be dealt with by its own limited method—neither of these men is a naturalist. Both of them fervently disavow, however, the classical Christian transcendence as primitive superstructure—as almost superstition! The *objective* world-view of the disciples, out of which came the New Testament writings, was not, according to them, the heart and reality of the *original* faith. Both of them, therefore, reject a God beyond experience and beyond our world who is the prime originator of it, but especially they reject an actually living, personal God who, from beyond the world, acts in history and in the world. Bultmann and Tillich both explicitly reject such classical Christian transcendence as outmoded thinking for modern man.

I

Rudolf Bultmann is right now at the forefront as a theological thinker, or at least he is a front-thinker who is deeply challenging and influencing theological thought. He has spent most of his life lecturing at Marburg University in Germany. At the start, he was deeply influenced by Karl Barth, and has continued a dynamic, antiliberal thinker. But whereas Barth had espoused, heart and spirit, the transcendence of classical Christianity and carried it, along with Søren Kierkegaard, to its most radical extreme, Bultmann, while granting the right of Barth's antiliberal crusade, went in the opposite direction with equal Kierkegaardian passion and conviction. At his side was Paul Tillich who for a while was his colleague at Marburg. Emil Brunner, in *Eternal Hope*, has suggested that Bultmann turned from Barth's complete objectivism to entire subjectivism. No term, of course, cuts quite clean with regard to these men, but there is a real truth in Brunner's suggestion.

It seems almost as though Bultmann had said to himself: "All right! Barth's transcendence is both unprovable and irrelevant [by his own claim] as dependable knowledge for this world. Then why should we keep it? Why not be honest, real, and accept the modern world of science and critical thinking? After all, Jesus found his victory in this world. His peace and power we need. He was authentic. In him, whatever is real and right took place once for all. What we must do is to analyze both our experience and the New Testament message to find this original good news for our day." Bultmann continues to ponder aloud, "I shall let everything go that is not consistent with hard thinking and competent knowledge. Supernaturalism is dead for modern man. The modern world, too, in that sense, is post-Christian. Why not release the saving truth of Christianity by radically disassociating it from all outworn thinking?"

The fact that Bultmann dared thus to think and to begin his radical demythologizing of the Bible is surely a most significant event in the history of Christian thought, and I believe, since Christ is the truth, that it is of immense importance to world history. We owe an inestimable debt of gratitude as a whole to

Bultmann for what he dared to do. For me, Rudolf Bultmann represents our greatest hope and our biggest danger among modern Christian thinkers. Before I try to explain these superlatives, we should take a closer look at what Bultmann teaches.

There are many sides to Bultmann. No one pattern fits him. For one thing, he is a devout Lutheran churchman. Long ago, John Baillie distinguished between religion at the top of the head and at the bottom of the heart. Sometimes we are intellectually caught in positions where, to be honest, we cannot see how we can keep the faith in the same way that we once held it, and therefore we take over the position that by now has come to be the most honest and real for us. At the same time, deep down in our lives, we may dwell in a persistent affirmation of the God whom we still know on a far more profound level than mere intellectual understanding. For this reason we can affirm that whatever else Bultmann may be or say, he is a great Christian who can proclaim the essence of the New Testament message in sermons that stir the heart and move the will. Both he and Tillich are great preachers of the Word of God who communicate far more and far more profoundly than their actual, final analysis of reality.

Second, Bultmann is a keen, critical scholar of the Bible, and even of the history of historical criticism. He may not continue the most radical line of Bruno Bauer in his denial of the historical Jesus, in the ordinary sense of history, but his application of existential ontology to the historical Jesus, whereby Incarnation in terms of classical Christian transcendence is denied, is almost equally startling for those who can really take in what that signifies for Christian faith. In any case, Bultmann continues the vigorous critical line of Ferdinand Christian Baur. The sheer vigor and rigor of his immense scholarship should be gratefully acknowledged and taken into full account.

In the third place, Bultmann is, foremost, a disciple of Martin Heidegger, one of the greatest existentialist philosophers of Germany, who has structured modern philosophy by his existentialist interpretation of experience. Bultmann's devotion to Kierkegaard and his respect for modern science, plus his liberating stimulus from Barth, contributed to his collapse into Heidegger's existentialism.

Beyond his deeply pious Lutheranism and beyond his immense, technical, biblical scholarship, Bultmann is overwhelmingly, in any case, the man who has equated Heidegger's philosophy with New Testament theology. Basically, Bultmann cannot be understood as anything so much as the grateful captive of a nonmetaphysical philosophy that equated existentialism with man's only honest and authentic road to truth, which is in effect the knowledge of his own self. All attempts to claim that Bultmann has done away merely with an outworn cosmology, leaving the ontology of the Gospel undisturbed, are stuff and nonsense. Bultmann is no liberal who is bringing Christianity up-to-date by differentiating between outworn and indestructible elements of the Christian faith. He is the pioneer of the most radical possible retranslation and transvaluation of the faith itself into existentialist categories.

Rudolf Bultmann is an antiliberal, antisupernatural demythologizer of the Christian faith. For Bultmann, myth is "the use of imagery to express the other worldly in terms of this world and the divine in terms of human life, the other side in terms of this side."[1] By myth we understand, if I may interpret Bultmann, the conviction that the origin, meaning, control, and destiny of life and this world are from outside this world. He writes: "Myth is an expression of man's conviction that the origin and purpose of the world in which he lives are to be sought not within it but beyond it."[2] It is the conception that there is a realm of being which affects man from outside this world. Thus, any change in this world described by science as caused by a power or powers not of or beyond this world would be myth. Therefore, for example, God's sending his Son to the earth to die for man and to rise from the grave is the kind of primitive, superstitious myth that Bultmann resolutely rejects as intellectually unworthy and, indeed, impossible for honest and completely educated modern man. Equally mythical would be any account of answer to prayer by a God who hears from beyond this world and then "interferes" with this world order.

Myth, to be sure, shows that man is not master in his own house. He seeks for explanation and help from beyond this world. The real purpose of myth is therefore, according to Bultmann, to indicate transcendence. Man is not master, and he needs help. Such help is to be found, Bultmann holds, but not in terms of primitive superstition. God is real and Jesus is Lord, yes; but in different senses from classical Christianity. There is transcendence, or else man is lost, but the transcendence that is real cannot be had within the framework of the old, outworn, objectivistic superstructure of classical Christianity.

This is the heart of Bultmann's theological thrust. This basic rejection of classical objectivity and this radical acceptance of

[1] *Kerygma and Myth*, H. W. Bartsch, ed. (S. P. C. K., 1960), p. 10.
[2] *Ibid.*

Kierkegaardian subjectivity, minus Kierkegaard's supernatural ontology, is the reason for Bultmann's enormous significance for contemporary Christian thought and for his heading the list of those whose positions are violently rejected or passionately accepted. For this reason, we repeat, he is either at the forefront of the destroyers of the Christian faith or else a giant pioneer in its retranslation. Personally, I believe that we can learn unspeakably much from Bultmann, notwithstanding the fact that his main assumption is the complete denial of Christian reality in the Christian Gospel.

As stated before, Bultmann took over, in general, Heidegger's existentialist philosophy.[3] Bultmann's key to the Scriptures is *Sein und Zeit*. Karl Jaspers complains that, in fact, Bultmann knows only one book, *Sein und Zeit*, and that he actually misunderstands it. In any case, Bultmann believes in philosophy in a sense impossible to Barth. Interestingly enough, Brunner and Tillich both come close to Bultmann's position, which is that philosophy can ask but not answer man's basic questions. Philosophy can analyze the nature of man's existence, Bultmann asserts, and thus clarify the issues, but the answers must come from the decisions themselves. Man finds his answers in his acts, not in his abstract thinking.

The real intention of the Gospel, according to Bultmann, is decision for the Kingdom of God. This is what Jesus preached. But since there is no Kingdom beyond this world for which to decide, man decides for what is basic in this world, namely, for his own existence. The Gospel has to do with authentic existence. Man is sinful, lost, full of anxiety. What these affirmations amount to is that man has failed to find self-realization. He is suffering from a "fallen" existence.

Man cannot be understood in terms of his possibility or his facticity apart from passivity. Decision for the Kingdom helps man find himself, to be sure. But man does not decide in the self-assertive way of the philosophers. Rather, he accepts salvation passively. He is saved, not by works, but by grace and faith. To be free from anxiety is to be saved. To be rid of the state of guilt and its entailed anxiety is to be "in Christ" or "in faith." Thus, the Gospel instead of being otherworldly is really the direct answer to man's basic need as he truly knows himself by correct

---

[3] John Macquarrie's *An Existentialist Theology*, in spite of its careful distinctions, well illustrates this fact. On reading Heidegger in the original after years of reading Bultmann, I was particularly struck by the general sameness of approach.

existentialist philosophy. The New Testament analysis and Heidegger's both happen to coincide, Bultmann believes, because both are true! Therefore, in his *Theology of the New Testament*, Bultman speaks of Paul's writings as being basically concerned with anthropology! Of course in his system they have to be. And when Bultmann writes in the name of Paul he means the verity of the Gospel.

Nor should we think that existentialism is all individualistic, because, with Heidegger, Bultmann distinguishes between the *existentiell* (individual) and the *existential* (common human experience).[4] In his Gifford Lectures, *The Presence of Eternity*, Bultmann treats human history. There he finds that "the subject of history is man. Secondly, *the relativity of every historical situation is understood as having a positive meaning.*"[5] "Humanity is always a whole in each epoch and in each human being."[6] Knowledge of history is self-knowledge. Self-knowledge gives rise to numerous *Weltanschauungen*, relative to, and reflective of, the human situation. Christian self-knowledge is through Jesus Christ as the eschatological event, "the action by which God has set an end to the old world."[7] This event becomes present over and over again in faith. Eschatology is no final cosmic catastrophe, but decision. This decision is not, first of all, for responsible action, but for a new understanding of man as free from himself by the grace of God. *Then* responsible action becomes possible because only he who is free from himself can be born of love and truly love his neighbor.

As a matter of fact, the heart of Bultmann's gospel can be summarized in his own words: the Lordship of Jesus Christ, for Bultmann, means just what follows: "In principle, the future always offers the man the gift of freedom; Christian faith is the power to grasp this gift. The freedom of man from himself is always realized in the freedom of historical decisions."[8] "Christ is an historical event which happened 'once' in the past; it is, at the same time, an eternal event which occurs again and again in the soul of any Christian in whose soul Christ is born, suffers, dies, and is raised up to eternal life. In his faith the Christian is a contemporary of Christ, and time and the world's history are

---

[4] For discussions of these terms see Heidegger, *Sein und Zeit*, p. 13; De Waelkens, *La Philosophie de Martin Heidegger*, p. 3; and Macquarrie, *An Existentialist Theology*, p. 34. The terms also have different spellings.

[5] Harper & Brothers, 1957, p. 143.

[6] *Ibid.*, p. 144.

[7] *Ibid.*, p. 157.

[8] *Ibid.*, p. 152.

overcome."[9] Thus, however, even man's collective history is reduced to a common human nature, ever facing individual existential decisions.

Bultmann claims that we know little about the human, historic Jesus. At this point he is at once vividly with Kierkegaard and Barth. The Gospels are the result of a mixture of influences: the mystery religions, Jewish legalism, and Stoicism. Bultmann's book *Primitive Christianity* is a shocker to an orthodox scholar. Later theology, in every sense of *Weltanschauung*, however expressed, even in creed, is the importation of Stoicism into Christianity. It is the ruining of Christianity by a denial of its nature as faith. It is making an existence-communication into an objective situation. That will never do. Even to ask if Jesus rose from the grave, for instance, is to show oneself alien to the nature of the faith which is subjective, immediate, existential.

Instead, we must start where the Church started, with preaching. The Scriptures, he holds, have a clear order: the death of Christ, the resurrection, and preaching. Preaching, therefore, to be biblical must start with the death and the resurrection. The death is a concrete or public event. The resurrection is a concrete event only as preached. Preaching does not destroy or eliminate myth, but rather gives it an existential interpretation. The central Christian myths are the death and resurrection which mean the dying of the old self and the rising to the new self, the free self, the authentic self. Resurrection is God's saying "yes" to Jesus. The resurrection is the Cross of Christ proclaimed. To believe in Easter is to have faith in the preached word.

God did something once for all in Jesus, in the central events of the Cross and the resurrection. Such a claim does not require that a personal God acted in history. A lonely affirmation of God as "a personal being" may be found in *Jesus Christ and Mythology*.[10] If correct exegesis could take this literally or nonmythologically as God having self-existent, supernatural being, Bultmann's whole impact would be altered. Nevertheless, for the record, the expression appears in the following sentence: "The so-called images which describe God as acting are legitimate only if they mean that God is a personal being acting on persons." The discussion that follows seems to give the context of God acting as a basic factor of the total existential involvement of persons. It means, as Bultmann writes in his *Essays in Philosophy and Theology*, that the stream of reality manifested its nature; it

[9] *Ibid.*, p. 153.
[10] Bultmann, Scribner, 1938, p. 70.

showed man how to gain authentic existence. What such a once-for-all act by God in Jesus means is that what happened in him when he became authentic can happen to all men. But it can happen only existentially, only for man's passive acceptance of authentic existence the way Jesus acquired it. The hearers of preaching are to die and rise, to open themselves freely to the future; they are to find their real selves.

All of time is in the present. What happened objectively is historical. What happened in such a way that it can be accepted by all in the present is what Bultmann calls *Geschichte*, or real and relevant history. Without such contemporary involvement, what happened is merely historical, but not timeful in the fullest meaning of that term. As I have said before, to ask if something really happened is to destroy faith, it is to choose unreality, it is to seek security in externals. The Gospel is the great, good news, and what God "did" once for all in Jesus, "he" can now "do" for us, delivering us from our guilt and "fallenness" and setting us free for fulfillment in forgiveness, whereby we become more than victors over sin, law and death, and rise to eternal life in our freedom for the future as authentic selves.

This is no place for a full appraisal of Bultmann's position separately. Nor is one needed. At the end of the chapter however, I shall give an over-all appraisal of neonaturalism and existentialism in which the theology of both Bultmann and Tillich will be included.

II

The most profound and far-ranging among contemporary theologians is Paul Tillich.[11] During the later years of his teaching career he has poured forth a vigorous and full stream of theological writings. It seems likely that he and Barth will leave behind well-fashioned theological positions to represent our day; and yet Tillich, in many senses, is beyond our day—the voice of the theological ages.

Tillich was born in Germany in 1886, the son of a Lutheran clergyman. When he was fourteen years old, young Paul moved to Berlin. He was trained in both public and private schools and, being typically German, he went to several universities in order to hear such men as Bornhausen, Haupt, Kähler, Kattenbusch, and Loofs. His own characterization of his life is that he has always lived on the boundary: between city and country, between religion and art, between church and politics, between theology

[11] For a fuller discussion of Tillich's thought see Chapter 11.

and philosophy, between the religious and the secular, for example.[12] In 1935, he went to Union Theological Seminary in New York. During the nineteen-fifties, his influence in America and throughout the world has catapulted, especially with the publication of his Gifford Lectures, *Systematic Theology*. At present, he is University Professor at Harvard University (a position of highest honor at that institution) where he pursues vigorously his teaching, lecturing, and writing.

Tillich's thought has deep roots. One root is in Friedrich Wilhelm Schelling on whose work Tillich wrote his doctoral dissertation, and to whom, in his Lowell Lectures of 1958, he attributed his main indebtedness. Boehme and Schelling, with their focus on the deep, dark abyss and with their understanding of man's going out from himself and returning to himself, have sired a large part of Tillich's thinking and have affected the remainder. The neoplatonic stress on the ultimately unqualified one of Jakob Boehme runs at the bottom of all Tillich's understanding of ultimates. In his book *Biblical Faith and the Search for Ultimate Reality*, Tillich simply assumes this unconditional, ultimate unity of being as true ontology. Ultimate reality is beyond all qualifications and descriptions. Even Being itself, which formerly could be ascribed literally to God, has now in the second volume of *Systematic Theology* become symbolic. A still later pronouncement is to the effect that he now holds Being itself to be both symbolic and nonsymbolic. Ultimate reality, in any case, never "stays put" within any subject-object relation.

The second root is in the biblical faith itself. Tillich has brilliantly understood and described the nature and history of the Christian faith. No one can understand him who does not see how deeply into his own being the Christian faith has penetrated. He is a great preacher, as can be judged by his books of sermons, *The Shaking of the Foundations* and *The New Being*. As a churchman, too, Tillich has understood and cherished the holiness and power of the Christian faith.

A third strong root is in Immanuel Kant's general critique of knowledge. Kant granted, in effect, that as far as knowledge goes, David Hume had shown the inadmissibility of dealing with the transcendent or the supernatural. Kant advocated instead our dealing with the universal necessities in and for experience that were analytically true of any and all experience, or of experience in general, forms *for* experience as real as experience itself and

[12] For a most insightful autobiographical account see Tillich, *The Interpretation of History*.

logically necessary for it in such a way that experience itself could not be conceived of apart from these forms. The scene became thus changed with regard to knowledge from a realm of ultimate reality to principles of validity for and within experience, from the supernatural to this world, from the transcendent to the transcendental. Kant lives in Tillich more than most interpreters see.

A fourth root of Tillich's theology is in existentialism. Søren Kierkegaard, of course, has affected Tillich profoundly, but so have the contemporary existentialists, especially men like Karl Jaspers. A recent reading of Martin Heidegger in the German has convinced me that Tillich also stands far closer to him than I had ever thought before.

For our purposes now, it will be necessary to confine our dealings with Tillich to his central category of history in its relation to the Kingdom of God. I have often felt that Tillich's thought could be best approached by the light that his God is the ground of being. He is the power for being and the one who makes for unity and harmony of being in history. History is the creation of meaning by freedom. The source of such meaning ultimately is God; and heaven is the unification and purification of meaning. God does not exist as a person or being outside of this world of history and experience. Such existence would make him limited, conditioned, localized. Nor does the unconditional as such ever enter experience or history, for then it would become conditioned, relative, and finite. There is, therefore, no such God as is assumed naively by biblical myth. God is, rather, the power for being and for harmony of being dynamically present *for* history and represented *in* experience and *in* history by partial embodiment.

Creation as a cosmic coming-to-be out of nothing by divine fiat is symbolic thinking. To accept this doctrine literally would be to deny the source of the creature.[13] Creation is, rather, the dependence of everything conditioned on the unconditional meaning and the power for being in the ground of being. Providence is not God's active, personal activity, the interference in this world from some fanciful other level of reality, but is, rather, man's capacity to adjust to the ground of being and to unconditioned meaning, and thereby to know himself accepted by God, rightly adjusted to the ground of being.[14]

---

[13] *Systematic Theology*, Vol. I, pp. 253-254.
[14] For Tillich's view of providence cf. *Ibid.*, pp. 266-267.
Tillich's view of providence is easy to understand only if the reader observes rigorous distinction between symbolic and ontological language. The classical Christian view of God's actual participation in human history through

History moves forward in epochs called kairoi. Chronos is clock time, or empty time, which when filled by human decisions becomes kairos, thus constituting a basic structure of relevance for individual and group decisions. The standard for historic decisions is Jesus as the Christ, *the right time*, the fullness of time, the logos of God. He is unique and nonrecurring, for in him essence became transparent to existence. To put it another way, in him the full ultimate meaning of existence can be seen by the daring eyes of faith. It cannot be seen abstractly, however, but only within the conditions of its original appearance and from within the perspective of the present kairos. All such general kairoi are ambiguous and never transparent to essence, for they are permeated by the demonic element of existence. This comes out of the abyss. All finite acts as soon as they become creative partake of a possession by the conditioned order to things which in fact denies the unconditional order of ultimate meaning.

Possibly the best way to describe Tillich's theology is by an illustration. History is like a sandy river bed. On this river bed men are living. The meaning of their lives is to build an edifice. This structure and the community engendered by the task of building it is the meaning of existence. The edifice is constantly being reared. It cannot ever be fully destroyed because of the drive within the whole situation, in material and men alike, to construct something meaningful. This drive is God who both maintains the situation reliably and urges material and men alike to meaningful fulfillment.

Individuals cannot start their own little buildings apart from the main edifice of their time. They live in the edifice, and whatever they do relates to that building. The building can never be finished, can never be perfect. If the building were ever finished the reason for existence would be gone. History itself would be finished. All men come from the ground of being and return to it—the totality

---

special providence becomes, in Tillich, "Providence is not interference." There is no "additional factor," and no "miraculous physical or mental interference in terms of supranaturalism." But "it is the quality of inner directedness in every situation." Prayer, according to Tillich, means not that "God is expected to acquiesce in interfering with existential conditions," but "the surrender of a fragment of existence to God." Prayers are powerful elements as "a condition of God's directing activity," but this directing activity is nothing but the "drive" or "lure" of the power for being and for harmony. There is no special or personal providence as God's initiative of concrete action or as concrete "over-ruling" of human history. What matters concretely in Tillich is, rather, man's adjustment to God's providence as a "quality of inner directedness in every situation."

of the situation in its ideal meaning and drive—when their own individuality is over forever. But since they come from this ground, they always feel within themselves the pull of its perfection, its infinity and unity.

Therefore, they spend their lives in trying to make their edifice embody their perfection, but unfortunately they never can. They never can do so because they, in becoming individuals, have become estranged from their true selves, which alone are perfectly united with the ground of being. But they spend their lives trying to return to it by living and working, in terms of their community and their edifice. Once upon a time, in one part of the edifice, one came who remembered and envisaged perfectly the true nature of the edifice and built perfectly, but his construction became so commingled with the building of others that it cannot be seen apart from the imperfections of the other building in and around it, and it cannot now be isolated and built over again separately by anyone or by any group.

The second reason the builders cannot build a perfect edifice or finish it is that water from the river bed is peculiarly and continually seeping into every material and into every part of the building, causing settling, erosions, washouts, and cave-ins. The edifice is a constant problem to the builders because of this evil that seeps into the building. Furthermore, it is not true that such destruction results primarily from the poor work of the ignorant and the lazy builders. No, on the contrary, the more creative and imaginative the construction, the more likely it is to be mixed with such evil seepage.

There is also a community of people who have made it their mission to see the building as envisaged by the perfect builder. They live in a constant attempt to live his kind of life and to build his kind of edifice. They help history the most by keeping ever fresh his vision and by seeking the power that came in this unrepeatable life. But they, too, all too often, grow vain and proud, and seek to build after him without partaking of the spirit of him who so forgot himself and his task as an individual that the vision and the power of the original ground of being came through in him. All people are related to him, however. Often some who do not confess to be his followers build better because they are more critical of themselves and of their work than are those who have a false feeling of superiority because they are the disciples of the perfect builder.

To build according to the pattern and the power of the perfect builder is life's best experience and history's highest meaning.

Deepest down, all men are free so to build. This freedom is the essential reason for their existence, but they become bogged down in and by the actual situation of their existence. Some, however, cherish beyond the frustration of not finding entire fulfillment of their purpose or of their life, the vision of what they essentially are and most meaningfully are doing. Therefore, they find joy even within and beyond their frustration—in the very depths of their being where true joy alone resides—by looking to an end which is not the finish of the building but the realization of the true meaning in the building.

Such is Tillich's system in an illustration. No parable walks on all fours, but in the main this concrete presentation gets at the heart of Tillich's theology. In a world where science and semantic philosophy have reduced men to objects and where existentialism has returned to a real, free and responsible self, but not to the full overarching meaning of man's creation by God and man's final fulfillment in him, Tillich's analysis of experience reaches out with much more hope than any other analysis, offering a meaning to the whole of historic existence.

Those, however, who have found the Christian Gospel good and true, no matter how much they may respect and admire Rudolf Bultmann and Paul Tillich, cannot substitute these theologies for their own faith in God the Father who has made us for himself and who will use the whole of life to prepare us for, and prepare for us, the indescribable realities and joys of his eternal life beyond this earthly preparatory school. Our Gospel centers in Christ who came to us from the Father, God transcendent, to save us by his own self-giving love, and who rose from death to throw open the gates to eternal life, now and beyond death. For sorrowing mankind, caught in the horrors of its own construction, no lesser Gospel will do.

The intellectual problems of "supernaturalism" are, of course, demanding. The word, too, is unfortunate. No one can merely bypass Hume, Kant, Bultmann, or Tillich. In *Faith and Reason*, in *Christian Faith and Higher Education*, and in our next chapter, "Three Critical Issues in Tillich's Philosophical Theology," I come to grips with the main assumptions of Bultmann and Tillich, and show explicitly that no way of looking at knowledge is more adequate than the classical Christian way and that Hume and Kant have not themselves faced in their antisupernatural analysis of knowledge the basic approaches, problems, or evidence now at hand.

Neither neo-orthodoxy nor neonaturalism can win the final day because their positions do not face the full evidence or build on the full meaning of the power of Christ. However much reinterpretation of historic Christian theology admittedly needs to be done, the Christian faith stands or falls with its indelible classical Christian transcendence: its faith in God the creator, in Christ—God become historical—in God the ruler and God the Judge, in God the completer of history and the bestower of life eternal beyond the narrow horizons of physical death. Such explicit focusing of the issue of transcendence is the only adequate way to appraise succinctly the works of Bultmann and Tillich.

Our existentialist neonaturalists, by whatever name, have helped us by a magnificent analysis of our human predicament and by their insistence that we face the problems of the mind of the modern postcritical age. We owe a deep debt of gratitude to both Bultmann and Tillich. They have also helped us by refusing the arbitrariness of the neo-orthodox, but they have not proceeded to that constructive center of the Christian faith where and whence alone lies and proceeds man's true hope. In order to see Tillich, perhaps the most disputed thinker of our day, in greater detail, I am including a special treatment of his thought in the next chapter. My own attempt at constructive theology follows that chapter.

Chapter 11

Three Critical Issues in Tillich's Philosophical Theology

PAUL TILLICH'S approach to theology is inclusive and open. Nothing seems alien to his spirit, but everything must be accounted for in its being, meaning, and context. Tillich is a scientist in his respect for fact, a philosopher in his demand for explanation, and a theologian in his insistence on relevance for life. Art and politics, depth psychology and cultural analysis, for instance, are amply and vividly at home in his thought. Such a comprehensive grasp, however, never impedes but actually abets detailed analysis. Seeing things steadily and whole does not prevent concern either for rich complexity of composition or for active decision, whether personal or social. With Tillich there is pressing need to synthesize rational and existential thinking, for his approach combines organismic wholeness with a clear recognition of the discontinuities of existence. Above all, however, Tillich is the profound wrestler with reality who refuses intellectual short cuts and spiritual sedatives. Even though he is easily at home both in the history of thought and in major contemporary problems, he is a scholar who, to borrow a phrase from Whitehead, is not fettered by "the 'l'arned' tradition," but is a seer of first magnitude.

In this chapter I want simply to raise three critical issues in Tillich's thought: (1) a personal God, (2) supernaturalism, (3) theological method. The order in which I present these issues has been chosen deliberately for the reason that I believe Tillich's theological method rests upon prior determining assumptions.

I

The issue of a personal God is not easy, especially for the philosophical theologian. It presents strong pros and cons. In the light of these, Tillich's contribution may become a bit clearer.

On behalf of those who hold the belief in a personal God it can be pointed out, *historically*, that all three great living religions of the West—Judaism, Christianity and Islam—are built around belief in such a God. Greek and Nordic religions, too, although not monotheistic, put ultimate emphasis on the personal; and even primitive religions, it is held from a good deal of evidence, often assumed as ultimate a personal God. *Metaphysically*, furthermore, belief in a personal God is not marred by reductionism, i.e., by ignoring the persisting problems of consciousness and of personal being; nor does it fail to interpret reality in terms of and within the context of the highest category of being we know. In the history of evolution each category of being becomes more meaningful and may be thought of as fulfilled in terms of the next. At least there is continuity of relation downward from the highest to the lowest level, but there is no necessary and predictable continuity in the reverse direction. Of this order, personal being is the climax that cannot be explained by, but may help to explain, the other levels. *Religiously*, moreover, faith in a personal God leaves the worshiper in no alien and hostile world. Rather, the ultimate has capacity for being known, is available to trust, and provides the ground for the persistence of finite personalities for fulfillment beyond death. Without any attempt at a comprehensive summary of reasons for belief in a personal God, we can nevertheless suggest that there is historic, metaphysical, and religious strength in such a position.

On the other side of the ledger, however, there is also strength. *Historically*, we are aware of the prior appearance of the impersonal. History may thus suggest that the personal came from, or is the product of, the impersonal. Moreover, some great universal religions, like Buddhism, identify the personal with separation and estrangement from reality. Such religions have an enviable record both for satisfying their devotees and for providing conditions for peaceful civilization. Many of the leading thinkers of the West, too—for instance, philosophers like Spinoza and Hegel —have accepted the impersonal as ultimate. *Metaphysically*, furthermore, the nonpersonal realms in their vastness make the personal seem most tiny; and, except for minor parts, they seem to have no direct relation to the distinctively personal. There is also a demonstrable dependence of the personal on the impersonal. How precarious and fugitive is personal life within the ongoing forces of impersonal existence. As a matter of fact, we can observe an impersonal realm existing apart from the personal, but not vice versa. The personal, again, seems always to be localized, i.e., to be connected with some specific body and with some selective span of attention, whereas localization is limitation. The infinite ground of being, it is suggested, cannot be localized, whereas we know no personal being that is not localized. Even though by consciousness and thought the personal can transcend precisely such bodily limitations, a person seems always to be connected with some definite place. *Religiously*, to continue, the problem of evil prevents any easy acceptance of a personal God. If a well-intentioned, competent, personal God is in charge of our universe, why, it may be asked, is there a world like this? Many people also report that they have genuinely tried to make contact with a personal God by prayer, thought and faith, but in spite of long persistence have had to give up the attempt as hopeless. If there is a personal God who is religiously available, why should he be so hard to reach? There are also subpersonal and indeed antipersonal forces at work, even within persons, for instance the death wish. Death of persons, in any case, is a constantly observable fact; fulfillment after death seems at best the inference of divided reason or the report of faith.

Obviously, I have no more than suggested some strengths and weaknesses connected with the intellectual acceptance of a personal God. For philosophical theology, in any case, it is a major problem. As an answer to this question, Tillich has suggested the category of the "transpersonal."[1] What is the value of this proposal with regard to the philosophical strengths and weaknesses adhering to faith in a personal God?

The transpersonal position affirms that although ultimate reality is not personal as such, i.e., although there is no personal God as *a* being who is the ground of all reality, nevertheless the personal is a veritable and significant ingredient in the ground of being. Only Being itself, beyond all finite qualifications and irreducible to terms other than itself, is literally to be ascribed final reality. God as ultimate, eminent being is thus not *the personal* ground of all else; but neither is he impersonal in Tillich's thought, for even as Being itself resists nonbeing and works everywhere for unity and harmony, just so that which makes for personal being and harmony is part and parcel of ultimate reality, receiving its power, indeed, through being part of, and participating in, ultimate reality. In a true though symbolic sense, it can therefore be said that God is living, personal, and loving. Even beyond justice and power God is symbolically and effectively love, fulfilling both.[2] But ontologically,

---

[1] See his vigorous treatment of this issue in *Biblical Religion and the Search for Ultimate Reality* (The University of Chicago Press, 1955).

[2] See Tillich, *Love, Power and Justice* (Oxford University Press, 1954).

Being itself is the ground of everything, not only of the personal; and therefore God is transpersonal in some such sense as red is truly in the neutral white where all the colors are. Red is, and is available for redness, in the spectrum for analysis, and, as a separate color, for beauty and function. Nevertheless, the white that includes the red is white as such without separate redness. Even so, God as personal does not lack status in ultimate reality, but the personal is never present as such in Being itself, even though it is religiously available as reality and as power for persons and for society in need of help and companionship.[3]

Three positive points at least can be made for Tillich's transpersonal position. First, it provides ultimate unity of being. At the heart of reality is oneness, harmony of being. Second, his position also allows for diversity of being and adequacy of description. He has not reduced history to maya, thought to nescience, or all reality to history. He never denies or belittles either the personal or the impersonal realms. He even allows for the full actuality of the demonic as an aspect of existence. Third, besides unity and adequacy, the transpersonal position of Tillich provides a religiously available God, for he is to be approached in biblical terms as living, personal, and loving. Tillich has presented us, consequently, with a view beyond most simply personal or simply impersonal positions. Because of his strong stress on history, his analysis cannot be, as it sometimes is, dismissed merely as neoplatonic or Hindu. The biblical insights in Tillich's thought are also too strong for such equation.

In spite of the strength of Tillich's transpersonal position, however, and without denying the need for taking into account both the personal and the impersonal aspects of our data, can it not be that the personal as such does not disappear ultimately by merger, but is in charge of the impersonal? Even hierarchically such a relationship would bind ultimate reality and our world of experience together more organically than does Tillich's position, and would strengthen our trust in the personal ultimate. Such a view, however, could hardly be sustained unless the control were to eventuate in some solution of our problems as persons. And such a solution, to be organic and consistent with our experience of freedom, requires time. If God as personal, then, is most real, cannot our world of experience be a pedagogical process that provides time, a process made possible, indeed, by the very existence of the impersonal as that passivity of God which makes our freedom real? Perhaps

[3] Cf. the God above all gods in Tillich, *The Courage to Be* (Yale University Press, 1952).

the fullest explanation of our existence as a whole does not demand some ultimately undifferentiated unity, but rather is obtained in the light and power of the selective, revelatory *personal* Event of the Christian faith. If so, the Cross can give us the clue to both the meaning and the conquest of evil (the fact of which often becomes the reason for not believing in a personal God). Then also, beyond our knowing and imagining, the scene for the solution must extend beyond our earthly life, making death not man's final frustration but a condition for his final fulfillment.

It may also be that personal existence does not involve the limitation connected with localization. If God is not a spiritual personality, but a personal Spirit, the ground of being can be living love, both having ultimate self-being and capable of self-manifestation in different forms for different purposes, although always present everywhere in some sense. Tillich presupposes limitation in metaphysical terms as the presence of relations. He takes it for granted that the absolute is never relative; the ultimate unity is also, mathematically speaking, never differentiated into the many. Could we not, however, start with distinctively Christian presuppositions, in which case God is not limited within or without unless he is limited in love or in the ultimate control of love? In such case, the absolute (agape) is not limited, but expressed by relations. As a matter of fact, perhaps the basic question, even on this issue of the transpersonal, is whether we should start with being and define God in its terms, or whether we should start with God as agape and define being, becoming, and even nonbeing in terms of God. Obviously an essay as short as this cannot more than suggest issues. Tillich has given us a strong position. There is also, I believe, a distinctively Christian position that, without denying the impersonal or without avoiding the discussion of God's relation to this realm, yet finds the living, personal God of love to be rock-bottom reality—a position that I, at least, have found to be open to increased intellectual confirmation and dynamic self-verification.

II

The issue of supernaturalism is, for modern man, both intellectually and emotionally confused. Intellectually, he often thinks of the supernatural as the preter- or anti-natural, and emotionally, as the occult. Writers like Karl Heim have therefore used the word "supra-polar," Reinhold Niebuhr, the "superhistorical," and Lionel Thornton, the "superorganic." The issue, however, remains the same: namely, does reality center in our world or in a reality more than, other than, and beyond it, upon which or whom, the world in fact depends? Is God other than, more than, and in some real and significant sense prior to the world rather than merely a part of it or even the whole of it?

The weaknesses of supernaturalism are basically that it seems to be a needless or arbitrary category and that it can occasion, or even be the result of, the desire to escape from the problems and responsibilities of this world. Aristotle and Occam have weightily reminded us that no referring away of our problems beyond the known world either explains them or solves them. Emotionally, besides, such otherworldly reference may even help us to avoid our real problems of personal and social demands. Tillich has pointed out, for instance, that those who refuse to believe that death is real and final for human beings do not take life seriously either.[4] They never face their real problems in this life because they have postponed their solution to some fancied life after it.

The strength of supernaturalism centers in the fact that it avoids naturalistic reductionism to sensation in epistemology and to the physical in ontology. For this reason it can help explain becoming. If the world remained steadily a mixture of good and bad without basic change, supernaturalism would be a redundant category. The evidence we have, on the contrary, is that there have emerged level upon level of new actualities, while these, in turn, as they ingress or appear in the cosmic process, are both organically and accumulatively related to it. Such an organic and accumulative series of becoming bespeaks prior creative ground.[5] In the light of the total history of nature and man, supernaturalism is, consequently, a strong candidate for the highest possible bestower of intellectual adequacy. Emotionally, too, it has been seen that the great reformers of men's moral and spiritual life have often been believers in a reality beyond this world. Socrates (in spite of current attempts to reduce him to an existentialist), Jesus, St. Francis, Schweitzer, and Gandhi, for example, cannot be read out of court easily. The experience of total religious dependence, history shows us, is capable of generating creative and responsible thought and action.

Tillich's usual position on this critical issue of supernaturalism versus naturalism has been a refusal to be bound by either position. In his earliest writings—of the first two decades of this century— he spurned supernaturalism with vigor on the ground that it was in fact determined by its reference to naturalism. Ultimate reality,

[4] In a sermon given in White Temple, Miami, Florida, January, 1956.
[5] For a detailed analysis see Ferré, *Faith and Reason*, chap. iv.

for him, could not be thus confined. At the same time, he has scrupulously avoided the scientific kind of naturalism with its usual methodological monism. In response to my direct question on the issues of supernaturalism in a previous book[6] he replied, however, that if choice had to be made he would be an "ecstatic naturalist," one who by the ecstatic reason goes beyond our limited methods and experiences but who will never allow the positing of a world beyond this world.

His own position can perhaps best be explained as akin to Kantian transcendentalism. He accepts the fact that reason never deals with *the* ultimate reality of some transcendent realm beyond our actual world, but rather that it works critically with the analysis of the world we know, finding, if we may use Kantian terminology, principles of validity. In his own, as well as Kant's language, "transcendental" necessity becomes *das Unbedingte,* the unconditioned (later "unconditional') beyond, before, and underneath experience, not as some transcendent realm, but as an analytical, universal necessity for experience and history. Mixed with elements from Boehme and Schelling, his ultimate category becomes some mystical Being itself, the unconditional that resists nonbeing and makes for harmony of being. Not a transcendent or otherworldly realm of reality, then, but a transcendental or unconditional necessity for experience and history—this is a clue to Tillich's thinking.

Transcendentalism—the unconditional *for* but not as such *in* experience—avoids several pitfalls and emotional drawbacks of both supernaturalism and naturalism and speaks, in addition, especially in Tillich's distinctive form of it, a vigorous, creative word. His use of symbols, within this method, as pointing to truth beyond literal language, while also participating in reality beyond direct expression, stays clear both of an objectivist position that equates knowledge with reality and also of a subjectivist position in which there is no objective counterpart in reality to the symbols employed.[7] His symbols both relate to reality and fail literally to indicate it. They have, nonetheless, a rare evocative power. They elicit lively subjective response to reality and appeal powerfully to religious apperception. Symbolically, Tillich's theological analysis

6 *The Theology of Paul Tillich* (The Macmillan Company, 1952), p. 341.
7 To what extent *das Unbedingte* is a limiting concept, or *das Ding an sich* is a nice point. There seems to be some sort of dualism in Tillich's thought whereby any transcendent realm is precluded by the fact that the unconditional cannot be related, while at the same time his system seems to indicate some transcendent power for existence and harmony of being.

is centrally Christian and potently needed. The real crux of
the adequacy of his position, however, concerns the nature of the
objective counterpart, ultimately, of his symbolic analysis of the
Christian faith. Especially is this question of adequacy a matter of
the significance and the permanence of the personal, to which we
now turn.

The issue of supernaturalism versus Tillich's kind of transcendentalism is not so much whether this world or a world of prior
reality is central for faith and thought, since Tillich's thought, in
its actual drive, never becomes a limiting naturalism; but the issue
is rather that of the significance and the permanence of the personal. With relation to God there is no problem as such in Tillich's
thought. Whatever is ultimately personal by its participating in
Being itself is, according to Tillich, everlasting and ever potent.
Nothing of personal significance, he holds, can therefore ever
be lost; it is permanent. One is strongly reminded at this point of
Whitehead's position.

The real issue is, to repeat, with regard to God's relation to man;
and with regard to the significance and permanence of the personal
in man. If God is not personal in the sense of conscious knowledge
and will, there can be no personal communion between God and
man. The subject-object relation is said to be transcended in reality,
but so is, in fact, the Subject-subject relation. Whitehead's stand
has at least the Fellow Sufferer and the Companion who understands. Nothing of this as objective, ultimate reality is to be found
in Tillich. However, I believe that the deepest significance of finite
spirit is its capacity to have intercourse with the infinite Spirit.
Being itself unfortunately affords no such significance, *really*, and
offers no hope or help for prayer as an I-Thou relation.

Neither can man count on the personal purpose of God in
providence. What happens to him is not, at the deepest, ordained
by a loving will who creates and controls, directly and indirectly,
human lives and the order of nature. We can participate in reality,
adjust ourselves to it by powers inherent in it and available to us,
but God never literally acts in our behalf, answers prayers, or
shares his purpose in special providence. The security, the intimacy,
and the fullest creative conditions for personal growth within the
eternal purpose are therefore gone. If such an impersonal unconditional is ultimate, we must, of course, face the fact. I believe,
however, that Christian supernaturalism is not only religiously but
also intellectually more adequate. In the next section this point
will be developed.

Even more important precisely for the nature and character of ultimate reality is the question concerning the permanence of the personal in man. Tillich is insistent that we must face the fact that death is real and final. He even believes that modern man is particularly hurt by his refusal to take death with full seriousness. But whether specially, as in the resurrection of Christ, or generally, as in the everlastingness of personal life, the issue of supernaturalism will not die. The Christian faith holds that man is created by God for God and for fullness of life in fellowship. It holds that death is not frustration but fulfillment. It holds that everlasting life is both a new kind of life in Christ, in agape, and a life that lasts. Such faith is not easy emotionally; intellectually it staggers the critical reason. Nevertheless, it is a firm implication, in some way, of the character of God as agape. Life everlasting, I believe, is a necessary condition for an adequate view of that ultimate which can account most suggestively for both origins and ends and offer, besides, a blueprint and power for the solution of our personal and social problems.

In Tillich's view, whatever is ultimately personal in man lasts because it belongs to Being itself. The personal, however, is effectively buried in the grave of the undifferentiated itself. The personal never remains beyond death as persistence of persons. The impersonal has therefore won. If Tillich were not explicit on the nature of his transpersonal ultimate, we could interpret his position to be that the persistence of the personal, though not persisting as individuality, is mostly an affirmation that our kind of personal existence, now, in this life, will be fulfilled in some new kind of being where the separations and estrangements of our finite existence are transcended, even while the kernel of self-being exists in such fulfillment. Or we could understand him to mean that we must leave this issue with faith in higher hands. As the case stands, however, there is a basic contention between Tillich's "transcendentalism" and Christian supernaturalism that will not down. All the same, Tillich's view will offer itself as a strong position for those who believe Christian supernaturalism to be primitive mythology and yet cannot acquiesce in the intellectual reductionism and emotional thinness of scientific naturalism.

III

It may seem a strange procedure to take up last the question of theological method. I do so because I believe that in Tillich's case method is the result of system. It is obvious that in theology, as Tillich himself says, "method and system determine each other.[8]

[8] *Systematic Theology*, Vol. I, p. 60.

For Tillich, however, the presuppositions of his thinking are the occasion for his method. "For systematic theology this means that its method is derived from a prior knowledge of the system which is to be built by the method."[9] Such is his avowal for the method of systematic theology in general inasmuch as it must necessarily center in its object of ultimate concern and revelation, concretely, explicitly, and totally. Yet beyond this specific consideration, theological method in general is determined, in Tillich's case, by his assumption that "our ultimate concern is that which determines *our being or not-being*,"[10] for this assumption gives actual content to the revelatory event or center itself. His systematic theology thus becomes filled ultimately by his philosophical presuppositions.

Let us once more look first through Tillich's eyes at other main choices for method. "Supranaturalism," as he calls supernaturalism —introducing thereby an unnecessary dichotomy by the very use of terms—gives us a "sum of revealed truths which have fallen into the human situation like strange bodies from a strange world."[11] If supernaturalism is accepted as meaning an arbitrary and unrelated body of knowledge to be taken on external authority, it should, of course, be rejected outright.

The second choice for method is naturalistic. This, Tillich teaches, makes the mistake of taking the answers from human existence whereas human existence itself is what needs both to be explained and to be delivered from its estrangement. Theology speaks *to* man, not *from* man. In this assertion, too, Tillich speaks acceptable truth.

The third method he surveys is dualistic, building a supranatural structure on a naturalistic basis. It involves natural theology, using such devices as proofs for the existence of God, derived from the data of man's situation. Tillich holds this method to be false, since man's situation states problems but never affords theological answers.

Instead, Tillich substitutes the method of correlation, wherein the intent of "natural theology" is accepted in the realm of the analysis of existence, and the intent of "supranatural theology," in the realm of theological answers. Existential questions receive theological answers in mutual interdependence. As a matter of fact he goes on, there is neither a basis of comparison between philosophy and theology nor a true possibility of conflict, since they deal with different spheres or operate on qualitatively different planes.

[9] *Ibid.*
[10] *Ibid.*, p. 14, italics mine.
[11] *Ibid.*, p. 64.

No more than with Kierkegaard is there any direct passing by discursive or synthetic reason from existence to essence. Philosophy deals with the structure of being by the analysis of existence; theology, with meaning—ultimately, unconditionally, totally and infinitely. Man's existence can be grasped in existential questions and analyzed by philosophy in terms of pure reason; then theology, from its full focus of the revelatory event, answers man's existential problems and offers solutions to his intellectual needs. Since the logos is on both the side of existence and the side of essence, and since essence and existence come together in the revelatory event, the method of correlation is not arbitrary but a partially confirmatory affair. This is so since no other answers can so well meet man's real needs of life and knowledge as the revelation of the concrete truth of Jesus as the Christ. Furthermore, there can be interaction between the two realms inasmuch as not even a theologian lives always within the theological circle, but must relate himself and his thought more or less to "the situation" of concrete experience.

At this point what, to me, is Tillich's chief difficulty becomes most clearly apparent. He presupposes that the problem of being versus not being is ultimate, that Being itself, as infinite, cannot ever be defined or contained within history and experience, and that, therefore, the most that can be said of revelation *literally* or *directly* is that it constitutes an unconditional demand for being and harmony of being. This basic assumption controls the content of the revelatory event. The interpretation of Christ, without historic justification, becomes controlled by the relation of essence to existence. This historical Jesus, consequently, in Tillich's thought, merely became transparent to the Christ by refusing to make infinite anything finite, and thus transmitted to us through a concrete life the synthesis of essence and existence, not in such a way that essence ever became existence or the infinite became finite, but in such a way that existence became perfectly transparent for essence, revealing for us the unique nonrecurring kairos.

When Tillich is thus understood, we can see why he can, at the same time, be rather cavalier about the historic Jesus and yet also be completely insistent that in him the Christ has come. With Tillich, Christ meets the demand for constructing a bridge between essence and existence as well as the requirement for a center of the theological circle that is both perfectly universal and completely concrete. Tillich's two definitions of the power of Being itself, namely, to resist nonbeing and to make for harmony of being, correspond respectively, I believe, to God's power of creation and his power of redemption. The power for such universal creativity and for unification and purification of meaning is precisely Christ as the agape of God.

If, therefore, Tillich had started with Christ as the agape of God instead of with a mathematical-metaphysical idea of Being itself, he would have started with a concrete Incarnation that affords the highest explanatory as well as saving power. The difficulty with his position, as I see it, is that he presupposes an undefinable, undifferentiated Being itself that cannot be incarnated as such in history. He inherits the problems of Aristotle's *actus purus*. Accepting as fact the claim not only that the transcendent cannot be known but also that there is no transcendent realm as such beyond, or other than, the world we know, Tillich operates, as we have seen, with a method akin to Kant's transcendental analysis whereby there are universal forms for experience that never exist independent of experience, but are nevertheless unconditionally presupposed by, and requirements of, experience. Actually this unconditional demand for being and for unity of being for Tillich has been revealed through the Christ, but Christ has not revealed a personal God or a supernatural realm beyond experience and this world.

This presupposition of Being itself as a transcendental power— God as the ground of being that does not exist as an eminent, transcendent person or realm—lies at the heart of Tillich's system and determines his method. I believe, however, that if he would begin with the concrete Christ as agape, he could through him find as ultimate the God who is personal Spirit, an uncreated reality, supernatural but not supranatural. He could also devise a theological method which, while keeping all of his positive insights, would at the same time allow for a more positive though dialectical relation to philosophy.[12] He could keep the ultimacy and distinctiveness of both his theological center and his circle, with their subjective demands for faith and commitment, even while having in Christ as agape a meaning that relates concretely and realistically to all of life and thought.

He could then keep Incarnation of being as well as of meaning, in the full, literal sense, and, with Calvin and Luther as well as with the Early Church Fathers, find a doctrine of the Church which in some real sense *incarnates* as well as *represents* the Kingdom. He could further arrive at a living faith in everlasting life not only as that unification and purification of meaning in which "the personal" participates in and beyond personal exist-

[12] My reasons for so believing are developed in *Faith and Reason*, chap. iii, and in *Christian Faith and Higher Education*, chap. vii.

ence, but also as the eventual and everlasting fulfillment of both the purpose of God and the life of man.

In his description of the Christian faith phenomenologically, however, and in his actual analysis of life and social conditions, Tillich has been profoundly motivated by the central Christian fact and meaning. For the most part, he need only accept as true what he describes as Christian. He has given us forefront depth and creativity of philosophical and theological analysis. He has also been unafraid and yet forbearing in his dealing with movements and issues unsympathetic to his thought, evincing that great and generous spirit that marks him as something of a saint as well as a prince of scholars. To acknowledge with gratitude both extreme and extensive indebtedness to him is only to declare oneself an active part of the contemporary world of theological formulation.

Chapter 12

Where Do We Go from Here in Theology?

AT THE General Assembly of the World Council of Churches held at Evanston, Illinois in 1954, many persons recognized the need for a more profound American theology. In Europe, I was once told by a group of Christian leaders that they looked to America for a revival of effective theology. Europe is too tired, they said, to produce constructive thought. Having lived through two world wars and standing on the edge of hitherto undreamed-of destruction, its more mature leaders are too shocked by events to think daring thoughts about God's ways with human history. Living in the shadow of frustration, the younger leaders also seem unable to create a theology of hope. These Christian leaders therefore urged American theologians to produce an effective Christian theology.

The embarassment at Evanston and the request from these European leaders coincide with a general turn to theology. To put it in the vernacular, a rush to religion is on. The more thoughtful in this rush are increasingly devoting their attention to theology.

Such a turn to theology is healthy, for theology is study concerning God. By God we mean the ultimate nature and purpose of existence. Therefore, the turn to theology is really a deliberate attempt to understand the ground of our being, the goal of our lives, and the direction which we must choose in order to fashion the goal of our lives in line with the ground of our being. The turn to theology is thus our deliberate confrontation of our most important decisons, whether as persons or as a society.

Fortunately, I can point without hesitation to a Christian theology which places full stress on objectivity, prized by fundamentalists and neo-orthodox, and on subjectivity, emphasized by liberals and existentialists. Both elements—objectivity and subjectivity—are within the organic necessity of truth. The Christian revelation alone can provide the whole truth for life.

The Christian faith is grounded in the bedrock of the *historic revelation*. The Christian faith therefore acknowledges a necessary mediate relation to God. This historic givenness of revelation has, furthermore, both an objective and a subjective side.

The *objective side* comprises God's own presence and work in the Christ-deed, the Holy Spirit, the Church, and the Bible. The Christ-deed is God's own incoming into human history as the Son. The Christian faith stands and falls with its affirmations not only of the power but of the presence of God in human form. In Jesus, the God who is love came, acted, and spoke. This does not mean that God was absent from history until Jesus came, but, rather, that then he came in matchless fullness as the turning point of all history. Then he came as eternity fulfilling time. The Christ-deed, the Holy Spirit, the Church, and the Bible. The Christ-deed is God's act of revelation and redemption in the fullness of time. The universal, unconditional, sovereign love, who is God, came, acted, and spoke for the salvation of all men, that whosoever believes and lives this Gospel of God's love may be saved and come to the knowledge of the truth.

The Holy Spirit, moreover, in one of his aspects, is God himself, God in the Church. As Jesus was born of Mary, yet became enmanned or indwelled, by God the Son, so the Church has its own authentic human side, as a human community, while yet indwelt by God the Holy Spirit. Revelation at its most intimate and real is always, as Robert Barclay pointed out, by "the inward and objective Holy Spirit." The Holy Spirit, like Christ, becomes organically, personally, united to the Christian community; Christ is the pattern, structure, and substance of love, while the Holy Spirit is God's energizing, whether for counseling, comforting, enlightening, sanctifying, assuring, or for establishing. Christ is ultimate to each new creature; the Holy Spirit is ultimate to the community of creatures in Christ. To receive Christ is to be born again as a new person, but also inevitably to be born into a new fellowship of the Spirit. Christ is the pattern of the unity of God *in* the individual believer and *for* the community of faith. The Holy Spirit is the energizer of Christ, the alpha and the omega of the new creature, for the fullness of self-being in Christ and in the Christian fellowship. The Holy Spirit is God *in* the Christian community and *for* each member of it. His presence and work are objective through and through, of God and not of man, but at the same time part and parcel of man's new creaturehood in Christ and in the Church. Thus they are genuinely and inseparably the decisive aspect of man's new subjective situation as an individual and as a social being.

The Christian Church is also objective. It comes from God. It comes as God. It comes for man. As a human institution it is of man. It is man's response to God in the Christian community. Yet, first of all, the Church is made up not of man's response but of God's gracious calling in Christ by the Spirit. The Christian Church is primarily God's presence and power for a new kind of community on the part of those who are new creatures in Christ. The Church is the extension of the Incarnation, of the atonement, and of the resurrection, not as a self-sufficient prolongation of Christ or as the vicar of Christ or as a substitute for him. It is Christ, present as "the head of the body." It is the contemporary Christ in human history. It is the Holy Spirit calling, winning, and perfecting saints, those called by God and justified by him. It is Christ giving himself ever anew in a broken body and the shed blood. It is the love who is God, caring in the Community of Concern. Still the Christ comes within the weaknesses of the flesh as the triumph of saving power, no longer in the physical body of Jesus, but now in the risen body of the Universal Church, in those who know the reality of his universal love to save, to create, and to promote community.

In addition to the Christ-deed, the Holy Spirit and the Church, on the objective side of the Christian faith, there is also the Bible. The Bible is an objective strand of history reporting man's response to God's Christ-deed, his sending of the Holy Spirit, and his founding of the Church. The Bible has its authority in the God who has thus acted to save mankind. The Bible is the exemplifying history of human experience interpreted by God's love in Christ. The Bible shows us God's preparation for the Christ-deed and the culminating revelation and redemption of man. When the Bible is read with dedicated intelligence as the living Word of God's universal love, we behold the glory of God in the face of Jesus Christ. "The truth as it is in Jesus" becomes our criterion of all truth and conduct, showing us both the nature and the will of God. The Bible becomes the objective rule of faith, the lamp for our feet, illumining the will and way of God with all men and for all times.

These four—the Christ-deed, the Holy Spirit, the Church, and the Bible—are the objective factors of the Christian faith in history that are permanently valid. They are the mediating realities through which we come to God. They determine whether our faith is genuinely Christian and, therefore, whether it is fully in line with truth.

The *subjective side* of revelation also contains four factors. The first of these is the response of the original faith-witnesses. They were real and free human beings reporting as best they knew. Because they responded as finite human beings, touched with sin, to the holy facts of God's saving presence and mighty acts, the biblical record shows us the absolute truth, but not absolutely. Even as the Son came incognito in order to preserve our freedom to find God in the fullness of experience—including after his coming, however, his very presence in human history—so comes the holy book, not as an errorless compulsion confronting finite man, but as the saving fullness of objective reality touched with the foibles and fallibilities of the original faith-witnesses. The truth to which they testified is altogether and absolutely true; the way in which they testified to that truth was to report what they saw and heard as they saw and heard it, and to report what was remembered through a period of oral tradition and through the fallible transmission of writings. The reality of the fullness of God's saving love in his Son, his universal concern for all men, thrusts itself upon all who are ready to accept and to walk in the light of the holy Incarnation, but amidst secondary contradictions and misinterpretations due to the subjective failings both of life and of light, on the part of the early disciples.

Secondly, the Church as the community of confirmation has not made sharp and constant the one and only criterion of God in Christ, which is holy and universal love. There is a whole history of subjective response to God's historic revelation. The original errors of the first faith-witnesses have persisted as part of the holy tradition along with the holy Gospel. The chaff has never been winnowed from the seed. These errors and misinterpretations have accumulated in Christian history, owing to the subjective and fallible nature of our response, and have become solidified in Christian theology, particularly as this has become expressed in terms of alien philosophies and divergent world-views. The community of confirmation transmits through history the reality of the Gospel, man's constantly vertical relation to God in acceptance, forgiveness, and fulfillment, but the confirmation has been through a glass darkly, a situation which has made it possible for many to worship the shadows as the light, either because they prefer the darkness to the light or because no one has trained them to distinguish true light from darkness. The whole history of confirmation has been a history conditioned by a subjective response on the part of the believing community to God's objective acts of salvation.

Third, our present knowledge of the historic Christian faith, the work once wrought by the Holy Spirit, is subjectively conditioned. How we know it depends upon the quality of our own response, both in intensity and in the kind of faith which is ours. Only those who were already translated saints could respond perfectly to God's historic deeds in Christ, the Holy Spirit, the Church, and the Bible. We therefore must be humble about our own reception and interpretation of the historic Christian faith. Our witness to others of our holy faith must be humbled by the consciousness of the forgiveness of our sins and of our failings because we are finite men. Even though God's part in the historic revelation is absolute, there is always our human side to it, which is relative and clouded by sin.

Fourth, man's creative response to God's objective self-disclosure is also subjective. History presents new situations. Revelation cannot be repeated exactly as it came the first time. History requires constant choice, the relating of the old to the new. The Church is not only the community of confirmation, but also, in some sense, a community of experimentation. History demands new thought. The new, while unavoidable, is always dangerous. We men are sinful and finite, and it is as such that we handle the immortal message of God's redeeming love. We sometimes essay creation without having been triumphantly redeemed or without being fully in the service of the Holy Spirit. The finiteness we cannot avoid; sin besets us too easily. Therefore, as the contemporary community of experimentation we actually impose a subjective element on the Gospel we present. Only a few in the community keep close enough to Christ and are sufficiently trained to follow anew "the pioneer and perfecter of our faith," and even they judge as creatures, not as God himself.

There is, thus, the mediate relation to God, presupposing the historic Christ-deed, the work of the Holy Spirit up to now, the Christian Church as the community of confirmation and as the community of experimentation, and the Bible. All of these involve objective and subjective factors of God's work and man's response. Without these mediate relations, there is no Christianity. The Christian faith is a historic reality which concerns us. It claims nothing less than the revelation and saving activity of the absolute God. Therefore, to accept the Christian faith is to renounce all other faiths as either inadequate or false at heart. There can be only one absolute revelation, whatever way God's wider work in nature and history be afterwards related to that revelation.

Nevertheless, the Christian faith is not merely *mediate*. It worships a living God. Man's basic relation in life is to God. The horizontal direction is ever under the vertical. Jesus knew that God is Spirit and must be worshiped *immediately* in Spirit and in truth. The four objective factors in history must therefore become objective for *present* experience, structuring God's immediate revelation. The Christian faith lives by such encounter of the living God. The content of the Christian experience could never be mediated without the historic faith, even as what we now experience could never be interpreted for what it is apart from the history of our experience. The Christian faith is *mediated immediately*.

Therefore, God must reveal himself ever afresh in the Christmen. The living Christ is God as Son conclusively fulfilling those who understand and accept him. God must become Christ in us "the hope of glory." He who once came to fulfill his eternal purpose in Christ Jesus must keep coming to fill full that purpose by his ingression organically—redemptively and creatively—into all men. Man finds fulfillment only when God becomes his true subject. The human self is not eliminated or curtailed by God's taking complete possession of it, but is fulfilled and made free. We are made for God and for his community; the more passive we are to him, therefore, the more active we become and the more real as human selves. The more we resist him, the more we are slaves to what is alien to our deepest selves. Therefore, God must continue his holy Incarnation to express himself and to finish in glory his own creation.

God also will enter us as the Holy Spirit, the guide and energizer of our new life in Christ. Christ is the perfect fulfillment of God's purpose for us and of our human natures. The Holy Spirit is the intimate companionship of God within that new relationship. We are not only born again by the revolutionary entrance of Christ into our lives, making us new creatures in him, but we are also allowed to grow in grace and in the fruit of the Spirit by means of the present objective work of God the Holy Spirit.

The Church also becomes, in the present, the creator of creeds, not the mumblers or even the repeaters of them. A creed is not Christian if it is other than a symbol which directs faith. Such a symbol is existential, the mediating context of an immediate confrontation. The early Councils wrote afresh the creeds. They were creative of new and better insight as well as defensive of false directions for faith and practice. Dark years and deadened periods of history imprisoned faith within the contexts of the past, putting the living heart of confession within the corpse of formulation. The throbbing life of commitment, which once created a symbol to match its information and decision, became embalmed within the cadaver of a former faith. God must work ever anew to write creative creeds that free the spirit, match its present knowledge, and serve as the occasion for its fullest commitment. The creed is Christian only when it is the declaratory statement of contemporary worship and theology. Although it structures faith, it is expressed by it creatively, not imposed upon it.

The Bible, too, is living light. Too often the Bible is only a book—dead fuel never catching fire. The Bible mediates God's objective self-revelation as the Son. There can be no other revelation that is real and final than God as holy love, conclusively and universally concerned for all men and sufficient for all needs. Yet such a God is present *now* as the author of his living word. The Bible cannot become a closed canon without denying the Christian faith at its very heart; that God lives and encounters us now for our salvation; prayer and worship are no empty rituals but living relations to the One Lord. The Bible is God's living speech to men, and therefore the Bible is buried in mediacy unless it is resurrected in the immediacy of the present revelation for contemporary needs. Revelation is not limited by mediacy but is ever open to the illimitable truth of God. God still publishes his Word; he will publish it to the end of time; and great should be the company of them that publish it!

There are, then, the following four objective, immediate revelations of God in the present: (1) through the God-men of every today; (2) through the Holy Spirit, not merely as a decisive event on Pentecost, but as God the present guide into all truth; (3) through the Church as the real presence in human history of the new creatures in the eternal Son of God and as the continuing community of the newborn; (4) through the Bible as God's living speech in direct experience, the kind of speech which generated the written Word.

The subjective side of this objective immediacy of God as universal love we may think of particularly, for our purposes, in terms of our response for one world in Christ. God wants to make of one spirit all the divided men of human history. He wants to create true, unlimited community to the utmost of our allowance. He never compels fellowship, but, as we let him, he breaks down barriers of religion, race and nature, and unites men in the unity which is ever creative diversity. Our role is to be open and effective

channels of communication for the grace of God, whether on the
level of creation or on the level of redemption.

God also wants intensively to renew the whole social order with
his healing freshness. Our opportunity in this sphere is to conse-
crate to him our every talent and attention. Under God, every
vocation becomes a divine calling. God today is calling plumbers
and preachers, economists and politicians, educators and house-
wives, to work, each in his own way, to make a new social order.
With our cobalt bombs and computing machines, our jet planes
and television, our general education and specialized social engineering, this job is too big for any one of us or for all of us—
except we understand and truly believe that ours is only the
subjective side of the great objective acts of God which have made
this new world possible.

Our response to God's act is even more for the sake of the
celestial oneness of the whole company of God on earth. The
Holy Spirit is one, and all in him are one. Therefore, the present
divisions and competitive wastes in Church life are due to man's
refusal to own the Holy Spirit. Sectarianism denies Christ. We
cannot picture the creative nature of the Church which the Holy
Spirit can effect, but we can accept him and start to build within
his creative design. He will himself unfold it, if with all our lives
we dare to trust him for a new day of co-operative concern for all
men. Man is made for the Christian kind of community, for
freedom and faithfulness in fellowship based on Christ's love,
and made possible only by that love. Our response is subjective,
and we weary quickly except as we venture out into the great unknown of God's creative will within the peace and power of the
Holy Spirit.

We need also the eschatological response to God's creative
Bible, the Bible of contemporary revelation read toward the future.
What God has done in the past is recorded for our decision *in* the
present *for* the future. The Bible, past and present, must be released as the full pattern of God's love for man, within which
man can creatively discover the unity of truth for all life and
thought, both theoretical and concrete, but only against the back-
drop—the widest possible that finite man can see or understand—
of what God is about to do to conclude all things in heaven and
on earth in Christ.

In conclusion, then, we need a Christ-centered, evangelical supernaturalism based on revelation, which can be found only by faith;
generating and sustaining freedom, open to reason and using it
fully; energized by the Holy Spirit of truth and a concern for the

individual and for society; made conclusive in Christian community, which lives to the glory of God and finds fulfillment only within his will. Against such a faith, alive in love, firm in God, and flexible within the humility of human finiteness, no power of evil can prevail. Such a faith has been given once for all as our own holy heritage. Let us arise to take full possession of it.

IV

NEW LIGHT ON OLD PROBLEMS

Chapter 13

Natural Theology and the Christian Faith

IT SHOULD be obvious that the question concerning the validity and value of natural theology cannot be approached competently from within any system. To do so is to beg the initial and the determinative question. The subject calls for a decisive examination of theological method as a whole. The aim of this chapter, however, is only to describe and to evaluate two common approaches, and to suggest a third. We seem to be on the edge of a reformulation of the basic approach to religious knowledge. In any rethinking of this sort, natural theology, in one form or other, should be given an important place, for Horace's contention will not die: *Naturam expellas furca, tamen usque recurret.*

I

The first approach to be considered is that natural theology is itself the only basis of faith, even of the Christian faith. What other data are there, ask the advocates of this position, than those of this actual world? If there is any reality beyond this world, as soon as it has entered our world and can be grasped by our reason and experience, it is natural knowledge. Whatever can be known, communicated, and tested by our experience is natural knowledge. All valid knowledge, according to this position, is limited by the very fact of our situation to natural knowledge. Therefore, there can be no legitimate theology that is not natural theology. David Hume and Immanuel Kant have shown once for all, the advocates of this view of theology contend, that no arguments from this world can attain to knowledge of reality beyond it.

Few theologians, of course, have been content to limit theological knowledge to the reports of scientific inquiry. Those who do, hold that science deals only with the description of facts and functions. It limits its field of knowledge to such data as can be described and publicly verified by objective means. The aspirations and "revelations" of private devotions and public religion can never claim the status of knowledge. Such theological scientism obviously results in a completely this-worldly theology.

Nearly all other naturalistic theologians go beyond scientism, but reject in the name of philosophy all theological claims to know God beyond this world, at least in the sense of the supernaturalism of classical Christianity. Kant's critical philosophy has usually been presupposed by their method. All proofs of a supernatural or a "transcendent" God depend in some way on the ontological, Kant claims, and this proof is in fact definitional only in nature. Existence is no predicate that can be added to a perfect idea, especially since such perfection necessarily lacks confirmation within the realm of the contingent, the perishable, and the evil. Furthermore, theologians of naturalism point out, knowledge is either univocal or equivocal. If, in speaking of the supernatural, we use words in the same sense in which they are used in our ordinary knowledge, we have not superseded it; merely to posit another realm of the same kind as this world, furthermore, as Aristotle and Hume both held, is in no way to explain or to account for this world.

On the other hand, if the words we use in seeking to go beyond this world do not have their ordinary meaning, we are appealing to ignorance. The transcendent world, in such a case, has no knowable nature and no ascertainable basis in fact. If appeal is made to analogy, even to the analogy of proportionality, such reasoning, in the final analysis, is subject to the same kind of demolition as that visited upon the proofs themselves if the analogy purports to leave the realm of knowledge to become informative of some superrealm. Therefore, it is claimed that the final result of the attempt to reach any supernatural order remains either mere anthropomorphism or mere agnosticism. Neither philosophy nor theology as knowledge can go beyond this world.

A modern form of this argument is linguistic analysis, by whatever name. According to this school, broadly speaking, science alone gives concrete knowledge. Philosophy is uninformative, dealing with the meaning of meaning and the clarification of meaning. Meaning is either propositional and analytical, as in philosophy, or else it is verifiable in some public manner by objective tests, as in science. Such verification is possible only in the realm of sense knowledge, or as this position has now developed, by the most stringent possible check-back of any inference to the sense data from which it was made. No other language is meaningful. Theology is meaningless, it is claimed, because it is neither purely analytical nor stringently empirical.

God as necessary being is either a statement that is guilty of logical confusion—since necessity pertains to propositions alone and being to contingent probability—or is a logically demonstrable falsehood. No growth of this analytical position can fundamentally alter its condemnation of theology, it seems, without destroying its original basis. In Ludwig Wittgenstein's later usage, philosophy makes language less a matter of convention and less subject to correctional manipulation, but its stress on legitimate usage has never included any realm beyond natural knowledge. Whatever may be said, furthermore, of the existentialist school, including such persons as Heidegger and Jaspers, its dealing with transcendence has never reached any point where even the phrase "natural theology" could be properly used as relevant to the classical Christian field.

It is fair to say that both scientific naturalism and verification philosophy (linguistic analysis) should remind us that we have no right to live in a pre-Humian and pre-Kantian age. The day of an objective, rational metaphysics, deductive or inductive, is over. There is no presuppositionless thinking. Thought concerning ultimates is basically decisional, having at its disposal no full rational proof. Man has, even, the freedom not to see evidence. Justification by faith is a matter not only of life but also of knowledge.

The most adequate methodological inquiry in theology within the general assumptions of this first group in America is the work of men like Alfred North Whitehead, Paul Tillich, and Daniel Day Williams. They all reject scientism. They all proceed from validity to adequacy, to use Whitehead's terminology. Whitehead believed that his best writing was on God, but the God he described is accessible to scientific and philosophic confirmation without recourse to any transcendence beyond the order of our natural world. Tillich likewise refuses to be limited to any scientific or even philosophic naturalism, in the narrow sense. He advocates instead "the ecstatic reason" as the door to legitimate transcendence. For the most part, Tillich's method of correlation elicits theological answers to existential questions. Williams believes that all revelationisms that are unchecked by science and philosophy become arbitrary and ultimately relative. For this reason, he feels that honest and competent theology should avoid appeal to arbitrary "revelations" and speculative theological extensions that lack full relevance and power for our actual human situation. For these three thinkers all valid theological knowledge is natural theology in the sense that they cast out the supernaturalism of classical Christianity.

From the viewpoint of those who no longer believe in any ontological reality beyond this actual world or who believe positively
that our theological task is correctly to analyze this world and to
prescribe remedy for it, natural theology, in the classical sense,
appears within a radically altered perspective. It is not right to
observe this view of natural theology from within the assumptions
of supernaturalism. Instead of being a realm beyond nature and
history where God basically is and works and whence he came to
reveal himself and to save us, the whole revelational content of
classical theology is, for these thinkers, simply part of the data
of Christian theology in the postcritical modern sense. Thus,
whereas those who hold to supernaturalism interpret as naturalism
all theologies that do not affirm supernaturalism, and consequently
class and compare these, in intent and field, with the historic doctrines of natural theology generally, from the point of view of
those who consider classical supernaturalism untenable, the old
naturalism is itself untenable because it was built upon a fallacious
dualism.

In general, the theological content of this position, whatever
its name, stresses dependable cosmic order and resources for human life. This theology is no humanism. It testifies to objective
powers that make for being and for harmony of being, to principles
of concretion, to streams of reality that afford victory over anxiety.
The human situation is accepted realistically and subjected to
keen analysis, with its hopes and frustrations, its fulfillments and
its demands. History itself becomes a matter of answering man's
basic questions of embarrassment, reason becomes ecstatic and
a question of problem solving. Needs reveal the resources in reality
to meet them. Usually the Christian content of love is accepted
as a way of believing and of walking, with powers available in
reality to answer such seeking for love. Christian words are taken
over with a fresh meaning. Although God is no longer considered
to be a supernatural, personal being, he is both the ground and
the goodness of life. Creation and providence are no longer deemed
to be due to God's personal initiative from beyond our world but
are rather conceived of as divine activity within our world and
history.

In these interpretations, Christ is still central to Christian
faith, not, to be sure, as the Son sent by God into the world to
save the world, but as the revealer of the true meaning of existence
and its saving power. The Cross and the resurrection are for them
still the power of God for salvation, not as God going literally to
his death and rising again a victor over it, and not as salvation

in terms of continued personal life after death, but as God's victory within history and human life over man's chief enemies and the tragedies of existence. God, in a new sense, is ultimate meaning and effective power for good. Natural theology, as traditionally considered, becomes within this context the general religious experiences of men, and is apart from the central revelatory and redemptive acts of the Christian faith.

The honesty of this position is unmistakable. Its advocates are among our most competent and creative thinkers. If the facts of the situation demanded that we thus reduce our faith, we should all be willing, I hope, to do so. My own inability to do so is due to an insight that has captured me, namely, that the history of creation when seen in the light of the Incarnation indicates a transcendent ground of creation and a transcendent goal of human history. Furthermore, when Christ as agape is taken univocally as the revelation of God, we have within human experience him who promises fulfillment of it, but who, nevertheless, cannot be accounted for by general experience. By situation, all men must live by faith; and this faith in the transcendent God, the God and Father of our Lord Jesus Christ, although unprovable, is for me the least arbitrary and the most convincing faith. An explicit or an implicit faith in the world we now know, apart from some explanation of the history of its long coming to be and the sudden appearance of the whole realm of life and meaning, would, for me, be begging the basic questions of ontology. This is my answer to the Hume-Kant rejection of all knowledge of the transcendent. It is not precritical but postcritical. In such a faith, meaning and mystery are both present; faith and reason join in the task of living. Within naturalism there is no real God as creator, no sovereign ruler, no ultimately inscrutable personal providence, no Cross as the identification in redemptive suffering of the infinite God with man, and no actual resurrection from the dead on the part of Christ or man, now or ever.

There is, therefore, no requisite answer within this position to the presence and power of evil in the world and no legitimate acceptance of the ontology of love as ultimate. Such is the case whether salvation be conceived of as a victory within man in this life or as some finding of final rest and fulfillment in the ocean of being. Every ocean of being ultimately drowns not only man's hopes but man. The accommodation of this position to our actual world robs faith of its power for the people as soon as they see through the richness of the language to the poverty of the promises. We turn, therefore, to another way of looking at natural theology.

II

The opposite way of looking at natural theology is to accept a self-contained, authoritative revelation. From this standpoint, the method for determining whether or not natural theology is Christian is to search the revelation. If it is Christian, the next step is to ascertain what natural theology means in the light of the accepted authority and what place it has in the faith. There are three ways of doing so: (1) to search the teachings of the authoritative Bible; (2) to search the teachings of an authoritative Church; (3) to draw legitimate inferences from the given revelation.

Biblical scholars find that God in the Old Testament works in nature—witness the testimony of the Psalms; and in general history—witness God's use of Cyrus. In the New Testament, occasional verses offer evidence for natural theology, as, for instance, in the statement of Jesus: "Why judge ye not of yourself what is right?" Similar testimony is Paul's explicit reference to the Gentiles' having a conscience whereby they judge what is right and wrong. Other suggestive statements may be added, such, for example, as that God has made himself plainly known through creation, "even his eternal power and deity"; or that the Gentiles worship the same God as the Jews, "for God is one." Against these verses must be balanced, of course, such a claim as the assertion that the natural man cannot know the things of the Spirit. Such an affirmation, however, refers not to natural theology, but rather to natural knowledge of revelation. Hendrik Kraemer's basic analysis of natural theology in *Religion and the Christian Faith* is weakened by his failure to distinguish between these two kinds of knowledge. In any case, biblical exegesis shows that what may be called natural theology is plainly though rarely present in the Bible.

If, on the other hand, the Church is accepted as authority, it is important to observe that most of the Church Fathers, not just writers like Justin Martyr and Clement of Alexandria, assumed some form or measure of natural theology. In Augustine, God's presence and work outside the Christian revelation is definite and large-scaled, and in Thomas Aquinas, natural theology is a twin pillar of faith. Should Rudolf Bultmann be right that such teaching is an importation of Stoicism and not a part of the original kerygma, those who depend on the authoritative teachings of the Church must, on the whole, consider natural theology a part of the Christian faith. Even the Reformers, as John McNeill has ably demonstrated, kept natural theology within their exposition of the Christian faith. Church Fathers like Tertullian, who in the main rejected natural theology, are exceptional. Thus, the Church has taught natural theology in some form.

In contemporary biblical and Reformation theology, however, there has been an outright denial of natural theology. This radical rejection has not come in the main from exegesis, but for the most part as a result of the acceptance of Søren Kierkegaard's dictum that there is a qualitative distinction between time and eternity. Karl Barth formulated radically the consequences of this thesis. There is nothing of God in man, in history, or in nature, Barth growled, nor does any revelatory or redemptive work exist there. Even after Barth realized that his extreme stand was due to Kantian philosophy and not to the biblical revelation, he nevertheless maintained it.

Barth, to my knowledge, has never indicated that he sees any organic relation between God's special presence and work in Christ and the realm of creation and history. In *Fides Quaerens Intellectum*, in *Christengemeinde und Bürgergemeinde*, and especially in *The Doctrine of Reconciliation*, Barth has begun to deal with the question of God's general work. His treatment of the Noachic Covenant in *The Doctrine of Reconciliation* is of real importance at this point, as are also his treatment of the Abrahamic Covenant, the Deutero-Isaiah Commission of the Suffering Servant, and the New Covenant of Jeremiah. But even in his frank and sweeping acknowledgment in *Die Menschlichkeit Gottes* of his definite failure at this point in his early writings, Barth is still so confiningly Christocentric that he does not begin to fathom the extent and importance of God's general presence and work in nature and history in preparation for the fullness of time in Christ.

What has obviously happened in Barth's case is that he has rejected so passionately the importation of philosophical considerations and conclusions that on the whole are unbiblical, that he has also rejected basically the minor allowance made for natural theology within the Bible. He has done so, evidently, on the ground that all natural theology is damaging to a vigorous and forthright Christian confession. In his main rejection, I believe him to be right. He is wrong, however, not only in his general neglect of whatever natural theology there is in the Bible, but, much more, in his narrow biblicism whereby he isolates Christ from God's comprehensive, indirect work pedagogically in human experience, in nature, and in history.

The approach of an authoritative, self-contained revelation threatens us with an arbitrary faith and therefore, ultimately, with relativity. Inasmuch as revelation, in this understanding of it, cannot by its very nature to be related to general knowledge, it lacks relevance for life and thought. Although there was decisive need for the emphasis on the primacy of revelation, the time is long since past, or should be, when scholars had to obtain knowledge of nature from the Bible or from theology, and when they were willing even to dispute the facts of nature for the sake of a self-contained fully authoritative revelation. Likewise, the time should be past when man's religious knowledge, on any level or in any realm, could be isolated from his total knowledge. For me, consequently, recourse to an arbitrary revelation to determine the nature and meaning of natural theology, if any, is anachronistic and unrealistic. Such a faith is arbitrary, relativistic, and solicits a capricious acceptance.

Thus, just as I could not find adequate the position that assumes natural theology as the only available basis for faith, no more can I accept what to me is an arbitrary and authoritarian position in this matter. I turn, then, to an understanding of natural theology that I believe accepts the distinctive truths of both positions while doing fuller justice not only to faith and reason but especially to the nature of the full Gospel.

III

We have now sketched possibilities for natural theology: first, from the standpoint of reason informed by general experience, and second, from the point of view of revelation. There is, besides, the Thomist position which holds natural theology to be accessible within the realm of reasoned experience, but which superimposes upon such theology the distinctive revelation of the Christian faith. Although the method of Thomism gives expression to profound truth, it is as a whole a convenient historic solution, not sufficiently integrated organically to serve as the most inclusive context for unified inquiry and as the definitive discourse of religious knowledge.

What I propose, in place of the positions we have discussed, as the correct approach to the problem of natural theology goes neither from reason to revelation nor from revelation to reason; nor does it require a separation one from the other as does Thomism regardless of the extent to which they point toward the same conclusions. My suggestion is, rather, that we rethink natural theology within the context of incarnational theology. The Incarnation is Christ as the Event-meaning of agape; it is the revelation, for the world's redemption and fulfillment, of the personal Spirit

who is holy love. Both revelation and reason then center in Christ
at the start, branching out afterwards into the supernatural and
the natural realms. We do not start methodologically either with
God or with man, but with the Godman. Incarnation is in, but
basically not confined to, the world. The new being of Christ cannot be accounted for by general experience, nor reduced to it. Even
so, he most fully gives meaning to experience, not only to personal
experience but to that of history and of nature as well. His origin
cannot be explained in terms of what we know, and yet he gives
both reason for, and context to, that origin.

While the Incarnation is in itself selective, it nevertheless involves all we know, even reorienting and reshaping aggregative
reality into an eschatological expectation by the power of the incarnational center. The Incarnation of Christ as agape has the
power of supernatural transcendence. While it can never be definitely limited to the observation of the actual, calling as it does
upon the illimitable mystery of the God of eternity, Incarnation
is not arbitrary, since it offers definable meaning that can be tested,
at least partially and secondarily, for its right to claim transcendence. In other words, Christ, the Godman of the Cross and the
resurrection, is the Event which gives us eternity in, beyond and
for time, which gives light for explanation, judgment and salvation, and which affords the power for the redemption and the
fulfillment of life.

Christ is therefore no bridge between the natural and the supernatural. He is the common corridor that must be entered and
traversed if either is properly to be reached. We can neither presuppose supernaturalism, unfolding thereafter its content in Christ,
nor assume naturalism while reaching the full meaning of the
natural in Christ. Instead, the only door to full truth is Christ as
the Event-meaning who is agape. In the light of the life, teachings,
Cross, and resurrection of Christ, we discover that no supernatural
order can be known decisively apart from Christ, while no natural
order of this world can contain and confine him. The supernatural order is the eternally transcendent reality and power of the
love of God revealed in Christ for our judgment, salvation, and fulfillment. The natural order is the realm of creation *in response to*
the realm of redemption: the conditions of nature and history that
make our process pedagogical.

Thus both the supernatural and the natural, to be correctly
known, must be seen in Christ. Accordingly, with the coming of
Christ, natural theology offers no realm of investigation apart from
him. Before his coming, the full scope of problems concerning

natural theology could not be understood. He alone gives the full context to God's plan and purpose for nature. Besides, natural theology cannot be carried on competently apart from the eyes of faith that kindle sight. Believing and knowing are twin requirements for theological adequacy. Discipleship and scholarship must be wed for legitimate theological children to be born.

At the same time, natural theology cannot be curtailed to the human nature of Christ, as Barth generally does. Even when he allows the Noachic and consequent Old Testament Covenants, thus providing more room for natural theology, even protesting, in his *Doctrine of Reconciliation*, a freedom to which he never gives content or concrete significance, Barth is still confined by his view of natural theology to a specialized biblical focus on God's activity. The study of natural theology can be carried on aright, however, only when the theologian, with the eyes of faith and with ungrudging allowance for whatever measure of objective investigation of nature and history is possible, faces and genuinely comes to terms with the facts and relations of the natural order, as a whole and in specific parts, and then places all his findings within the context of God's eternal purpose in Christ.

Christ as theological context alters no fact *as fact*, but the Christian pattern involves change in the meaning and the relations of the facts. The configuration of Christian revelation, Christ as Event-meaning, rearranges, revalues, and reconstitutes facts. Christian theology can never impose its truth; it cannot lord it over any other subject. Christ, when rightly known and accepted, sets men free to study the orders of nature in history. Christian love as *context* gives ultimate meaning and motivation to both life and study without distorting or prejudicing any content of knowledge in any field. Where the Spirit of the Lord is, there is complete freedom of mind, of task, and of field. If we abide in him who is the truth we shall take the way of meaningful but open inquiry and be set free by the truth. Only against the background of such natural theology does revealed theology display its more ample truth and relevance. Only God's patient work on the level of creation makes intelligible, in the face of evil, the claim of God's self-revelation to be from the beginning creative love.

In our day, there should be no need for a reminder that the supernatural is not to be thought of directionally or geographically. The eternal Spirit does not relate himself to his creation or creatures basically in spatial terms. Supernaturalism should be considered not directionally but dimensionally. Wherever God is, he is incomparably more and other than his creation. Even in his presence with nature, he is completely transcendent of it. Similarly in his presence with man, even in Incarnation, God retains his unbridgeable, qualitative distinction from man. Even when "filled with the fullness of God," man never becomes God in the slightest bit. Whether in his deity or in his humanity, God remains forever God. However much "in, with, and under" any creature God may be, he is wholly other and entirely transcendent in the sense that, while truly present, he never becomes part of, or commingles his nature with, any creature. Thus, no matter how fully God is present with a creature and no matter how fulfillingly he participates in its life, God remains God without localization or limitation.

Dimensional transcendence has been brilliantly and weightily treated by Paul Tillich as categorical necessity (nonexistent as a realm of transcendent being or of pure being within existence), the impingement of the unconditional on the conditional for the sake of being and harmony of being. Dimensional rather than directional transcendence in my understanding, however, presupposes difference of being from our time-space existence, but not the absence of transcendent being. The clue to such an order of being is God as Spirit. Theological content and context come together is Christ the Godman. Such supernaturalism as results from this conjunction is subject to no demythologizing. Such naturalism as results can have no limits of investigation set for it by revealed theology. The contents of the orders of redemption and creation are different, needing distinctive methods; the context for the knowledge of both is the same.

Simply to go from revelation to reason is to fall prey to the problems of an arbitrary faith; merely to go from reason to revelation is to center revelation in the natural order and, therefore, never decisively to rise beyond it. Rather, we should so start with Incarnation that the special revelation of God's self-disclosure is related to general revelation as its fulfillment by transformation while the general revelation becomes secondarily a resultative check on the special, delivering the special from the charge of arbitrariness. Revelation should disclose to the trained eyes of faith at least the proper nature and meaning of the order of creation. In this way faith and reason, for us finite creatures, become dynamically interrelated, neither ever reducible to the other or independent of it. In the primary revelation of Christ, the agape of God, has come the full light. This light has not come apart from either man's realms of darkness or the faint lights of God's preparatory dawn; it is a light which, when rightly seen, cannot be dimmed by the natural order, but can be seen only in richer rays when reflected and diversified in God's glory in creation.

Chapter 14

Notes by a Theologian on Biblical Hermeneutics

IN THE March, 1958, issue of the *Journal of Biblical Literature* appeared four articles on the question of hermeneutics written by biblical scholars James Muilenburg, J. Coert Rylaarsdam, Krister Stendahl, and G. Ernest Wright, the last named being, however, only indirectly concerned with hermeneutics. Stendahl suggested that, as far as hermeneutics goes, the "principles belong to the discipline of theology, not to biblical studies as such." As a theologian, I shall limit my discussion to constructive comments.

I

Although the purpose of this chapter is centered in its third section, the level of total context, there should be no bypassing or short-cutting of either the level of fact or the level of the principles of interpretation. At one time the question of fact seemed relatively simple. A primary scholar in the field of the history of religions, for instance, once said in conversation that "he worshiped at no altar except the holy altar of fact." And fact he defined as "actual archeological evidence," like monuments or physical objects used by the people under study. In a letter to the author, a prominent American physicist writes that all facts "have in them elements which are essentially pre-assumptions; i.e. there are no 'pure facts' in the old sense. For some 'facts' the observational elements are relatively weaker, and the presuppositional elements relatively stronger, than for others. In some the presuppositional elements are relatively unimportant while for others they are almost decisive." He even goes so far as to call attention to the danger of "the assumption, rarely explicitly stated that the laws of nature are independent of time, i.e. the same in the past as in the present, and therefore essentially unchanging." Careful science, he contends, is at best only some three hundred years old.

We need to be warned at this point! Nevertheless, we should be under tutelage to all objective evidence and, without placing blind trust in the scientific method, we have to assume, I believe, the general reliability of such means, for instance, as the carbon test for dating material. Fact should be at least one stubborn pole aiding exegesis within the principles of interpretation.

Obviously, manuscripts and tradition are far removed from primary fact. Even so, they must be accepted and used if there is to be any exegesis, however thin and tenuous the result. In addition to all the cautions and precautions which are demanded by the next level of approach, there are original factual risks connected with the handling of any manuscript. Although it may be established that the manuscript itself is genuine, questions remain as to the bias, the competence, and the position for observation on the part of the writer. At best, in all areas of remote historical investigation we have only a thin, subjective strand, a hair-thin thread binding us to an unimaginable wealth of past events and attitudes. Even so, such evidence can be indicative of the happenings and feelings of an age.

When several manuscripts relating to the same period are available, the problem of the correct interpretation of words and symbols increases. If we interpret words according to their usage contemporary with the period of the manuscript itself, we become guilty of the reductionist fallacy, or we may read too much into the manuscript, whereas if we do not make use of contemporary meanings at all we may become involved in the falsification of the past in terms of our own age or of some other age.

The discussion of adequate exegesis is not the purpose of this chapter, however, for that would involve all the internal problems of interpretation and all possible techniques for checking the meaning of any manuscript in the light of external aids. The reason for mentioning manuscript problems here is to affirm, for common understanding, the need for the maximum regard for fact insofar as this can be had at all, with no illusions or pretensions regarding the possibility of arriving at any objective portrait of the past as such.

Furthermore, tradition as history is at once subjective and objective. Any one piece of tradition is historically so vague and unestablished that it is practically worthless. Occasionally its information might provide a clue to other evidence and thus play its part in the interpretation of history. On the other hand, when there is a strong tradition available, it might constitute an informative continuum of consolidated material as a broad history of background. As almost a history of history it can become objectively weighty. In the case of biblical hermeneutics I take it that apart from the oral tradition and certain Jewish and other background material, tradition is not a major factor.

II

When we move up to the level of the principles of interpretation, the correct rendering of historical data becomes severely difficult. The levels of the data to be interpreted and that of interpretation or of the interpreter cannot be isolated, of course, except for analytical purposes. All knowledge is had within a synthesis of subject and object which cannot be torn asunder without some violence to itself. Modern theories of knowledge, beyond mere linguistic analysis, stress the creative or distorting involvement of the knower in his knowledge. The more personal and value-weighted the object of inquiry, the more important becomes the personal angle of vision. Some have gone so far as to declare that all such knowledge is through and through subjective and altogether relative. If this be the case, the personal angle of vision becomes mere preference or bias. Others have at least so minimized the objective element in the fields of value or of the interpretation of faith-judgments that all possibility of reliable common knowledge is precluded. At best what is known, within these theories of knowledge, are concrete events, separate facts, plus severely limited relationships. For knowledge, history can then have neither universals of meaning nor ultimates of purpose. Such an understanding of the knowledge situation makes mincemeat, of course, of most biblical scholarship.

Add to that the Christian understanding of the sinfulness of man—within which man distorts by his rebelliously and faithlessly warped vision whatever affects the basic meaning of his life, all judgments upon him, and the nature of his salvation—and the plight of the biblical interpreter becomes hopeless in the sense of any adequate dealing with the heart of the biblical message. The limitations of the field, the finiteness of man, and man's sinful drive to distort combine to draw the curtain between the interpreter and all meaningful history, including, of course, biblical interpretation.

Another blow to the aspirant to objective biblical interpretation is the obvious presence of divergent assumptions on the part of the various schools of biblical interpretation. Both the nature and the perspectives of these schools are complex and hard to determine. For one thing, there is a natural progression of attention from one item to another in the process of scholarship. Only thus are the separate items developed and given their chance to throw light or context on the larger body of material. This is the positive side of the question. The negative side is devious and treacherous. Within the scholar's drive for professional recognition, even legitimate scholarly creativity usually receives distortion of emphasis. No field of scholarship, moreover, is devoid of compelling personalities who distort knowledge and who help pervert less forceful and often less competent colleagues in the discipline. But the most determinative side of this situation is the psychological need of the professionals in the subject to say something new. There is an ennui in teaching and a constant longing for creative relief. Accordingly, the new scholarly insight often comes with more emotional impact than with intellectual conviction. Under these circumstances, the primacy of the prophets in the Old Testament eventually becomes an old story, while the prominent role of the cultus is new and exciting. The discovery of the Dead Sea scrolls has released research from the continual commitment to well-traveled roads.

Particularly welcome to one drive in human nature is over-againstness. The Hebrew and the Greek views of time are consequently distorted or oversimplified, not alone because of ignorance but because of the in-group psychology which variously affects the different interpreters. In addition to this temptation, there is the overagainstness of one school of interpretation to another. Entwined within the whole problem of interpretation, moreover, is the emotional continuum of conflict and approval among primary personalities with regard to each other and to their followers; and among the disciples with regard to conflict and approval. Thus the drive and drift of interpretation is due both to the nature of creative progression and to the emotional entanglements of professional life itself, whatever be the relation between the need for the new as such and the temptations and sins of overagainstness. And through the whole process, besides, lurk the pitfalls of human creatureliness.

In addition to the personal and the professional angles of vision there are the general presuppositions of an age, so presuppositional, or perhaps post suppositional, that neither the individual interpreter nor the schools are aware of them. Paul Tillich has told us of the general kairos of an age from which it is almost impossible to stand apart. More than we know, the age in which we live predetermines by its very nature not only the questions we ask of history but the way in which we put our problems. Only a few great spirits can either undercut the general assumptions to see the deeper continuities of history before the age or sense and help bring in the questions of a new age. But whether these exceptional interpreters be Schlegel's "retrospective prophets" or Nietzsche's prophets "born posthumously," they are not and cannot be understood from within the dominant assumptions and attitudes of the age. They are therefore generally ignored or rejected, but always more the former than the latter. Since they do not seem relevant, they seem unimportant. A safe and cautious generalization is, then, that the more popular or even the more dominant in scholarly circles the point of view is, the stronger is the likelihood that it is the fullest expression of the particular questions of the age. The deeper unity of the continuum of interpretation usually lies buried by the age or else speaks a quietly strong but unheeded voice into the clamor of contemporary interpretation.

There are three sources for corrections of these three kinds of distortion: the personal, the professional, and the cultural. The personal bias due to sin can be mitigated by the effective life of worship. The prayer of a surrendered life to God's will for the common good is the strongest antidote to personal ambition and to the distortion of vision that comes from sin. Forgiveness, trust, and concern for truth are engendered and obtained by the right relation to God. For most interpreters at least, this medicine is at best only a partial remedy, but to whatever extent it is received, it is important. Even the self-knowledge that is afforded is corrective of distorting prejudice. In the second place, there is recourse to diligent, open-ended study of contemporaries. All differing from other competent and dedicated scholars ought to hurt. All argumentation of overagainstness widens the distance between the interpreter and the adequacy of interpretation. The humble wrestling with divergent positions can deliver a scholar from the complacency, premature certainty, and insecure aggression of the personally ambitious and partially oriented interpreter.

Third, the history of interpretation can help correct not only the personal imitation of vision and not only the false importance of a professional school or position, but also the cultural presuppositions that are most difficult to penetrate. More and more I am convinced of the need to listen to the long history of a subject in order to see the narrowness of one's selection of items for emphasis and the ease with which distortion of combination can be made. When life before God in humble worship, when life before our fellow scholars in diligent learning, and when life before the long, twisted ribbon of the past in patient tracing, are simultaneously accepted and pursued, there is available a genuine measure of deliverance from the prejudice of personal factors, the bias of professional belonging, and the presuppositions of the age. There is thus hope within the high hopelessness of rigid and committed scholarship, even within the field of the principles of interpretation which affect exegesis.

III

The third level, that of total context, is of special concern to the theologian. There is, however, a new understanding of the importance of context in the fields of knowledge generally. When physics passed from thinking in terms of isolated particles to field physics, when biology accepted more of the organismic approach, and when the insights of Gestalt psychology were appropriated, a new understanding arose not only of the importance of pattern for interpretation but of the impact of the whole on the parts. In philosophy, the struggle has been largely between the powerful new proposal of organismic philosophy by men like Alfred North Whitehead and the attempt to rule out as meaningless any recourse to the whole, as in most of linguistic analysis.

But both verification philosophy and usage philosophy have been backing away from the extremes of logical positivism into a more constructive confrontation of issues. Although theology itself has suffered in some quarters from a relapse into an extreme nominalist position, the attempt to deal only with concrete particulars, this trend is so contrary to its own nature and function that it is more a sign of borrowing from contemporary philosophy than of a healthy condition. Theology *is* the interpretation of all of life in the light of God.

I think it is correct to say, in any case, that most theologians now see the inescapable nature of some governing context, of some presupposition for thought, of some stance for seeing, of some position for perspective. In any case, since I have undertaken the responsibility of making these comments on hermeneutics from the point of view of theology, I confess that I am constrained and convinced by the fact that there is no presuppositionless reasoning, that we have to have some context for thought, some configuration of interpretation, and that such a context affects our total understanding as well as our view of the parts.

The Christian faith should use history for its foundation. The Bible records this history. Only by the use of history can the Christian interpreter avoid the danger of a speculative transcendence. Revelational supernaturalism is vulnerable unless it centers in history. Otherwise, philosophy can show that we use terms either univocally or equivocally. In the former case, using language in the ordinary sense of terms, we never get beyond what we know in this world. In the latter case, using terms to mean something other than what we know, we are still left ignorant of the other world. When we start with history, however, there is no such problem. How we then arrive at adequate transcendence, without which there is no Christian faith, we shall consider later. But even while starting with the Bible we should remember that the Bible centers in the Christ. The Scriptures at their height and in their basic direction tell of him. To this claim all true Christian history of interpretation attests.

By starting with Christ as Christian context we avoid the danger of an arbitrarily selected history. Christ as the center alone provides the context for Christian interpretation. Therefore, no Christian interpreter can go to the Bible aright without going through Christ. Christ is the Event-meaning who is agape. The personal Event is primary. The meaning derives from this Event of Christ, the truth known through the Holy Spirit, the Spirit of truth. Objectively and subjectively, historically and personally, the criteria for Christian faith are thus provided from within the faith itself. Christ as context claims unequivocally to be God's final and full truth. In his life we see light. From him all true understanding proceeds because all knowledge is made obedient to him, or put into its true context apart from which it neither is as it is nor is known as it is.

Up to this point, the biblical scholar can proceed from within the presuppositions of his own field. Since, moreover, he has to have some dominant stance, the Christian perspective should be openly acknowledged as necessary for Christian interpretation. There is no Christian exegesis without Christian principles of interpretation. Such a context, although it cannot or may not be meaningful outside of faith, nevertheless provides a unity of discourse for Christian communication.

The real question of ultimates, of the legitimacy of the position for truth, lies beyond this point of analysis. The final problem is whether this Christian context is optional as one way among others to look at the world, whether it is necessary as ultimate truth, or whether there is some other real and relevant choice. The first two I cannot accept. The first would imply a complete relativity, at least of knowledge, and a complete arbitrariness of choice of context. The Christian faith itself, on the contrary, claims to be universal both in reality and in truth. It claims that all ultimate reality and knowledge so center in God that in some sense men are responsible for not knowing as well as for not obeying, or perhaps more accurately, for not obeying and knowing him. The second position would involve either the falsity or the forfeiting of man's freedom. The Christian context cannot be necessary as ultimate truth for man's knowledge or else man would not have to be justified by faith in knowledge as well as in life. There would then be no freedom not to believe. In such a case, knowledge could be coerced and faith not free. We turn therefore to another choice which I believe is both real and relevant.

In the final analysis, since there is no presuppositionless reasoning and since no ultimate presupposition can be proved, the Christian context is and remains a faith-stance. Ultimately we all live not by sight but by faith. Nevertheless, this faith-stance is not arbitrary, both because there is no other perspective which more fully accounts for what we know and because the Christian context affords a maximum of coherent organization of our total experience and knowledge. Moreover, for reasons soon to be offered, it cannot be said that every ultimate context determines the criteria by which its adequacy and that of all others are measured and that therefore every context turns out to be best merely for its own world of organization and explanation. For the same reason Ruth Benedict is wrong when she says that every absolute is the defensive and aggressive rationalization of an in-group which has no validity beyond the group.

At least the positive affirmations about to be given are true for those who accept the legitimacy of any knowledge and the desirability of life as such, understood at its best. The reason such positive statements will be made with conviction is that human nature and history come together in the realm of need, while need points organically to its source and fulfillment. Obviously, within human history and cosmic process we cannot have proof from the proximate to the ultimate, a logical inadequacy, but we can have reliable pointings in the direction of the solutions which endorse the truth of the Christian context and claim. Thus we are left with faith requiring commitment and study. Only the final consummation, however, can validate the Christian claim.

Man's deepest needs come from his total situation within the world, and they reflect the nature of the reality which has produced him. If man's basic need for creative life and for community, center in Christ's kind of love, the love that God prepared for with power in the Old Testament, and revealed by his own enmanment, or becoming man, in Jesus Christ, then that need indicates the heart of reality. If human history finds its meaning in the fostering and fulfillment of a certain kind of community, the inclusive, creative community of concern which is the true nature of the Christian Church, then history helps authenticate the Christian revelation. If nature discloses a relation between the kind of predictability and precariousness which are the conditions for human initiative, responsibility, and growth while also allowing for the constant need for faith, nature strengthens the case for the Christian context.

If moral and natural evil yield significant meaning most fully within the context of the Cross of Christ, then one of man's deepest needs to know, to believe, and to overcome indicates the centrality of the Christian context. Obviously there is no place here for a lifetime of investigation along these lines, but the Christian context has captured my mind by its adequacy to minister to the facts of experience, history, nature, and evil. Such seeing may, of course, be convincingly meaningful only within the gift and power of faith; it may presuppose commitment, but it offers the kind of organization and explanation of experience that can also be meaningfully offered to others for conviction and conversion as well as for study and growth. Thus the Christian faith is and remains a posture of faith, even while it also secondarily offers both a unity of discourse and a context for communication. Humanity is collectively related through basic need with regard to both history and nature to its common origin, point of reference, and power for fulfillment.

Possibly we can point out or at least hint at the way from the foundation of the Christian context in history, in the Bible centering in Christ, to the classical biblical and Christian transcendence. The first is the way of protology: The history of creation, life itself, the preparations for Christ in experience and history, and finally Christ, cannot be adequately accounted for either by a reductionistic naturalism or by considering our present world to be ultimate. Since we must have some context, configuration, or presupposition, a transcendent ground of creation is the least arbitrary explanation of these beginnings and developments. In the second place, the Christian context provides the kind of organismic potential for human nature, history, and nature itself which best organizes and explains these even while transcending immeasurably the actual world we know. The love of Christ both indicates that all things consist in him and also goes beyond present actuality as an ideal, a potential, and a locus for the solution of our needs.

In the third place, Christ as agape most severely shows what is wrong with us, judges us, and affords power for forgiveness and transformation. Thus there is an existential transcendence as well as the transcendence of protology and of organismic requirements. Fourth, the main transcendence of the Christian context over our actual historic and cosmic situation is the eschatological. We live mostly in the world of not yet. Christ as the end and ending shall draw all men unto himself. The end of history is present in its midst, promising and pointing to its fulfillment. Even these embryonic suggestions may show how we can start within history, with the Incarnation at center, thus both avoiding the problems of speculative transcendence and arriving at real reasons for an adequate, classical Christian transcendence.

In this chapter we can do little more than propose that the Christian principles of biblical interpretation which are presupposed by exegesis center in Christ as the context for the total task. Historical scholarship and textual exegesis have their own distinctive tasks up to the proper limit of the efficacy of their methods. But since no part is ever separate from, nor without influence from, the total context, there must be a constant checking back and forth from fact to faith and from faith to fact, each illuminating and correcting the other. The more the interpretation enters the realm of meaning, the more necessary it is to be both critically competent in technique and competently critical of one's own assumptions and attitudes. Since, however, the Christian context is one of Christ as concern, under the Holy Spirit as truth, the more the interpreter commits himself and lives his faith, the less biased he will be and the more ready for objective seeing, especially for self-correction. The total task is difficult and dangerous, probably far beyond the awareness of most interpreters, but, within the resources of historic data and of personal preparation and discipline, there is yet some real ground for confidence that the task not only is worth attempting but can be done with some sense of objectivity and real community of seeing. Such long labor of biblical interpretation is invaluable for the Church and for the believer as well as for the theologian.

Possibly the main contribution of the theologian to the total work of biblical interpretation can be his seeing that the selection of Christ, the revelation of God as universal love, creative, redemptive, and fulfilling, although a stance of faith, is not arbitrary, but instead meets strikingly man's common need for the fulfillment of experience, for meaning in history, and for the interpretation of nature with reference to both experience and history. Thus the Christian context is not arbitrary either in its selection from within the Bible and Christian history or with reference to ascertainable truth. In Christ as context, criterion, and dynamic for faith, center the principles of biblical interpretation.

Chapter 15

The Bible as Authority

We MUST return to the Bible. There is no hope for man outside the biblical faith. The Bible, rightly interpreted—that is, from its own highest peak, God's actual presence as holy love in Jesus Christ—is man's final revelation. I do not know and cannot imagine any other God, or to phrase it more explicitly, for me there is no other God than he who has disclosed his will and way in Jesus Christ.

The Bible should be not a problem but a power. It should be the light of the world and the light for life. It should be our proud possession. We should live by it, grow by it, and become glad and strong by it.

Nevertheless, it is a problem to numerous people, both inside and outside the faith. It is a difficulty in people's lives because it has been abused. It has been used wrongly. It has been sinned against by both enemies and friends. The Church is confused, divided, and enfeebled because the Bible has not been allowed to to be the Bible, the living Word of God.

Two dangers beset the Bible, one from the left and the other from the right.

From the left, we have a group of scholars who want to demythologize the Bible. They mean to remove from the Bible the primitive myths which modern man, trained in science, can no longer believe. This group is led by Rudolf Bultmann, the most prominent theologian in Europe, and Paul Tillich, who is in the opinion of many the most weighty theologian in America. Both leaders are able, profound, and dedicated, but they believe that science has forever destroyed legitimate faith in the supernatural world and in life after death.[1] These men have among their followers a number of determined spirits.

[1] Without life after death there can be no adequate solution of the problem of evil. If this life is all, faith in the Christian God of sovereign love is illegitimate. Hence the decisive importance of this criterion in this book.

I believe that this movement constitutes a threat of life or death to everything that the Bible affirms at its very center. This movement will be defeated because the Bible is true, and, ultimately, we do everything for, and not against, the truth. God's truth will prevail.

The threat from the right has made the threat from the left possible and indeed necessary. This is the threat unintelligently and immorally to flatten out the Bible, putting all of its material on the same level, rather than putting God in Christ as the center and the heartbeat of the Bible. Gerald Kennedy calls this "the crime of the levelers."[2] This devastating attack on the Bible which drives the intelligently alert and morally sensitive people away from it, falsely, is due, all too often, to a zeal not according to knowledge. The Bible must be rescued from its unintelligent friends and be allowed to speak its sovereign message to a needy and waiting world.

Let me illustrate what I mean. An executive of one of the major denominations in the United States went to Principal Nathaniel Micklem, of Mansfield College, Oxford, with a problem: the Church official's daughter, a high school student, had gone to her father asking him whether to believe her preacher or her teachers as to the age of the earth. "I myself," said the churchman, "can get along by believing, when I am in Church, that the world is only six thousand years old, while believing, when I am with educated people, that the world is much older, but I don't want my daughter to have to grow up a split personality."

There is no need for a split personality on account of the Bible. I want to point out the full biblical faith, in its own light, for the world, with no sacrifice either of honesty or of competence. We shall consider first "The Bible and Christ"; second, "The Bible and the Holy Spirit"; and third, "The Bible and Experience."

The Bible is indispensable as the original record of the constituting events of the Christian faith. The Church without the Bible is like a person with amnesia, i.e., without memory. Such a person lives, sees, chooses, but he does not know who he is or how he became what he is. The depth and riches of his experience have dropped out. Everything for him is flat and thin. He has no secure sense of self-being. The Church without the Bible is unthinkable. The Bible is the original self-attestation of the Church. It is the founding deed of the Church.

Even such a state of complete forgetfulness would not be disastrous if the Christian faith were a matter of correct ideas or a

[2] *Have This Mind* (Harper & Brothers, 1948), p. 172.

matter of prescription for right living. But it is not primarily either of these. The Christian faith is a historical religion that is more like a personal life than like any system of ideas. It is rather a matter of a living relation between God and men, which God has brought about by his mighty deeds. The Christian faith is a matter of God's showing his will and way, first in "a people prepared unto the Lord" and then in a Person. God reveals himself through mighty events. To be sure, these people, these events, this Person must be known through ideas and be communicated by means of ideas. Life is impossible on any developed level apart from ideas. That is the reason why I am so appreciative of the position of my conservative friends that the Bible gives what they call "propositional truth," i.e., definite ideas that one can nail down, can fix as definite meaning. But all of these ideas tell of God's mighty deed, they tell of a chosen people, of a Person who came in the fullness of time, and of a new kind of community that God has created through him.

The Bible is, then, first of all, the record of God's mighty deeds to show us his salvation, to show us ourselves and how to reach heaven and home. As such, the Christian faith is through and through historical and is dependent upon the historical record. To be sure, these saving deeds, this Person, must be capable of being described. Where are we then? If, on the one hand, our interpretation of the Bible will not take us to the place where God's self-disclosure through his saving deeds and his own coming to us is primary, then we are wrong and in need of correction; if, on the other hand, we arrive at God's deed and personal presence without being able to tell the old, old story of Jesus and his love in terms of such ideas as to convict us of sin and failure and to show us the way to true salvation, then we, too, shall have made a mistake. We shall, however, arrive precisely at such a combination.

Christ and the Bible are inseparable. Martin Luther said that he did not believe in Christ because of the Bible but that he believed in the Bible because of Christ. He said that Christ was the Lord of the Bible. When we come to the Bible we are confronted with the act of Christ at its very center, and Christ is not the whole Christ apart from the whole biblical faith, of God the creator, the God of history as seen in the Chosen People, and the God of the Church. But Luther was right in his order of stress: the Bible tells of Christ. It is Christ that gives the full meaning to the Bible.

Christ, the holy love of God come to earth, is the Word. John of Damascus said that God is never without his Word. God is never Wordless. But that Word has become flesh in the fullness of time, full of grace and truth, through whom we have seen the Father of glory and our own true selves. Christ is the Word of God and therefore we sing: "O Word of God Incarnate, O Wisdom from on high," referring to Christ. Henry J. Cadbury has said that wherever the New Testament speaks of the Word of God it refers not to a Book but to a Person—it refers to the eternal Christ who became incarnate in Jesus Christ.

This is of utmost importance. Paul had trouble with legalists and literalists who did not know the truth that only the Spirit gives life, even to the letter, and the Spirit is the Spirit of Christ, the living love of God in human history. The very earliest of all Church Fathers, the blessed St. Ignatius, had the same problem in the first century of the Christian faith:

When I heard some people saying, "If I don't find it in the original documents, I don't believe it in the gospel," I answered them, "But it *is* written there!" They retorted, "That's just the question." To my mind it is Jesus Christ who is the original documents. The inviolable archives are his cross and his resurrection and the faith that came by him. It is by these things and through your prayers that I want to be justified.[3]

Luther also said that the Bible was the cradle in which the child was laid. We are saved by the child, not the cradle. The cradle is necessary, but we must distinguish between the straws of the cradle and the holy child. Our problems are not new, but neither is the power of God to save. The Bible consists of many words, of which Christ is *the* Word.

I want, however, a yet closer relationship between Christ and the Bible. I want even the straws to be of intrinsic importance to the Christ. I want the whole Bible to be purposive. How can all the truths of the Bible fit into the Truth of the Word of God in the fullness of time? If we can be both honest and competent at this point, we shall have succeeded in meeting the needs of every age on this question.

I believe that Christ is the Word made flesh, while the Bible is the written word for the preparation and for the exposition and development of what Christ means for us and for the world. The written word contains the whole range of human experience; it consists of the whole gamut of human life. It is composed of the total spectrum of human colors from black to white. It is all

[3] Cyril C. Richardson, "Letter to the Philadelphians," *Early Christian Fathers*, Vol. I, p. 110.

there—from the murder of Cain to the sacrificial death of Jesus Christ and his glorious resurrection. In between are all the shades of human deceit and human devotion. The movie magnate justifies before Congressional inquiry the depiction of sex abuses on the screen by saying that they are in the Bible. The total spectrum is needed, for here is drawn for our benefit the whole history of the human race, the entire record of man's experience in microcosm, and this history is an experience organically related to God's mighty deeds of revelation, and in the end to the figure of the Christ.

The Bible is a realistic book. Therefore it is wonderful. It is genuine and open, but withal it is not a discouraging book, for in spite of all the sins and failure of men therein portrayed, there emerges the even truer picture—truer because it is eternal—of God's saving mercy and faithfulness. To place everything on one level, stories of rape and the Sermon on the Mount, songs of hate and the Cross of Christ, is to be guilty of what Gerald Kennedy calls, I repeat, "the crime of the levelers."

No, we need a criterion, and the only criterion for the Bible is Christ. Christ is the Incarnation of God, the personal Spirit who is holy love. He is not a glorified X, the representative of the unknown God still a mystery, but God revealed in personal form in the fullness of time. Christ is God come to earth to save man by enlightening him, judging him, forgiving him, correcting him, and fulfilling him. Christ is "the true Light which enlightens every man who comes into the world." He is the love of God who is "full of grace and truth." Christ is the universal love that God is, who alone can fulfill every person and all people. He is not a theoretical or abstract universal, but a concrete embodiment of God who is the reality and the full potential for all fully personal and universal relations. Christ is, at the same time, person and actuality, standard and potentiality for community. He is the Head of the Church.

He is the perfect truth who is also sovereign grace. He is the changeless absolute who yet relates himself in love to every changing person and condition. He is the living soul of the Bible who inspired the preparation of the fullness of time and is thus the beating, waiting heart of the Old Testament. He is the reality of the New Testament, person, and Church, and the criterion and dynamic of all the truth into which the Holy Spirit is to guide all who accept the Gospel and expect his coming again in glory. His coming in glory to put all things right, when even the Son will be subjected to him who put all things under his feet, alone gives the Bible its full convincing power, for it proclaims that the sovereign Lord is saving love.

Everything in the Bible contrary to this criterion is judged by it—from black to white with all gradations of color in between. The very purpose of such gradations is to show us vicariously and authentically in human experience and history what is right and what is wrong. Everything consistent with the criterion makes rich in human experience and history the meaning of truth, and serves as example and encouragement for us.

The Holy Spirit, too, is defined as the Spirit of truth, and the witness to him who is grace and truth, in such a way that everything that is true in the Bible is true because of him and everything that is false, is false in relation to him. The Spirit of truth works through many channels and in many ways. When the scientist or the historian or the psychologist discovers a truth, he does so only because *truth is* and because truth is made possible for man in a spiritual universe. The final truth is God a Spirit, the God who came as savior in Christ, and the Holy Spirit who communicates Christ to those willing to accept him, whether as creator, sustainer, or redeemer of man and of his world.

The Word of God then is primarily the Word Incarnate, Jesus as the Christ, the enactor in full humanity of the holy love which God is. But the Bible is also a trinitarian book, not arbitrarily, not in terms of three Gods, but in terms of the nature of God in his relation to the world. For the Word of God is also the continual offering to each receiver and reader of the Gospel. The Word is also the present imparting of the Holy Spirit to give light, warmth, and power to the Incarnate Word in relation to the written word. Without the presence of the Holy Spirit, the Word is never fully proclaimed, read, understood, or accepted. We must always listen to what the Spirit says to the churches, whether by man or book.

We need the letter; the Word must become flesh in a person, be enmanned; the Word needs also to become nature in the Bible to creatures of and in nature; but the Spirit must yet breathe life into nature and into flesh. The letter without this Spirit is death; but the Spirit needs the letter of communication. No letter can, however, communicate in any fullness, nor can the letter give life. To substitute the letter for the Spirit is therefore death, but the Spirit without the letter is that neutral white where all the colors are or that silence which is the source of sound; most of the time we mortal creatures must live by color and sound. Such is the function of the letter.

To use another figure: the written word is the riches of all stained-glass windows, for it is the full story of human life in one painting: this painting revolves around its central theme: the Christ, his life, ministry, teaching, crucifixion, resurrection, and the consequent spreading of the Gospel and the waiting for the consummation in glory. The meaning of the multitudinous and varied subscenes find their explanation only in terms of the central theme. Nevertheless, the whole painting is in shadow and undecipherable until the light is turned on it. Then its momentous and all-important message shines forth. The light that is turned on is the Holy Spirit.

Or, to use still another figure: a diamond well-cut has innumerable facets, but it never glows with fascinating sparkle until the light strikes it. Even so the Bible is the condition for Christian radiance, but until we seek and find the light of the Holy Spirit, we are unable to discern that radiance.

This light of the Spirit will come when we are willing to be led into all truth. Central to such truth is God's own universal love, this inclusive and yet full, intensive concern for each and all. The Bible is read in the Spirit only when it is read from God for the world. This Spirit is One who so loved that he gave his own Son, his very life, for the world. Unless we so read the Bible as a self-offering unto God for the world, the Bible will remain a closed book to us. Only when the Bible is read in the spirit of agape, or Christ-love, can the Bible open up to us its unsearchable treasures and offer through us and to us its riches in glory. John Woolman said that where there is great treasure there is also great trust. Treasure and trust go together. Only he who will live the Bible can rightly read it and fitly teach it.

Such reading in the Spirit will also mean that we are open to all further truth. As John Robinson of the *Mayflower* said: "God has yet more light to break forth from his Word." That Word is inexhaustible. The truth of the Bible is God's own self-disclosure as holy love, and not through all eternity shall we be able to comprehend fully what that means, for we shall remain men and not God. Over and over again we must study and obey, obey and study, thank God, and receive, knowing full well that we know not yet as we ought. What a treasure of grace is our precious Bible.

The Bible is also God's living speech to men, and we must be open to any and all truth from whatever quarter it comes, treating it with reverence and holy respect. *All truth is of God and we do insult the Spirit*, as John Calvin stressed, *when we refuse to accept the self-disclosure of that Spirit in whatever form and in whatever subject.* Humble openmindedness along with a critical care to test the spirits whether they be of God is the only attitude to maintain toward such truth as is not developed in the Bible. We can trust the Spirit to be our helper as we have need and to guide us into all truth as he will. The Spirit is never defensive but always open and creative. In him we believe all things that are true and of a good report, in that he is himself the love who abides in faith and hope. Biblical truth comes then, even as Jesus, not to destroy but to fulfill. The Bible judges what is untrue and evil while enriching and giving new context to whatever is true and good.

The Holy Spirit makes the biblical faith a reality in our lives. He provides the immediacy for us. He gives us the click of conviction. He wipes the dust and the tears from our eyes and makes them eyes of faith. Assurance never comes from self-assurance. Assurance of self is brittle and easily shaken. The assurance which is mainly subjective is fugitive and fleeting. The assurance given by the Holy Spirit is deep and continuing. As long as we remain in him our faith is strong even within our own weakness. The biblical faith is assurance through the Holy Spirit who provides all joy and peace in believing, making us "to abound in hope." There is no strong approach to the Bible as the Word of God that does not make indispensable the Holy Spirit as interpreter and as giver of assurance. Christ as the given light precedes it, as does dedicated study and self-offering; but as Christ, the study and self-offering are carried on, within the larger orbit of the Spirit's reign and agency, until finally there must come an intimate understanding and assurance of the Word of God made possible only through the power of the immediate work of the Holy Spirit.

We have now considered the Bible and Christ, and the Bible and the Holy Spirit. It remains to mention the Bible and experience. This third part should not equal in length and importance the first two, for they are foundational. However, the subject of experience has come under a cloud lately and needs to be cleared. We must stress biblical experience, for Christ and the Holy Spirit have come that we might enter into a living experience of God. All of God's work in creation, history, and redemption is for the sake of experience. Experience is man's side of the picture, and, even though it is not primary or original, it is part and parcel of God's plan and work.

Christian experience is biblical experience. Christian experience is fellowship with God on the basis of his own grace and full acceptance. It presupposes the biblical world-view. With such a view we do not mean a world only six thousand years old, having corners, and with the sun circling around it! The biblical world-view is the understanding that in the beginning God created the heavens and the earth. Eternity we cannot understand; we must leave that in the hands of God. What we can understand, to a significant degree, is the reality of God as the creator of the universes. He is also the controller of the endless distances and of the submicroscopic spaces. Even man's history although partly free, is yet as a whole under God's sovereign planning and constant supervision. God is no absentee landlord; he cares for his land.

According to the biblical world-view, God is also the finisher and fulfiller of his work. This world is his; our lives are his; all is therefore to be accepted with thanksgiving and prayer and to be used within the framework of a free and responsible stewardship to God's glory, for our own growth and for human helpfulness. Our lives here are only part of their endless existence before the face of God. What such a promise means we cannot fathom, but we can trust him who has himself come into human life and history to show us his will, to make a way for us to himself, to our own true selves, and to right relations with him and with each other. All meaning, significance, and decision are to be seen in the love of God in Christ Jesus, who is our Lord precisely because he enmanned the universal love which God is. He is our only Lord in that no other love can ever be absolute or hold claim over us. The Son, life, and love thus go together inseparably in the biblical world-view. Such is at least a minimum but central statement of the biblical world-view, which is presupposed by all Christian experience.

Such experience is through and through supernatural. Words get in the way, and so we must explain "supernatural." The Christian experience is altogether natural in the sense that it belongs to man by his deepest nature. God made him for it. God gave himself in human life and death for it. God works to make it real and permanent in man. Christian experience is man's proper nature, and in this sense is natural to him. By supernatural we mean that what is potentially natural to man can never be had by man apart from God's presence and gift of himself. It is not something man can work out for himself. It is a relation to God which can come only by the work of God. Supernatural is therefore not over against, or contrary to, nature, but rather, is indicated by nature and is longed for; but it is impossible apart from what is more than nature as we know it.

Christian experience is a new relation into which we must be born by God. God accepts us freely because of his own work, by his own love, and insofar as we are ready to understand and accept what he can mean to and for our lives. Jesus was a complete realist when he insisted that we must be born again, from above. Natural man has a spirit centered in himself and in his own ideals and interests. Such self-centeredness is necessary to an individual who is to become real in freedom and responsibility. But since what is natural to us as we are is not natural to us as we are to become, our ideals and interests fail to satisfy our deepest longings. We shall never find fulfillment and satisfaction on the deepest level of our lives until we find the reality for which we are born, namely, to be born again into the fuller presence of God with new ideals and interests, even of his own inclusive and intensive love. Christian experience is finding the love of Christ and living in a constant acceptance of God, oneself, and others. It is therefore also a being born again into a new kind of community, the holy fellowship of the Church.

The Bible describes the Christian experience and how we can acquire it. The Bible shows us God and all his work on our behalf. The Bible shows us the conditions that must be met if we are to receive and live such an experience, but the Bible also feeds such an experience. We are born and therefore live. All life requires nourishment. The Bible is the proper food for Christian growth. Biblical experience is growth in grace, growth in the love of God which surpasses knowledge, growth in the community which builds itself up in love. The Bible contains milk for babes and meat for men; it also satisfies all the stages of feeding required in between. Those who feed on the Bible wisely and regularly show the growth of Christian experience. Christ, the Bible, the Holy Spirit, and Christian experience ought always to be held together within our thinking and seeking.

Therefore, let the Bible be a power not a problem. Let it unite by its love, lead by its light, and save by its spirit. Let us all honor the Bible by using it at its highest: God's love in Christ, its truest light of God and leading for man.

Chapter 16

A Definition of God in the Light of
Twentieth-Century Knowledge

I

MY TASK in one sense is impossible, for God alone can define God. Why should a human being presume to tell others who God is? Why, particularly, should a twentieth-century man dare to do so in terms of his own time? Suppose God had been defined a hundred thousand years ago. What kind of standard would that have been? Suppose someone should define God a hundred thousand years from now. If we may use James Bryant Conant's prophecy, even cautiously, to the effect that the next fifty years may see more basic change in thought, especially in scientific knowledge, than has the last five hundred years, how ignorant, dull, and primitive may not the thought of our century seem then.

On the other hand, we all have a God inescapably. In *fact*, there are no atheists or agnostics, but only true worshipers or idolators. God by definition is whatever is most important and most real. All of us have to have some way of organizing experience and directing behavior. There is no presuppositionless thinking. All of us have some presupposition, not only for thinking but for living, that we cannot prove. If we could prove it, it would no longer be our presupposition. Thus we all have a god of some kind which or whom we cannot prove. He can be proved only in terms of what is more real than he; and then *that* is our God. Yes, we all live by faith, worship some god, and are in this sense unavoidably religious. Religion is nonoptional because it is situational. We must choose some position, some way of standing, or some direction, some way of walking. Our dominant drive discloses our worship. The question, then, is not: *Shall* we believe? *Shall* we be religious? Or, *can* we believe in God? Rather, it is: Is our God a private necessity, to help or to hurt, or is God also in some sense public? Is religion merely *existentiell* or is it also *existential*? Can this inescapable faith-judgment, or the choice that we must make of presupposition for life and thought, be understood and communicated, and are there any reasons at all why one god can be called better or truer than any other? Reason serves our dominant drive; can it also check its truth and change the drive?

Alasdair MacIntyre of Manchester University, England, once said on the Third Programme of the BBC that for civilization to become meaningful we need a metaphysics. He avers that the modern revolution in philosophy has made metaphysics based on reason impossible (and I agree with him if by reason he means rationalism), that we are now consequently caught in Meaninglessness with a capital M, to the point where men no longer communicate with each other. What he is really saying, I believe, is that we need God, but we do not know how to find him. Is MacIntyre right? Is *he* speaking for twentieth-century man?

I have shown that we have gods inescapably. The real question is, therefore: Can we know at all who God is, who the right God is, and can we know him together? To answer this question, I must admit that knowledge can never give us God. At most, knowledge can give content to a response that we must make. Knowledge provides us choices for decision. I shall try to show that it can also help check and help change our faith. As knowledge grows, that is, we might be helped by it to outgrow certain immature and inadequate ideas of God. Only because of this fact is our task at all worthwhile. How then can twentieth-century knowledge help us? How can it inform our existential decision and improve it? How can reason serve faith?

Unfortunately for me, in this task, there is no one twentieth-century man. Some of our contemporaries are affected scarcely at all by modern knowledge. They have fixed their faith in some part of history, in some institution, or in some book. Since faith cannot be forced, only changed from within, what I am writing is not for those who wear dogmatic blinders. Others want to flit around from one shrine of authority to another or from one wilderness of negation to another. My definition, however, is for the sake of those who are intellectually trained in modern knowledge, who dare to see that they have to have some faith-stance or other, and who want their response to reality to be as true as possible.

Such a person, of course, cannot bypass Copernicus. Earth is no longer central to his thinking. Darwin has moved into his home. Man is somehow, in some real sense, a slow product of the patient ages. Marx has taught him about sociological knowledge, and Freud has introduced him to the perilous power of the subconscious depths that enter unbidden into man's best thinking.

The twentieth-century man is aware of amazing dimensions of thought and consequently is rightfully wary of all claims of faith. In our century, radical changes of thought that once were new and startling have become domesticated and enter into the very presuppositions of modern man's thinking. Added, however, are the facts and implications of atomic science, the messianism of the social sciences, the long tendrils of cybernetic inquiry, and the naked memories of world conflagrations that have unstrung man's moral muscle, unnerved his intellectual fiber, nearly crushed his spiritual backbone, and left him, in the main, defeatist with a will not to believe as well as with an accumulation of reasons for not believing.

The philosophical revolution that MacIntyre takes for granted I believe to be mostly the result of the incapacity of man to think as a whole. His inner unity is broken. Therefore, he splits knowledge as an escape mechanism into logical necessity and existential contingency, which even at their most abstract and unworkable are poles apart from each other. Thereupon, meaningful knowledge of God within this field comes to an end, but not man's personal need and necessity to respond to God, nor the need and necessity for God in life and in civilization. However, the intellectual revolution, so-called, could be constructively fulfilled if there were a will to believe strong enough to dare to see. As it is, the deeply seared conscience of our century tries to cover up its guilt by its outright denial of the God who can be known and, also, of those standards of right and wrong that must be honored if life and community are to be real. Confusion, nihilism, and convention cannot take the place of God in any century. And many are beginning to see that this is a fact.

II

How, then, can twentieth-century knowledge give content to faith in God, and what right has it to check faith or to change previous concepts?

In the twentieth century, energy is a basic way of understanding the world in which we live. The sciences deal with energy whether in terms of atoms, molecules, organisms, or galaxies. Sometimes whirl seems to be king and all seems ultimately to be flux. Yes, whirl appears to have killed Zeus and energy to have replaced God. Suppose, however, we employ *Spirit*, which suggests potential and active energy, to define God? Nietzsche may not have been right in his claim that whoever first defined God as Spirit killed him.

Energy, however, is not what we really observe. We arrive at energy as an abstraction of science and thought. What we do see is an actual world of interacting and changing phenomena.

Two observations must be made concerning this world: (1) It is a world with enough unity to be called a universe, where diverse aspects like the salinity of the ocean, the laws of gravitation, the speed of light, entropy, and life all affect each other. A critical work like L. J. Henderson's *The Order of Nature*, or his *The Fitness of the Environment*, with its strong stress on lack of purpose in the universe, has to admit the basically organic way the world hangs together. The sciences presuppose a dependable universe and predictable relationships; and philosophy presupposes that the rules of entailment are universally valid, not merely arbitrary and unpredictable conventions. Edmund W. Sinnott of Yale has shown in *The Spirit of Biology* how the organismic drives are unimaginably intense, as, for instance, when a sponge although pulverized through a nearly microscopic screen and thrown into the sea, comes together again in the ocean. Objectively, then, not only must we respond as total human beings, but we must respond, for ourselves and together, to a world which in some sense has the unity of a universe.

Not only does energy thus have pattern and appear in diverse forms, which nevertheless, in the large and surprisingly, involve each other; but (2) this unity of the universe, science tells us, has come into being through various stages over billions of years. If we were confronted merely by a ready-made world, we should have the right to say that out of an infinite number of possibilities this world is as likely as any other. But no! We live within a series of becomings, of novelties that insofar as they are genuinely new, cannot be accounted for in terms of previous existence. This series of novelties adds up to a universe that increasingly reveals its fuller and richer nature. Such a universe cannot have become by chance over such a long stretch of time, unless, of course, no thought counts. It definitely cannot be accounted for from below, or in terms of first beginnings, without denying the whole history of evolution; nor can it be interpreted in terms of present existence without our becoming intellectually presumptuous by freezing the process. Why should this series stop with us?

Our knowledge, therefore, operates with energy, but with patterned and interactive energy, that is, with relations that either are organic or analogous to the organic, with its parts interrelated, like tides, vegetation, and the salinity of the ocean. We work also with an accumulative series of novelties, of becomings, unexplainable and unpredictable from below, that have come together to constitute and increasingly to disclose a unity of a world we call a universe.

Even so, the most important fact is not the mystery of nature or of creation. It is history. Man's history is a cosmic swoosh, a blitz-emergence within the mystery of creation. Sir James Jeans has compared the time since creation with the height of Cleopatra's Needle, man's existence with a penny on top of it, and man's civilized history with the additional thickness of a postage stamp. On the scale of three billion years to thirty days, man's history, roughly, is ten seconds. But the next half-second may, at that, show more rapid changes than the last five seconds. Whence this swoosh, this blitz-emergence, unless reality is far different from, and more than, our actual world? It looks as though someone had shifted the gears of time from beyond the order of our time.

What of history itself, however? Has this thin edge of time any meaning to suggest? Through man's relation to nature in terms of need and nature's capacity to meet these needs, especially through technology, man has developed ever wider media of community and means of communication. Not through choice or conscious planning has man changed from a food-finding to a food-producing animal and from a localized wanderer through clans, states, empires, and the United Nations to a citizen of the world, in need if not in fact. This lightning-quick change has been due to the push of the process. Man has been driven indirectly by his needs and the history of meeting those needs into ever wider ways of togetherness. At the same time, ideal ways of behaving in his environment and of interpreting it have grown along with, and in response to, this push of process. Man has been drawn by this pull of purpose as well as driven by the push of process.

History, as Arnold J. Toynbee holds, has been a challenge and a response, a challenge of the push of process and a response in terms of the pull, to whatever extent faltering, failing, or prevailing. Thus indirectly, through man's relation to nature, history has been fashioned in accordance with man's conditioned freedom.

Right now we sometimes hear the claim that man through automation has become free from his previous dependence on nature. On the contrary, nature in the form of nuclear weapons now threatens our destruction unless this particular form of the push of process is answered in terms of an adequate pull of purpose, in terms of the responsible, concerned, co-operative community that lies at the heart of our definition of God and his purpose. Or we may think ourselves free from nature through medicine, but such power over nature fails to cure the diseases of civilization that involve our minds and spirits. We have, then, a world of energy basically organismic in nature, or analogously so, a unity of a universe due to an accumulative series of becomings that fit into and fulfill what was there before, a blitz-emergence of history as such, and a pattern of history calling for a matching of the push of process by the pull of purpose.

This pull of purpose, some of us believe, has been seen climactically in Jesus. His life, his willingness to forgive and to die in the interest of truth and people, suggest God as the inclusive and unconditional concern, who is the ground and the goal of creation and of history. They point to the God who is the power for the pattern of the process that seeks co-operative community. In Jesus we see exhibited that creative concern for community that constitutes our peak understanding of God.

Our definition of God as the creative and reconciling love is centered in Christ, but it is also definitely suggested by the main direction of knowledge and its incredibly sudden spurt; and it is to be filled in, corrected by, and verified by future history. The knowledge that we have is but a swift, flaming arrow across a dark sky. God is the Spirit of love and truth.

III

Since we must make some whole response, I acknowledge that such a God best satisfies my own deepest need both to know and to live. This definition of God, I believe, helps us find out what is wrong with us as well as providing meaning to life and to civilization.

The need for mystery is also met. Alfred North Whitehead suggests that not ignorance but the ignorance of ignorance is the death of knowledge. Evil is too real and too deep to be ignored with integrity. The shifting of history's gears is perplexing. Time and eternity are too much beyond us for us to have either easy or complete answers. While evil is real and sin is serious, the suffering of the Innocent for the guilty is at least a clue to love's use of evil. The Cross of Christ fascinates as well as frightens mankind by its truth, and finds deep echoes in all religions. Natural evil, on the other hand, begins to acquire meaning as God's means to frustrate man's self-sufficiency in sin through the control, indirectly by nature and particularly by death, of the consequences of man's deeds.

Of course, if God be this unaccountably great, eternal Spirit, our lives here on earth witness only the beginning of his pedagogy.

Neither good nor evil can be meaningfully discussed, let alone solved, on man's scale. Only the scale of God's eternity will do. Thus, knowledge finds meaning only within the fuller context of faith. If God is to be real, let alone meaningful, to twentieth-century man, our understanding of God must grow apace.

One more mainly practical suggestion: If God is ultimate love, his true worshipers cannot become fanatical. The more that genuine love is practiced, the more is identification made with concrete need. Attitude cannot take the place of needed study or of study of action. Love is a built-in, self-correcting pedagogical principle; it employs the true feed-back mechanism. Some American social scientists are saying that this is the generation that has discovered love as basic for life, personal and social. Now the concept is being used in, for instance, depth psychology, sociology, and penology. But most such discoveries, I believe, are yet to be made.

All that I dare to say in the light of twentieth-century knowledge is that since we must have some faith, since we must accept some God, the choice for me is God as love, made known and to be made known in concerned, creative, and co-operative community. Non-Christians and Christians can learn together what such a God means in the face of an avalanche of new knowledge and a prospective united world. Both church people and so-called secularists can find open communication and increasing community if they will direct their steps in the way of nonsentimental and inclusive love. The way is narrow and long, but I find that it provides enough light and meaning to walk by. My experience is that only according to our working faith shall we be given to find existentially who God is; for no one can choose the way of knowledge, in any century, without discovering that the way of faith is a way of darkness as well as of light, a way of trusting beyond our clearest seeing.

The Nature and Power of Christian Experience

WHEN science, the historical consciousness, and skeptical philosophy made more and more difficult a precritical acceptance of the Bible as the sole standard for the Christian faith, Protestantism veered sharply, among its advance leaders, toward experience as the ground of validity. J. Clifford Hindley has shown with care how much John Wesley was indebted in the case of his experimental theology, to Peter Browne in particular and to John Locke in general.[1] The Moravian influence, to be sure, should not be underrated, but Wesley's whole casting of his thought is sensitive to claims for experience and criticisms of "enthusiasm" on the part of Browne. Friedrich Schleiermacher later formulated religious knowledge as such in terms of "the feeling of absolute dependence." He did so, however, within the total aura of what Alfred North Whitehead has called "the subjectivist bias."

This radical turning away from the towering heights of classical objectivity by the breaking of what Arthur O. Lovejoy has termed "the great chain of being," namely, the general equating of the outreaches of mind with reality, began with Descartes, curved away rapidly with the British empiricists—Locke, Berkeley, and Hume—and eventuated in the basic redirection of assumptions in Immanuel Kant. Reformation and Renaissance, however unlike in some respects, shared not a little of the spirit of subjectivism; and the close following of the major turn in philosophy upon the Protestant Reformation witnesses also to a general turn inward. Martin Luther's justification by faith strikes a stronger note than his sole reliance on the Bible, which was not a little compromised in his own thinking. John Calvin's stress on the internal witness of the Spirit and his existentialist preference for singing to reciting

[1] "The Philosophy of Enthusiasm," *London and Holborn Quarterly Review,* April and July, 1957.

the creeds testifies to the same trend. Kant formulated, in general, a philosophy opposed to all external standards and especially opposed to all metaphysics and to every theology that claimed priority of knowledge for supernatural or transcendent sources. By so doing, Kant expressed the spirit of his age, a spirit that had originated centuries before and had culminated in more than two hundred years of crescendoing subjectivism. Albrecht Ritschl's reliance on a special religious faculty and Rudolf Otto's resort later to the numinous experience of the holy are merely the further exemplifications and outworking of this total drive.

In one sense, Georg Wilhelm Friedrich Hegel's metaphysics would seem to have gone contrary to the trend, but his method of making the reasonable the real and then equating the whole of human experience and history with the true (*das Ganze ist das Wahre*) in effect deified the cosmic process. Thus, he too continued and did not break with the basic tradition of this-worldliness. Søren Kierkegaard, on the contrary, in spite of his stress on subjectivity as truth and on the centrality of the individual to knowing, revolted profoundly against all stress on experience as continuous with reality, and proclaimed instead the infinite, qualitative distinction between time and eternity. Between all human thought and God's revelation, he held that there was an unbridgeable gulf.

Karl Barth incarnated the spirit of this revolt and let it loose in his famous second edition of *The Epistle to the Romans*. In one sense, of course, he fought "against the stream" of centuries of subjectivism in terms of methods and systems which centered in experience and history, but in another sense he exemplified and articulated the deepest revolt of a whole new age against making man's experience central to knowledge, particularly with relation to God. Kierkegaard has flashed and Barth has thundered that the less certain cannot prove the more real. How can man's experience prove or even enunciate the reality of God? Only revelation can do that. Only man broken of his pride can receive the high and holy self-impartation of God in Christ as the basis from beyond this world of biblical revelation. Barth's cry for rending the veil of man-made systems found electric response throughout the world. Storms of neo-orthodoxy, as many called the revolt, uprooted theologies of experience, leaving them withered if not dead. The atmosphere and assumptions of a new age were both hostile and haughty with regard to any reliance on Christian experience.

Several times, however, Barth has gone back on his extreme stand, as in the first volume of *Church Dogmatics* (1927) and later in *Fides Quaerens Intellectum* (1931). In *Die Menschlichkeit Gottes* (1956) he repudiates his own extreme position, calling it heretical and saying that it was called forth by the enemy at the time. His retraction is wholehearted, but guarded. Unfortunately, it is also as yet without sufficient insight into the nature of his "heresy." The fact is, of course, that unless God can be known in experience in some way, unless he can be related to life organically in some manner, and unless God authenticates his own presence by some means, revelation becomes both relative and irrelevant. There is then nothing left for us except some completely arbitrary choice on God's part, working faith in us directly, or some entirely capricious faith-judgment on our part.

Possibly the problem that is set for us in this chapter, even by this historical sketch, is, therefore, as difficult as any problem of human thought. The question is this: Is there any way that we can find a distinctive Christian experience sufficiently valid to allow us to return to the power of the classical Christian faith without landing in the pitfalls of irrelevance and arbitrariness? Can objectivism and subjectivism be synthesized constructively even by the correct understanding of Christian experience?

I

The problem of experience is that we have to be ourselves. We cannot escape this our privilege or our plight. At the same time, the hardest thing in the world is to be ourselves. How can we become ourselves, and are we potentially better and more than we know? How can we live our true life *now*, and is there beyond our every now some fulfilling *then* and *there*? Are these not the basic problems of experience? First of all, then, self-acceptance is most difficult. We did not choose to be born. Nor did we choose the circumstances into which we were born. We cannot even honestly say that what we are is mostly of our own making. We have drives from within, physical, psychological, social, and spiritual, that we cannot explain, but they are there. They are somehow ourselves. When we can control them, we usually suffer and labor in so doing. Somehow, too, we become alienated from ourselves in struggling with the self that we never chose to be. In the same way, we have received hurts or helps from the outside, not of our own choosing, and we find ourselves craving and striving to be the selves that we want to be; yet we find ourselves seemingly caught in something we have to acknowledge as ourselves but against which we nevertheless rebel as being ourselves.

Self-improvement is a strong desire that engenders a wide response; the hope of it gives confidence to many, yet countless people live on the edge of despair, knowing themselves controlled from within and by circumstance rather than being in control. Some lose the battle of the mind, becoming statistics of mental illness. Others seek escape in death. In any case, life generally is hard, and heavy is the battle of and for the self. Well have our existentialists called anxiety a characteristic of human experience. Martin Heidegger describes experience as man being ahead of himself, or possibility; being already in the world, or facticity; and being involved in the world, or fallenness. Anxiety, for him, is merely a special case of man's *Sorge*, his being caught in the despair of death. Paul Tillich knows that even if the essential self is free, the existential self is bound. Deliverance for him must be eschatological, an entering into the "*Gestalt* of Grace." Rudolf Bultmann, too, knows how dark and deep is man's natural predicament, how besetting his sin. He offers decision for the Kingdom, faith in Christ, as victory over anxiety. All these men know the dread of existence. They advocate authentic experience. How can we become real, and what of hope happens when we do?

The problem on the level of experience seems to be as follows: Is there a normally attainable experience that *as such* can witness to any reality capable of offering a fulfilling and authentically satisfying life? Or is all general experience so beset by anxiety, strife, and despair within, or at least by chronic dissatisfaction, and some such pressures and conflicts from without, that we go on living, having moments of enjoyment, hoping always for better days, feeling responsible for work and family, and dreading in our depth consciousness to die, not knowing for certain what is ahead if we do? Is much of our unhappiness a matter of being too busy with the things that have caught us to the point where we have no time to be or to become ourselves? Or are we thus busy because we dread being ourselves?

Are even our pleasures in food, sex, and sociability substitutes for genuine well-being? We cannot feel others' physical pain; we cannot enter into their mental anguish; we cannot plumb their spiritual cravings. Those whom we know best are still strangers to us as regards their deepest feelings about ultimates. Some of the most popular and seemingly happy people we have known have taken their own lives in the midst of what we took to be highly satisfactory living. What, then, is normal experience that can be held up as something possible of attainment? And what relevance, again, does it have for those whose structures and drives are not normal and who have tried beyond belief to become so, only to be defeated and to keep being defeated indefinitely? Life for most people seems to be too complicated; there seem to be too many choices where often even taking a good choice brings hurt to the self because it cannot also take the other choices. Is suffering our lot, and learning to suffer our best lesson? There seems to be no end to such questions and no way of settling them.

The problem of experience is that if we stay within its confines, for the sake of reality and relevance, we find no high hope for knowledge and salvation from beyond it. If we leave experience behind, all promised power seems arbitrary and unfounded. Some lives, to be sure, seem to find more serenity, confidence, sense of achievement, and satisfaction than others. But are the sources of these lives public and can they become standard for human life in general, or are they to be explained in terms of their own givenness and circumstance? Many of these persons claim help from beyond our ordinary experience, but how can we know that there are realms of reality beyond what we experience?

The Christian Gospel speaks directly to these problems. Some of us have to admit to only a partial understanding of its nature and to a most fragmentary realization of its claim. Yet what we know, what we have seen and have experienced, we dare not deny. We have discovered, too, that the Christian claim is far more real than our experience of it. What is this claim? It is that Christ delivers us from the morass of subjectivism without hanging us on the high cliffs of arbitrary objectivism; that Christ comes beyond all theoretical solutions, besides, as the healing and helping Savior whose presence and power are man's final and fulfilling Good News.

II

The claim of Christ is that he is from beyond this world, that he came into it, yet is of such a nature that he truly fulfills what the world needs. If his claim or the claim made for him is true,[2] then we know from within our world what is more than the world. Then we can experience in him what is yet more than ordinary experience. We then have a light and a life that can radically change what is in this world. In such a case, we have in him a remedy for our situation and the power to solve our problem.

The claim of Christ is that he is the Son of God. God is the creator, ruler, and finisher of this world. Christ is the very presence and power of God on earth. God is love. Technically speaking,

[2] The truth of Christ's claim I have tried to work out in a series of volumes beginning with *Faith and Reason*.

love cannot be qualified by anything real and good as external to itself in ultimate source and status. We cannot say high, holy or wise love, except colloquially, for God as love is all these by his very nature. There is no real and full love that is not of God; God is the only source of love. Man's "possession" of it is at best but participation in the life of God. Man has in creative altruism a reflection of this reality in his need for love. Love is God and of God; he who remains in love remains in God and knows God. Apart from love no one can know God, for God is love. Therefore, the Son of God is the Son of his love, and this is life eternal to know the eternally begotten Son of God, the love who goes out to create and to redeem, to produce community and to perfect it. God is Spirit; love is Spirit and can be known, therefore, only as we receive the Spirit, the Holy Spirit, the Spirit of Christ, the eternal love who alone is and gives eternal life. "Love only comprehendeth love and knoweth whence it came."

Thus, Christ is not of and from this world but of and from God. He is the Incarnation, revelation, redemption and resurrection of eternity in time, of God in man. Him we know, and knowing him we know God. Thus, within history and by means of experience we know God who is both incomparably and immeasurably beyond this world and beyond all full understanding. The reason that we know him, however, is that although he is from beyond this world he is yet in the world revealing to man what he most needs. Man needs God. He is empty at the center of his life. This emptiness makes growth possible. Man in himself is more empty than not, for fullness of being is of God alone. Man in himself is made for God, but man never is God or in any part a bit of God. The emptiness in man craves filling. Only God can fill the emptiness of man, which is the hunger for love. The fact that God made man in his own image comes out in man's capacity to carry on the imitation of love. God's agape is reflected in man's altruism. Man loves with a small "l." But such love leaves man still empty and hungry.

The claim of Christ on us is that he is the enmanment of the love for which man is made. Therefore Christ is God's answer to man's need at the center of his life. Man craves love and carries on a search for it. He longs to be accepted and known. He craves to be respected and admired. He longs for the community where he can both be himself and be fulfilled beyond the self. Man needs freedom, for freedom is a need for self-being. Man craves freedom, for freedom is also a condition for satisfactory community. But freedom in either direction becomes unconcerned and irresponsible unless it is motivated by love. Man's motivation in himself is at best "a drive" of love in the human sense. Such love is a distorted reflection of the love whom God is. Therefore, such love meets only partially man's need for reality and fulfillment. Man needs the fullness of love that comes only with the fullness of God.

Man needs also to be able to accept love. Many shut themselves off from what they most want and crave. They have to be themselves and yet fail to be. They want love so much and have so often been hurt by what passes for it that they dare not open their lives to reality. Thus they have to be, and yet dare not be, themselves. They know not how to become real. Man's niggardly and besmirched love has so hurt the self who needs God's presence and power that he dares not believe that God is real and can fulfill him. A. H. Maslow has well written in *Motivation and Personality* that love is as much of a necessity for man as salt. Actually a person can get along, however unsatisfactorily, on a comparatively salt-free diet; but without love the soul shrivels, it hurts, and harms others. In order to give love, man needs to receive love. Man needs to become lovable by letting God love him. He needs God at the center of his life. Man's misery consists mostly in being starved for the only full and final medicine for his sickness and for the true nourishment for full health.

A need shows the nature of man with regard to his origin, environment, and end. A value is a way of meeting a need. It is a guide to the fulfillment of need. Nothing is essentially valuable which does not fill a genuine need. Man's need for love is a universal need. It is as wide as the life of man. Therefore it is also as high as the heart of God. A universal need reflects back on the creator of that need, or on the origin and source of man. An authentic need also reveals the nature of the environment which produced the need, and which offers directives for its fulfillment. A true need bespeaks man's fulfillment and thus his destiny. If God's presence in Christ provides the potential fulfillment of man's basic and universal need, then the Christ is both the answer from beyond our partial vision and our bungled attempts to fill those needs, and also the fulfillment within the world of its deepest lack. Christ, being the presence and power of God from beyond our world, is the power for its salvation, for as a true man of earthly existence he is through and through relevant to our human situation.

God's Gospel is therefore both sufficiently powerful and relevant to meet us where we are and to give us radical help. The Gospel of God's grace in Christ is neither arbitrary nor impotent. It is *in* but not *of* the world. It is from beyond our world and yet all for it. Therefore, the experience of Christ is at the same time our present need and our ultimate hope. Christian experience is both a universal need and a true potential. Christianity as the proclamation of the Gospel of Christ, of the universal love of God for which we are all made, by which alone we can be fulfilled, and within which alone is perfect freedom, is therefore no in-group religion, no faith among faiths, but the realism of reality as the illumination of life, the judgment of wrong, and the power to become right.

III

The nature of Christian experience presupposes its power, namely, to find the fulfillment of life in the love of Christ which passes knowledge. To know is not man's basic need. Of course he needs to know, but knowledge is not the heart of life. Nor is man's deepest need to do. He certainly needs to act and to feel sure that his activity is both important and right. But man is not made for action. He is made for love. Love includes but goes beyond all aspects of self. The power of Christian experience comes, in fact, through forgiveness. The validity of Christian experience depends on its capacity to fulfill man's central need for life. The power of forgiveness is had as man becomes able to accept what he most needs.

Man suffers from ignorance. Knowledge is power to explore nature and to exploit its resources for meeting human need. Man cannot get along without power of knowledge. The full order and meaning of nature cannot be known or appropriated apart from God's purpose with it. Christ shows us this, especially in our precarious and perilous age. Man also needs to act on what he knows, for without such action his knowledge lies impotent and his spirit lies frustrated. Ultimate concern, the love of God, is man's fullest motivation for creative and co-operative personal and communitarian relations. Above all, however, man needs to be forgiven, for guilt more than anything else separates man from God, from others, and even from his true self.

Guilt results from wrong relations at the heart of life. The feeling of guilt reflects the inner sense of wrong. Guilt oppresses man by the registering of reality in his inward parts of his false choices and his wrong relations. These threaten the moral integrity of the self. The experience of guilt reflects the awareness on the part of man's most sensitive self that it has forfeited its integrity and lost its true self. Guilt gives rise to the experience of man's inner self-punishment, a fleeing of the sinner "when no man pursues him!" Guilt eventuates in the disquiet of evil forebodings produced by an inner understanding of the right relation between choices and consequences. Guilt feelings unmask the anxiety of the self that tries to own up to its own past and even to right it, but that cannot cope adequately with that past. Guilt occasions the crying of the soul for forgiveness. Guilt engenders the suffering of the self that shuns right relation and runs from God, from others, and from the true self. Guilt paralyzes man's spirit and robs him of vitality; guilt drains what vitality is left by excessive defenses or by foolish aggression. Guilt distorts knowledge, misdirects action, and robs the self of life itself as well as of the sense of reality and importance.

Guilt indicates the failure to love. It is the witness within to the sin against the Spirit. It is the drowning of the soul in the poisoned pool of self-concern. Guilt shuts the self in on himself. It makes life seem hopeless and without luster. Guilt makes life a burden to be borne or a threat to be escaped. Guilt is the groaning of God in man, the call of God's Spirit to man's spirit for right relations. At its deepest, guilt is understood within the context of the suffering of love on the cross of man's lovelessness. Guilt is man's central problem, his strongest enemy, and his deepest enslavement.

Therefore, man needs, above all, to be forgiven of his guilt, because forgiveness is the only way for man to God, to his deepest self, and to the filling of his central need. Man cannot accept himself, live freely with his neighbor, or live fearlessly before God until he is forgiven by God. God's forgiveness, however, waits for man's wanting to be forgiven. Forgiveness never violates freedom. Forgiveness by God that is apart from man's full acceptance of it is no real forgiveness. God is kept from forgiving until man forgives himself. The sign of such acceptance is whether or not the forgiven in turn forgives all others. God's forgiveness is always *universal in character*. It is a state of reality in which we participate. There is no reality in partial forgiveness; God's forgiveness is full or not at all. To be sure, we appropriate or actualize God's forgiveness in proportion to our actually forgiving others. The understanding, experience, and social effectiveness of forgiveness vary with moral sincerity and with spiritual maturity. But until total forgiveness is intended by faith, God is not personally present as power for Christian experience.

Only full surrender to God's forgiveness in integrity of intention lets in the love of God. All partial surrenders achieve only grades of human reflections of love. They may not be inconsiderable to experience and to effective living, but they never bring full forgiveness by the presence of God. They never let love in to rule. Here is man's most insistent and constant spiritual problem. He wants something of God, but not God himself. He wants to be saved, but not entirely and immediately. Narrow, indeed, is the way of Christian experience and few there be who find it.

The power of Christian experience is the freedom of the forgiven man. Man's two strongest enemies are guilt and bondage. The Gospel is not first of all an explanation of, or a direction for, salvation. It is primarily the power for forgiveness and for freedom from bondage. This truth is the reason that the Cross has had, and always will have, the place it has within the Christian faith. Only what God has done and will do avails. Whatever doctrine of atonement is accepted, none will ever suffice that does not place grace, as God's work, and faith, as man's response, central in the relation between God and man. The atonement, at its heart, is the message of how God made forgiveness a reality and how man accordingly can become free through forgiveness.

Man is guilty through and through. Therefore, he fears God. Fear has torments. Fear holds man in bondage. Man flees freedom as long as he hates God. Freedom before God comes only when, through forgiveness, man knows that God has accepted him and when he, in turn, is able to accept others and himself within that forgiveness. Freedom comes only as love throws out fear. Freedom comes only from fulfillment of life. Only God can fulfill the life he has made for himself. Guilt makes man shrink from God and suffer within. God is not the hope of his life and his portion forever. For the fearful man, Christ has not come to set him free, because he feels that God threatens the very way in which life is meaningful to him. Freedom in God is freedom through the forgiveness of guilt.

Again, freedom from others is the result of forgiveness. Fear of others and the resultant slavery of man-pleasing turn through forgiveness to the freedom with others and for others. Man longs for conformity because he is afraid of God and feels a degree of confidence in the community of guilt. Even the ordinary church life is insurance against God. There, guilty man finds that most persons who claim freedom before God actually fear him; and therefore he justifies his state as natural, and wants to consider it safe. But even in the crowd, man is lonely, and as Kierkegaard avers, the depths of man know that the crowd is untruth. Community of guilt, therefore, turns out to be no reliever of it. There is no freedom in fellowship that is not the result of the community of love.

Christ alone affords man true liberty. The Church is best defined
as the community of effective forgiveness, for it is the locus of the
operation of effective grace. The community of forgiveness, however originated and constituted, is the community of Christ who
is the source on earth of God's love shed abroad through the Holy
Spirit, the presence of God in the community of his Son. There is
no final power for freedom in community that does not stem from
God's love actively operating in human togetherness. Forgiveness
is the key to the power to love, the power of the presence of God
who is love. Thus, Christian experience is the forgiveness of God
that lets love loose. Love let loose always breaks down barriers by
effecting degrees of supergroup community. Forgiveness is the way
to community through the Cross by the power of the resurrection.
Christian community fulfills man by the God-centered community
in which he participates.

Forgiveness alone ensures fullness of life. Guilt dams up life.
Guilt leads to lessening of life. God is gone. Relation with reality
is broken. Or a fever of life tries to substitute for its fullness. Thus
lassitude or nervousness, spiritlessness or activism, sometimes expressed in sensuousness and sometimes in asceticism, become the
expression of the failure of life. Forgiveness restores the relation.
It sets the self free for fulfillment. The full life of forgiveness involves uninhibited self-acceptance. The self no longer wastes itself
in fearing God, in defending itself against others or in fighting
itself.

The Christian experience is thus the finding of the love of Christ
that shows the self reliably its own true situation. The problems of
selfhood and of community are made clear by seeing them in the
light of the needs of the self, as it in turn is seen in the light of the
source and the destiny of man. But experience alone can effect such
a living, forgiving, and empowering revelation. Teaching and
preaching can give prescription for the solution of life's problems, but they cannot afford conviction. Conviction results only
from the testing of the prescription. Most people, unfortunately,
never dare take with full seriousness the whole prescription. Therefore, there are few who can witness firsthand to the nature and
power of Christian experience.

Our age is more and more coming to appreciate how right
Kierkegaard was when he said that life's hardest task was to become a Christian. Hegel spoke of "going beyond Christianity," and
he produced a learned interpretation of the nature and course of
world history. Kierkegaard revolted against the superficiality of
Hegel's understanding of Christianity and taught, instead, that

the way of Christ is "an existence-communication" that is narrow to the point of despair. Only a few dare go on beyond giving up all to the finding of all in God. And those few in history exemplify the power of Christian experience: the St. Pauls, the St. Francises, and the Albert Schweitzers. But beyond all the towering figures of Christian experience stands the strange figure of Galilee through whom our very age order was changed. Mysterious and miraculous is the power of a life concluded on the Cross but consummated by the resurrection where God as love once for all became manifest as man's ultimate source, present power, and true destiny.

The New Testament promises that of Christ's *fullness* his followers are to partake. Only the actual experience of the dependability of this promise can ground man's faith in God rather than in theory. Only such knowing of the presence of God in one's own life can give one the right and the freedom to speak at all of the nature and the power of Christian experience. Our faith must become more personal, more intimate, more real and rich in experience. The more it does, the more we shall reject the subjectivism in religion that starts and ends with experience. The more, instead, the experience itself will point to the Godman through whom Christian experience once became actual and is now possible for us.

Christian experience is, in fact, the presence and power of God in Christ, of God made flesh; only as Christ becomes incarnate in us as the hope of glory, therefore, can the nature and the power of Christian experience become real for us and through us. When it does, we shall turn away the more readily from mere theory. We shall point with conviction born of experience to "the medicine of immortality" without which life can be neither free nor whole, and without which the problems of life must prevail, if, indeed, the world perish not entirely.

The claim of Christ remains: to meet man's deepest need, the need of God, the need for love, the need for meaningful existence and community. Only as the power of forgiveness through God's grace and our faith becomes the power of Christ for new lives and for a leavened world shall we grasp in grateful confirmation the nature and the power of Christian experience.

V

THEOLOGY IN EDUCATION

Contemporary Theology and Christian
Higher Education

HIGHER education is especially important during periods of rapidly changing culture. Then, teachers of higher education have a peculiar opportunity to help chart civilization. Major discoveries of fact and decisive new contexts of interpretation eventually remold the basic assumptions for culture. In both manner and intensity, our age is exceptionally transitional and consequently open to significant impact from higher education. Our assigned task is to survey and to appraise the field of contemporary theology for its capacity for constructive impact on higher education. Even a sketch can be of value if it highlights what is important; conciseness can gain the power of concentrated focus.

I

Farthest on the right stand the fundamentalists. A few years ago even to mention this position might have seemed quite irrelevant to the problem of higher education, both because of fundamentalism's external standard of authority and because of its belonging to a bygone era. As far as the first of these liabilities goes, there is always a natural chasm between fundamentalism and higher education. Fundamentalism accepts literal, biblical authority; higher education requires an open inquiry. No cleft was apparent, radically and finally, until scientific method and the historical consciousness showed us that truth separates literalism and open inquiry. No matter what minor concessions it might make to the historic conditionedness of the Bible, fundamentalism's basic position must remain because of the nature of its authority: "We know what we believe; don't confuse us with facts!" But fundamentalists are changing rapidly. They are giving up fundamentalism with its inflexibility and becoming what they call "evangelicals."

In a fundamentalist periodical, *Christian Life*,[1] a strongly representative group of young conservative leaders signed an article saying that they no longer want to be called fundamentalists or to be tied down to a narrow interpretation of inspiration but that they want to be called evangelicals, who make Christ as holy love their final authority. Similarly, in *Christianity Today* article after article disclaims obscurantism and calls for an honest facing of intellectual issues. Insofar as this tendency continues, we can conclude only that fundamentalism as a position shows itself less and less tenable to those competently educated. Resurgence to conservative Christianity in our day seems to be accompanied by its maturation. While respecting its devotees in higher education for their intention of integrity and for their loyalty to an intrinsically difficult situation, we must nevertheless maintain that there is an inherent tension between higher education and fundamentalism: external authority and open inquiry are hard to reconcile.

Let it be said, however, concerning fundamentalism, that with regard to its main positive Christian contentions it stands in the solid line of historic Christianity; and it may even be that in the far future we will come to see that liberal accommodationism could not get rid of true, evangelical supernaturalism because of the intransigence of fundamentalism. Therefore, we honor it while we recognize that our task goes beyond it: to find a theology that both maintains the heart of the full Christian faith and communicates constructively in give and take with higher education.

II

The theological tendency that is the strongest throughout the world today is Kierkegaardian neo-Calvinism as represented in different ways and degrees by Karl Barth, Emil Brunner, and Thomas Torrance, among others. Basically, this position is Calvinism as reinterpreted through Barth after his immersion in Kierkegaard and consequent conversion by him from liberalism. Actually, through Kierkegaard it is also touched by a strain from Martin Luther as well as by existentialism. This drive differs vitally from other returns from liberalism, for instance from that of P. T. Forsyth who maintained throughout an understanding and appreciation of God's work in human reason, in human conscience, and in the

---

[1] The issue of March, 1956. Illustrative of the best offering of this group for higher education is *Christian Education in a Democracy* by Frank E. Gaebelein, and, on a more popular level, his *The Pattern of God's Truth*. Both books should be taken seriously by open-minded educators.

order of creation as a whole, which neo-Calvinism rejects.

Nevertheless, this leading theological position is both right and needful in its main affirmations. It claims at its center that the Christian faith in its biblical position is ultimate and cannot, therefore, be classed as a religion or compared with other religions. In the Bible, and only in the Bible, God, focused and fulfilled in the Christ, has revealed himself. This revelation is not a matter of ideas but of God's mighty acts, of saving events. Revelation is not propositional truth. Neo-Calvinism furthermore claims that such faith cannot be verified in terms of reason, experience, metaphysics, or history. The less certain and the less real cannot demonstrate or prove what is absolute and eternal. It proclaims that God is not to be found in man or in nature, for God is "wholly other," eternally different from these, and is in no way part of what is created. Barth has backed away from his own extreme position, and some of his followers have also become modified "Barthians," but the movement as a whole owes its distinctive nature and power to the emphases we have noted. Throughout the world, it is maintaining and in some places gaining strength.

While right and essential in its main contentions, neo-Calvinism suffers from a false all-or-none analysis. Its primary either-or lacks a secondary both-and. The Christian faith *is* ultimate; revelation cannot be reduced to propositions; God cannot be proved by anything less than himself; and God is ever other than the creature. Therefore we must ever live by faith in loving obedience. On the other hand, neo-Calvinism is wrong in its repudiation of reason in its rightful place and legitimate manner. Albeit revelation is a matter of God's self-revelation in events, in history, and supremely in a Person, yet that revelation by its very nature cannot be equated with propositional truth; nevertheless, revelation must be apprehended, understood, and communicated by means of concepts and propositions. How can people believe unless they have heard, and heard the proclaimed Word? As we said earlier, Barth's theology can perhaps best be called the Theology of the Word, the Word transcending all meaning, surpassing all understanding, and yet also it must be recognized, communicable within and for faith by means of inescapable concepts and sentences.

As for reason's incapacity to prove God, reason does not exist either to create or to establish revelation but to find it, to clarify it, and to apply it. God reveals himself; that is God's part. Man responds to revelation in faith by reason; that is man's part. Revelation and reason are on different planes. One cannot take the place of the other. There is a positive relation between revelation and reason or between reality and man's need. In order to discover this relation man must first decide for, and develop integrity of, the whole man in actual life and thereafter study as best he can to find what is true and false revelation. In his able *Fides Quaerens Intellectum*, Barth goes so far as to accept the inferential use of reason from the basis of revelation. Such acceptance assumes that revelation has a nature that lends itself as a total context for knowledge or to a central focus of perspectives.

Beyond this expansion of his standpoint he should have gone on to see that from within this perspective man has the competence, by reason on its own plane, to check and to challenge candidates for revelation and even to be creative in the interpretation of truth. Unless this is so, the cord between revelation and all other truth is cut, and we are left with completely arbitrary faith-judgments or with a Spirit of Partiality who gives revelation to some and withholds it from others. Man's reason then cannot either create or establish revelation. But reason can help "test the spirits" whether or not they be of God. Similarly, by means of experience, history, and nature, man cannot prove God, but God's revelation can be self-authenticating in terms of these, providing for us the only true light of what ultimately is, what ought to be, and providing the road between them. God's revelation through events can therefore provide a meaningful total context for interpreting our existence, values, and aims not only intellectually but especially in terms of judgment and salvation.

Similarly, neo-Calvinism is wrong in its denial of God's presence and revelatory work on the level of creation. Its transcendence does not allow for God's both being himself in a peculiar way and coming into history in his unique Presence while also being present in man and history in a preparatory and pedagogical way. This all-or-none view has too little understanding of the nature of Spirit to remain one unit and yet be capable of different modes of adaptation by means of which God creates and preserves inviolate the conditions for man's self-being and freedom.

The main contribution of this group to higher education is the existentialist grasp that truth in terms of ultimates or of over-all contexts is more decisional than informational. It cuts to shreds the pretexts of an objectivist, rationalistic metaphysics or of any system of ethics that fails to see and to heed the fact that there is no presuppositionless thinking and that in matters of total contexts, configurations, and dimensions of knowledge we live more by faith than by knowledge. This genuine and vital contribution we accept gratefully. All-or-none transcendence, however, pulls down the curtain of irrelevance between the Christian faith and higher education. Higher education cannot by field or function deal with revelatory realities within a merely redemptive context. It deals with a world of actualities and problems which it must interpret and on which it must throw specific light. There must be a real measure of continuity between revelation and education or else they are unrelated. Complete or even basic continuity between them, however, is not necessary. It is not even possible if revelation is on a different plane from reason.

Neo-Calvinism lacks contextual relevance (in terms of explanation) as well as a relevant standard of judgment. There is no organic relation between revelation, redemption, and creation or between faith and reason that allows for a fruitful exchange between the Christian faith thus interpreted and higher education. Brunner's *Christianity and Civilization* comes the closest to providing a meaningful focus for looking at the problems of civilization and to offering concrete help. But even here Brunner fails to make available a central Christian pattern and to depict over-all organic relations. With his comparatively recent acceptance of agape as the distinctive and determinative motif of the Christian faith, he is in position to move into such relevance, but if he does, he will also leave with finality a position to which he is even now only ambiguously related.

The leading theological tendency of today has sacrificed far too much relational truth to social and religious relativism. When reason is repudiated, the result is relativity among claimed authorities. Therefore there is no basic hope for higher education from neo-Calvinism. There is much activity within this position and many vital things are being said by its adherents about higher education. But at its heart neo-Calvinism stands with fundamentalism in creating an unbridgeable gulf of irrelevance between the Christian faith and higher education.

III

Another movement that has been gaining ground in recent years is the Lund school, the kind of Swedish theology advocated especially by men like Gustaf Aulén and Anders Nygren. This theological position is best known in America through Aulén's *The Faith of the Christian Church* and Nygren's *Agape and Eros*.

Nygren shows us how Kant's Copernican revolution of critical philosophy was decisive for consequent thought. Critical philosophy after Kant was seen to deal not with realms of ultimate reality but with principles of validity; not with the region of the transcendent but with the reality of the transcendental; not with a supernatural world beyond this one but with necessities and universalities within experience and for experience. Critical philosophy deals with the preconditions for experience, those necessities without which experience itself is unthinkable. As unconditional necessities, they are not beyond our realm of experience because they do not exist, nor can they be *in* experience and remain unconditional; they are rather the presuppositions unconditionally *of* and *for* experience. Immanuel Kant found three such realms of experience: the theoretical, the practical, and the aesthetic, each with its own kind of transcendental forms. Not all normativeness for experience in his thought, therefore, was rational, but there were different types of unconditional categories of and for experience. Nygren accepts Kant's position and builds on it. He goes back of Kant's analysis critically to a category of categories, to an ultimate unity of logical necessity, "the category of eternity." The all-inclusive, ultimate presupposition of experience is, therefore, the religious category of eternity.

This category of the absolute presupposition for experience, however, is forever inaccessible to rational metaphysics. Reason cannot deal with ultimate reality, only with principles of validity; not with any transcendent realm, but only with transcendental necessity. Therefore, according to Nygren's analysis, choice of ultimates must be made from within experience, from the stuff of history. In history, choice must be made among religions that are seen to be organic wholes, with centers from which each religion must be understood. Each religion has a regulative pattern, an organic wholeness from a center, a foundational pattern, or *Grundmotiv* in terms of which alone its distinctive and determinative nature can be understood. The center of Judaism is nomos, or law; of Hinduism, karma, or deed (and consequence); of the Christian faith, agape, or God's unconditional, spontaneous, uncalculating, groundless love creative of fellowship, centered not in the worth of the object but in the unceasingly forgiving nature of the Subject, pictured most vividly in the forgiveness of and redemptive love for enemies.

The task of Christian theology according to this method is not to build a system of search for God from experience, not to construct a metaphysics nor an apologetics but to find in history, by a faith-judgment which is invulnerable to reason, the *Grundmotiv* of the Christian faith which actually is agape, and to describe the implications of this motif as they have been developed concretely by the faith of the Church throughout its history. Theology according to the Lund school is as objective, scientific, and intellectually acceptable as physics or biology. The theologian never judges what is ultimate truth or reality, nor does he ever defend the faith rationally, but merely describes it as competently as possible. No concrete confession of faith as such can be proved necessary to history, but faith itself is inescapable. Therefore, faith should choose true revelation by the eyes of faith, but it should never make the mistake of thinking it can or ought to be proved by reason. Can any method be more scholarly and congenial to higher education?

The strength of this position is obvious. Kant rightly pointed out that the traditional arguments for God rested ultimately on the ontological in some form, which simply assumed the identity of thought and being in line with classical thinking.[2] The evidence, however, does not support conclusively such an assumption. Therefore, rational metaphysics in the traditional sense, especially theological metaphysics, is impossible. At this point the Lund school stands on firm ground. It also maintains correctly that faith selects its religious content from history. Decision among historic faith-judgments is determinative for faith. Practically always, however, except in the case of the founders of new religions, the contents of faith are found in concrete historical religions. The Lund school contends convincingly that religions are organic in nature, having concrete centers from which they must be viewed, and that therefore theology in a decisive sense is the description of historic faiths from within their own distinctive and determinative natures.

The faults or shortcomings of this method are grave. As in the case of neo-Calvinism, the method severs all rational relation between the transcendent and the transcendental. The filling of "the category of eternity" by content from history becomes entirely an arbitrary affair. We are once again left with complete religious relativity in the realm of knowledge. The living cord between religion and truth is cut. Consequently, higher education is left with a choice for or against a religion that has no rational claim on education and provides no empirical foundation for it.

Then again, although the distinctiveness of faith is valuable for the contextual ordering of knowledge and communication, the distinctiveness of the Christian faith according to the Lund theologians consists in God's revelation of agape. This is a heavenly reality come into history. But no account is taken of the realms of eros or philia (seeking and mutual love respectively), the realms

[2] See Arthur Lovejoy's excellent discussion of this assumption in *The Great Chain of Being*, (Harvard University Press, 1936.)

of our actual problems, and no way is opened to account for these realms or to relate the heavenly to the historic. The relation is cut between the realm of redemption and that of creation. The whole aim of the Lund school is to distinguish the Christian faith at its own genuine center from all other religions and human thinking, *not* to relate the faith by providing a context of explanation, judgment, or renewal. Therefore, this method does not lend itself naturally to become the framework of meaning for Christian higher education, but it *could* if the aim of the method were to become relational, contextual, and renewing.

It should be added, moreover, that the new generation of scholars, with Gustaf Wingren as their leader, are cutting off the philosophical preamble to Lundensian method.[3] Dew-fresh creations, moreover, are still possible from within this movement. It has much to offer contemporary theology, but apart from its radical reconception it is hard to see in it a real hope for a full and organic relation to Christian higher education.

IV

Analytical linguistic philosophy or verificational analysis is not theology! Even so, it should be included because of its immense importance for both modern theology and higher education. It has challenged us to a radical rethinking of Christian language, method, and the relation of Christian faith to other subjects in the curriculum. Incidentally, it has kept countless good students from entering the ministry or has undermined the vigor of their faith. The preministerial students have seen no way around its claims that theological language, if not the whole enterprise, is meaningless.

Nevertheless, we must understand this movement sympathetically. It seems to have arisen primarily because the special sciences took over all the fields of knowledge. In giving birth to and bringing up these children, philosophy made itself a superannuated mother with nothing to do. For these thinkers, Kant's critical philosophy debarred it from metaphysics; and plain humility (or loss of nerve) kept it from tackling the job of synthesizing all the data from all the sciences. Analytical linguistic philosophy that actually started as logical positivism accepted as its premises that philosophy is empirically uninformative, that it deals with meaning as its sole province, and that meaning is not to be dealt with psychologically as the denotation of particular words as such but logically within propositions. The task of philosophy became the

[3] Cf. his *Theology in Conflict.*

analysis of the meaning of language, for language was its field and analysis its method. Meaningful truth, this position claimed, must be either certain, that is, totally analytical or tautology, or probable in terms of experienced sense data. Verification by sense data became a basic principle, even a criterion, of true philosophy. The ideals of mathematics in analysis and of inventory in the realm of experience underlay the whole movement. It is nominalism carried to its full extreme. A. J. Ayer's *Language, Truth and Logic,* especially in the first edition, and Ludwig Wittgenstein's *Tractatus Logico-Philosophicus* illustrate generally the earlier stage of this point of view.

In the second edition of his book (1946), Ayer has come out for a different kind of verification principle. He now admits a permissible inference from sense experience, such as the study of the past from manuscripts and all the necessary inferences of modern physics. "Tough" verification has given way to "weak" or "soft" forms of it. Wittgenstein, again, has shifted from verification to "usage" philosophy in his posthumously published *Philosophical Investigations* (1953). In this view, language is not so much a convention to be cleansed by analysis as an organic growth which must be considered for legitimate use. Verification is only one test and kind of usage. The disciplines of analysis and verification, in other words, have taken on wider contexts.

The appraisal of this point of view in relation to Christian higher education is not easy. It has done us all a service by cutting the ground from under a rationalistic, objectivistic metaphysics which illegitimately assumed the role of theology. It has also focused philosophy on its main task: the study of meaning. But above all, it ought to help us cut down much unfounded and foolish theological speculation. A flabby faith uses much slippery thinking. Most Christian apologetics is too weak-minded and softhearted to pass the bar of competent, fair-minded thinking. We should be well and lastingly rid of it.

On the other hand, linguistic analysis provided a convenient refuge from the kind of faith that is properly related to reason. Men seek concealment both against and through their own knowledge. They found it in logical positivism and its successors. One way of reasoning God away, for instance, was the following: Certainty has to do with logical propositions or with analytical truth only; all existential truth is contingent; therefore the claim that God exists, that a necessary being exists, confounds logical categories and is literally meaningless. Some even tried to prove the nonexistence of God by such logic! Philosophical analysis, in the second place, also removed faith from truth, religion from knowledge, and led to the full extreme, the split between the realm of form or thought and the realm of fact or experience. This bifurcation is perhaps the gravest cause today of our lack of religious and social leadership in intellectual realms. Christian higher education with its need for synoptic vision and contextual wholeness is therefore definitely threatened by this severing of faith from truth and by this depicting of religion as entirely arbitrary and not subject to knowledge and legitimate education.

What can we do about this position with reference to theology and higher education? The answer is partly that it is itself changing, and becoming self-critical. Its advocates need only keep on extending the realm of experience to be explained far enough, and they will find themselves right in the midst of theological problems and methods. The experience out of which the analysis comes in the first place is contingent. Therefore the all-or-none split between logical certainty and empirical probability is itself impossible for human beings. With that insight, the brittle bifurcation withers *at its heart.* Or we can show not only that we cannot experience "the whole," the world, God, or any other such category completely (one of the main contentions against theology on the part of verificational analysis), but that no scientific theory is ever experienced completely. The position has the appeal of the cleanliness of limited data and of a preconceived and confined method, but after its first, intoxicated blindness to the fuller problems of truth, it is already beginning to sober up and will doubtless gradually return to the central concerns of the relation of man's meanings to his existential problems. Christian educators can learn much from linguistic analysis without being either floored by it as the destroyer of theology or fooled by it as a revolutionary reorientation of man's total knowledge.

V

Liberal theology is presently under a cloud. It should not be so, more than others. Its advocates were great in faith and scholarship. Little apology needs to be made for old-line liberals like Walter Rauschenbusch, William Newton Clark, William Adams Brown, and Edgar S. Brightman or for new-line liberals like John C. Bennett, Robert Calhoun, and Walter Horton. Liberalism is characterized by an openness of spirit that is urgently needed. My former colleagues, Roger Shinn and Langdon Gilkey, have pointed out how dangerous can be the people who pass from fundamentalism into neo-orthodoxy without the mellowing influence of liberalism.

Liberalism stands for fairness, for understanding and appreciation of positions other than one's own. Liberals at least profess to believe that we are to learn from others, not just to oppose them. Liberalism stands also for unity of truth both within and between all levels of it, as, for instance, between faith and reason and between confession and conduct. Liberalism has also evinced an emulative social concern. Men like Rauschenbusch, Washington Gladden, and the Niebuhrs in their early years illustrate this natural combination between the liberal emphasis on truth, reason, experience, love, and social responsibility. Evangelicals of the middle of the nineteenth century evinced both social vision and concern, but the overwhelming credit for the acceptance of the organic relation between Christian faith and social ethics must be given to the liberals. For them social improvement, especially through education, became second nature. What are more important to higher education than an open spirit, respect for truth, and concern? Christian higher education owes a debt of gratitude beyond estimate to its liberal spirits, even its radically nontheological liberal spirits like John Dewey and Alexander Meiklejohn.

Liberalism failed, all the same, because of its omissions and mistakes. Idealistic in attitude, the liberals for the most part never took keenly enough to heart man's actual sinfulness. Therefore, they developed a theory of objectivity of knowledge that fails to take into account the fact that, as far as ultimate and personal involvements go, men tend to rationalize rather than to reason, that is, to use reason primarily as a means of self-justification, defense, and attack. "The cult of objectivity," as we now see, was largely an ideal. Men will not readily see the saving truth when it is also the demanding judge. There was also a false continuity of method in liberalism where the ultimate nature of faith (of there being, for instance, no presuppositionless thinking in ultimate matters, of selective truth being more real than aggregative truth, of decision often being more important than information to education) was not clearly perceived and applied.

Nor was there a vivid, positive zeal among most liberals. They were more interested in fighting backwardness and narrowness than in paying the costly price of positive zeal, particularly when this meant resolute opposition to partial and killing causes. Liberals were too willing to please. They lacked an effective principle of exclusion. To oppose, to refuse, to deny, to take the persecution for the commitment to absolute causes—such decisive action seems, to easygoing good will, to be intolerance. But at many of these points the neoliberals have changed while also preserving some of the best features of liberalism. We can hardly be thankful enough for its good points, but, educationally, we never dare to forget that an absolute demands *decision* for the pursuit of a certain course, no matter what. Educationally, too, growth is mostly the persistent following of such a course.

VI

One of the most important theological movements for Christian higher education is neonaturalism. In one form or another this drive in theology is best represented by men like Alfred North Whitehead, Daniel Day Williams, Henry Nelson Wieman, Paul Tillich, and Rudolf Bultmann. These men accept the best in science, and aim for adequacy of thinking through philosophy, acknowledging besides the need for mystery as the penetrating counterpart and the constant companion of knowledge. Whitehead, Wieman, and Williams believe that religious thinking must wait on scientific data and philosophic interpretation for intellectual adequacy. Tillich and Bultmann also insist that religious knowledge must not be prescientific. For all of them, the organic and relational stress of knowledge is of critical importance. Religion as an evaluative response to reality is part of personal, social, and cosmic experience. The stress of the first three thinkers on the organic nature of reality and of knowledge, on the fact that no subject can find its fullest truth apart from the consideration of its relation to other subjects and to the whole, on the togetherness of reality and of value, and on the synoptic approach in general, have made their thought of inestimable importance to higher education, while their stress on integrity of knowledge, life, values, truth, and the religious life has resulted in the creation of a very high form of religious thought.

Along with Whitehead, Tillich is at the very front of constructive thinking. Tillich's elucidation of the Christian faith, his expounding of philosophy, his grasp of historical thought, his understanding of non-Christian religions, his at-homeness in art and culture generally, his immersion in depth psychology, and his capacity to communicate with even hostile spirits in a secular university set him apart as a minister to higher education. Nathan Pusey, president of Harvard, has related how completely Tillich won over a group of Harvard professors who met him with pronounced skepticism with regard to his religious position. Tillich is more than a profound thinker, however; he is both a prophet and a systematic pioneer.

At a time of confusion or regression in constructive thinking Tillich has forged ahead with both deliberate care and accelerating speed. The center of his position is the relation between the unconditional and the conditioned. Religious reality is the dimension of the unconditional. God does not exist as a Being among beings, but is the unconditional reality, nowhere existing as such, yet everywhere available as the power to resist nonbeing and to make for harmony of being. The central scene for Tillich is history, where meaning is translated into concrete experience through freedom. Christ is the center of history as the picture in history of the unconditional. Thus, essence and existence meet in him, not in such a way that the unconditional becomes conditioned but so that the conditioned becomes completely transparent to the unconditional by the full acceptance of the right relationship between the unconditional and the conditioned. The Cross is the symbol and power of this relation; and the resurrection is the declaration in history of the victory in life of eternity. Eternal life is the releasing and creative participation in this reality. Love is the symbol that most fully explains and makes available true power and justice.

Protestantism is the realistic power for self-criticism and creative renewal. The Church is community in the full, inclusive sense revealed in Jesus as the Christ, but all community, whether secular or non-Christian, exists and has its reality in the true community of the Church as the representative of the Kingdom of God. The theologian must live and think within the circle of a concrete religion, but he lives also in the total life around him. Therefore, he mediates between religious and secular thought. The secular world has enough moral and spiritual sense even to be the conscience of the empirical Church which is always tempted by idolatry and self-adulation. Between theology and the secular world, therefore, there can be creative co-operation.

Tillich's theology relates itself exceptionally well, by its very nature, to higher education. His exposition of the faith is centrally Christian in a descriptive and creative sense. It has a piercing quality of firsthand insight. His faith in the general presence of the logos provides us with unitive meaning and synoptic vision without reduction of differences, and yet, even so, all meaning is subject to the infinite mystery of the unconditioned. Few theologians have fuller or truer appreciation of secular learning and culture than Tillich.[4]

[4] Surprisingly, Karl Barth also has such appreciation, but it does not come as the natural outgrowth of his central theological position.

Bultmann represents the existentialist kind of neonaturalism. Ontologically he is basically at one, he claims, with existentialist philosophers like Karl Jaspers and Martin Heidegger. The real difference between them consists in the fact that, whereas the philosophers believe man can make a free, positive decision, Bultmann understands that man must accept passively "by grace" the working of God in human life. God is the power available to man in the ultimate mystery of being who through man's acceptance of grace can relieve him of anxiety and give him a free decision for the future. Christ exhibited this reality in the Cross and in the resurrection. These are not objective events in the sense of bare, historic occurrences but are, rather, meaningful events that can and should be re-enacted in the present in response to the proclamation of the Gospel.

Christ saves insofar as we know for ourselves the present reality of the losing and finding of self by the overcoming of anxiety and the reception of faith freely open to the future. Insofar as they are meaningful, past and future are both part of the present tense, of the moment for acceptance. Those who have found this reality of overcoming anxiety by a power not of themselves are "in Christ," "in faith"; what counts is the original reality of the experience of Jesus and of his disciples. They interpreted these experiences, to be sure, in objective, supernatural terms of a God beyond this world who literally came to earth and paid for man's sin by the shedding of his own blood and by literally rising from death. Modern man trained in science, Bultmann holds, rejects such primitive thinking, but the *original* rather than the *objective* reality of the New Testament Gospel remains: "to offer man an understanding of himself which will challenge him to a genuine existential decision."[5]

The early Church succumbed, however, to Stoicism and made a world-view out of the Christian faith. This intellectualizing of the faith was a basic mistake. The New Testament speaks genuinely of a Gospel of Christ's death and resurrection as the power, of a new kind of life and community "in Christ" or "in faith." *Weltanschauung* is no part of the Gospel. Bultmann's theology, therefore, has no contextual capacity for higher education; its power, rather, is to break down static structures of interpretation imposed on experience in the past that hinder the creative activity of the spirit in its constant need to appraise happenings, to decide concerning their significance, and to provide freedom from anxiety and the motivational connection with "the stream" of

[5] H. W. Bartsch (ed.), *Kerygma and Myth*, p. 16.

reality of which Bultmann speaks in his *Essays, Philosophical and Theological*.

What should be said of neonaturalism in its relation to Christian higher education? Already we have stressed its high and significant relevance. We have also emphasized how profoundly and seminally Christian it is on its descriptive side, especially in the case of Williams, Tillich, and Bultmann. Why, then, can we not come to rest in the neonaturalist position? The real problem is created by Christian theology and concerns the nature of transcendence. This term or its obvious equivalents can be found in the writings of the men just mentioned. None of these men is a humanist. Saving reality, God, is radically more than human experience or effort. Nor are they reductionistic naturalists in the sense of employing a limiting scientific method. The closest to such a view of science is Bultmann's, but he goes beyond scientific naturalism in the narrow sense even in his ontology. They all reject unequivocally, however, the supernaturalism of Christian classical theology. God, for none of them, is the supernatural creator, the self-sufficient ruler of plants and planets who is other and more than the best we know both in human experience and in cosmic description, the One who from beyond the world became incarnate in it, who died for man's sin in his full identification with man and who rose victorious over sin, law, and actual death by the deathless power of his supernatural love. Classical Christianity with its objective supernaturalism can be treated as symbol or myth but never as factual history or as true ontology. Tillich and Bultmann are most emphatic on this point.

Is this shedding of supernaturalism, however, not a riddance and relief for honest faith and competent education? Does it not remove from the Christian theology of today the largest false obstacle separating it from higher education? Has not the demythologizing of the Bible been our biggest task for several generations, now at length recognized and effected? Is it not also true that many who confess to belong to other theological tendencies in fact belong here ontologically? Modernity of assumption is more pervasive of the inner man of education than appears on the surface of confession.

VII

Admittedly, the real problem is not whether neonaturalism is genuinely biblical or Christian in the historical sense. If it is true, we should all come to it. Radical translation of terms is then justified and we have no right to accuse these men of dishonesty in their use of them. Has not Kant, furthermore, made it impossible ever again to show critically that supernaturalism is true? Kant himself, of course, is a complex problem at this point, considering the whole history of his writings, and to try to refute him easily is foolish, but the following line of reasoning makes me believe that at its heart classical Christian supernaturalism is not only biblical and historical but actually true. At least, I find no equally convincing alternative for faith.

I grant that along the usual lines of thinking, naturalism has a right to say that any thought, experience, or fact, human or cosmic, may be defined as natural. Aside from these facts, we can know nothing. What is revealed, naturalists say, is only the fuller dimensions of human nature and of the cosmos in which we live. In terms of human experience or thought as such, therefore, there is no proving of a world beyond this one or of a being beyond natural beings. Naturalists also have a right to say that trust in unexamined revelation is completely arbitrary and eventuates in intellectual relativism, a choosing of ultimates at will, without check or challenge from evidence or reason. Along such lines of procedure the Kant of the first Critique remains unanswered; and supernaturalism is mere primitive thinking or, at most, precritical philosophy.

There are objective facts, however, that Kant was in no position to consider. We are not left with the choice of either disavowing the cosmological proof entirely or of assuming the ontological along with it. This Kantian cornerstone of modernity is not hewn out of the granite of fact nor is it built on the marble of reasoning. The facts, according to science itself, are that we live in a cosmic process that has come to be in the course of unimaginably long ages, by means of new levels of development which, as they become added to previous process, are found not only to fit into it organically but to fulfill it. To believe that such an accumulative series of appearances that have added up to an organic unity of the universe and of the universes has come to be and has come together without cause and without reason is to believe in miracle with unrestrained credulity. When there is added the astounding fact that from the point of view of life, personality, and creative community (our relevant data for the criterion of meaningfulness) this process is almost brand-new, the abruptness of the process becomes overwhelming.

However many ways there are of approaching or of explaining these facts, they are pivotal for any thinking concerning ultimates. They break all reductionistic naturalisms except as these are accepted either as ignorant assumptions or as credulous faiths. These facts also forbid all easy assumptions that the description of present process best indicates the nature of reality. Such a freezing of the process goes contrary to the overwhelming indication of process as on the move, awaiting further development. There are, therefore, solid facts which bridge the gap between the cosmological reasoning and the ontological.

Where, however, does this insight leave us? There is no returning to a rationalistic inductive or deductive reasoning that "proves" God. Kant is right that all reasoning from experience to ultimate reality does in the end in some way use the ontological "proof." Kierkegaard also correctly contended that nothing relative (historical, ethical, or metaphysical) can ever prove God. That the less certain should prove the more certain is obviously logically false. Dorothy Emmet, therefore, in *The Nature of Metaphysical Thinking* has properly dismissed deductive and hypothetical analogies, retaining only those that are existential and co-ordinating. However, she dismissed projective analogies too quickly. In case the projective analogies are merely the absolutizing of something in history which is obviously relative, Kant and Kierkegaard stand guard against such projective thinking. When the actual bridge between cosmological and ontological reasoning stands forth strong, then projective thinking changes its intent, status, and effectiveness.

In such a case, the entire problem is altered. To make no deliberate choice of ultimates if a person is mature enough to make such choice, is to retreat from reality and from responsible intellectual and religious leadership. But all *thinkers* have assumed presuppositions, some posture toward reality, some configuration of experience that indicates what they actually consider to be most important and most real. The right response to reality is consequently to have as true and effective an interpretation of ultimate reality and meaning as possible.[6] All must live by faith, the only question is by what *kind* of faith they live. William James is right that there are live, forced, and momentous options among which we must actually take our choice.

Brand Blanshard in his presidential address before the American Theological Society in 1956, made a strong reply to William James, however, to the effect that it is unethical ever to go beyond the facts or to make any leap of faith at all not warranted by the facts, for such choice is actually the confusion of faith with, or the substitution of faith for, knowledge. At this point, we all have to be utterly scrupulous and critical. No leap into ultimates gives us new

[6] This argument is worked out at length in my *Faith and Reason*.

knowledge, but such a leap may put us into position to receive new knowledge from beyond present process. After all, new knowledge *has* come into process in the past, and we are in no position to deny that new facts do appear or that new insights might throw fuller or different light on ultimate questions. Since no leap gives us knowledge, however, we can say no more than that we *must have* some co-ordinating presupposition or presuppositions for thinking, for the total configuration of life, and that therefore we should choose the one that seems least arbitrary.

We are then led back again to our facts concerning the origins of the world we know. Not to acknowledge a creative ground of cause and reason behind, before, or inexplicably within process which is more than present process and which accounts the least arbitrarily for it, is to be facing the past by infinite reduction or to be parochially frozen within the present. When our faith stands on whatever best accounts in process for its development, its unity, its meaning, and its fulfillment, it is the least arbitrary. Not that we have therefore cleared up the mystery of the new or of creation. But transcendence[7] becomes the least arbitrary content of our faith if it can be shown to have organic relations to the other levels and if it can be seen to explain inclusively the meaning of the total process with the richest explanatory adequacy we can find.

Translated into theological terms, this means that incarnation and eschatology are primary to thinking. Knowledge of ultimates must be had from within experience and process. God becomes man, enters human experience and process to reveal himself. It means also that knowledge is eschatological in the sense that incarnation points forward toward the consummation of creation. The redemption of creation by means of incarnation takes place in time directed toward the future. Such theology springs out of our actual knowledge situation. We as Christians believe in the Incarnation, that God came in Christ as the fullness of time. In such a case, eschatology becomes the fulfillment inclusively of what has come once for all conclusively in Jesus as the Christ. God is the personal Spirit who is holy love. We do not know him in his eternal glory, but we do know him as such love from within our bounds of time and space. Furthermore, it is important for education that the Holy Spirit is biblically defined as the Spirit of truth. When God came in Jesus Christ as the personal Spirit who is holy love, he came as the personal event that is also the center of

---

[7] Obviously, transcendence need not be conceived of *directionally*, only dimensionally, or even in nonspatial terms altogether.

meaning. The living Christ then becomes the context, judge, and transformer of all knowledge. If this is correct theology, how does our analysis refer to all the contemporary tendencies we have described and evaluated?

VIII

In the light of our analysis we can see that it is possible to keep the fundamentalists' emphasis on "evangelical supernaturalism" without their obscurantist literalism of biblical inspiration and of propositional revelation that shuts them off from the open inquiry of higher education. We should also rejoice in the neo-Calvinist stress on the transcendence of God and on his revelation in event, particularly in the history of salvation and in the Christ, without accepting its pitting of redemption over against creation, and event over against meaning. As a protest movement to establish the primacy of the transcendence of God and of his self-revelation in the Word, we have needed this movement, but now it is time to see how transcendence and incarnation are related to God's ubiquity and to his work in creation and history. The Lund school of theology can teach us about the distinctiveness of the Christian faith by means of its dominant and determinative motif, agape, and the need for patience and critical care in the description of what is truly Christian, but we need not with them deny to reason its proper place of interpreting and of relating the faith. If we release the full power of the Christian faith, however, we shall in all three of these movements find a classical Christianity which, while remaining itself, can be related both contextually and motivationally to the needs of Christian higher education.

In the case of the last three movements discussed—linguistic analysis, neoliberalism, and neonaturalism—the problem has been a forfeiting of the transcendence, or the distinctiveness of the Christian faith. We have seen, however, how it is possible competently and honestly to go beyond the strictures on faith inherited from Kant. We share with the linguistic analysts their revulsion toward slippery Christian apologetics, and we covet their drive for cleanliness of thought. We believe, too, that the day of an objective, rationalistic metaphysics as a legitimate approach to ultimate questions is over, but we know that the position of linguistic analysis is the extreme illustration of a false bifurcation between thought and fact and that fact cannot be tied down to sensationalism. We are therefore hopeful that beyond their function as a cleansing fire, the linguistic analysts will become creatively constructive within the bounds of their genuinely critical insights.

The liberals need to encourage us to openness of spirit, breadth of view, and unity of truth both in thought and in life. Their accommodation of spirit makes for co-operative inquiry with those in higher education, but we need not on that account lose decisiveness of truth or distinctiveness of theological method.

The naturalists we have already appraised by means of our own constructive analysis. What they lack is an effective method for understanding of, and pointing to, adequate and effective transcendence. They, above all others, are offering higher education relevant stimuli and contextual suggestions. Whitehead's influence should grow in the field of higher education, and there are some indications that it is growing. Tillich's *The Dynamics of Faith* shows how much a dynamic and creative religious thinker can offer motivationally as well as intellectually to Christian higher education. We share with these thinkers their horror for an arbitrary revelationism, unsupported by genuine data or by reasoning from within the processes of our modern educational activities. These processes can be opened up to the truth of classical Christianity precisely by the use of legitimate reasoning about the facts already established by modern educators. We need primary thinkers for this task.

Creative Christian higher education is a noble challenge during these days of rapid intellectual and cultural transition. No facile solution will do and no fixed formula will ever satisfy the constantly dynamic enterprise of education. I am convinced, however, that a new age of constructive leadership for civilization can come if we appropriate the universal truth of the Christian revelation in Christ and apply this with both experimental caution and bold creative courage to the ever expanding and deepening problems of higher education. Only such a constructive undertaking can entitle us to use the term Christian higher education.

Higher Education and Values

I

THE crisis of our times is the crisis of values. The Harvard anthropologist Clyde Kluckhohn is only one strong voice in a mighty chorus thundering this truth. Values indicate how we try to meet our needs. Human needs are what human nature requires. Our basic needs are universal to human nature. Human needs, as Rignano observed long ago, are also the expression of the necessity for human beings to be in the right relationship to their environment. They are, in fact, elicited by that environment. Therefore human needs reflect, beyond their own nature, the nature of the reality that produced them. The understanding of what human values are, consequently, involves the interpretation and the evaluation of what is beyond man. Inasmuch as religion is man's evaluative response to reality, the right religious response offers the answer to our crisis of values. What chance is there, however, that the nature of such a response can be established, and, if established, made?

Higher education is itself in a state of crisis. It is, at least, undergoing drastic reexamination. Many of those responsible for charting its course are in a flexible mood. They are ready for change. Development requires reappraisal, the discarding of unfortunate features of present practice and the discovery and incorporation of new methods and contents. For such constructive change, there is great pressure. One force for change is the inescapable fact of failure on the part of the present kind of democratic way of life in America to meet the demands of a new era, within and without. In a television series, for instance, in which outstanding Americans weighed the strength of their national life in its major areas, there was a frightening consensus that Americans are falling short of the requirements of the present day. Such searching judgment, however, can also be the proper prelude to a new fulfillment. A second force for the renewal of higher education is the focus of attention and of effort which is now put upon it all the way from the federal government and secular agencies to the National Council of the Churches of Christ in the U.S.A. and separate denominations. Our present topic, "Higher Education and Values," therefore combines two main areas of concern.

In order to furnish a constructive approach to the subject, I shall focus our attention on three areas of need: the trusting of truth; the freedom of fulfillment; and the creation of community.

The thrust of Western civilization originated in the trusting of truth. For the Hebrews, such faith meant obeying the source of trust, the living God. He was the author of dependable order. "Shall not the judge of all the earth do right?" Is not his judgment the plumb line of righteousness? The authors of the Books of Kings were the first historians of note; and for them history exhibited the faithfulness of God in punishing the wicked rulers and their nations and in rewarding the righteous. For the Greeks, also, the trusting of truth underlay their rise to creative civilization from Parmenides' equating of thought and being through various approaches to the trustworthiness of reason, such as Anaxagoras' identification of mind and reality, up to the magnificent systems of Plato and Aristotle. With the Greeks, it was reason and natural knowledge that delivered them from bondage to fate or from the fickleness of the gods. For the Hebrews, the trusting of truth was mainly obedience to a faithful God; for the Greeks, such trusting was largely the acceptance of the regularities in thought and nature disclosed by reason.

The strength of the Hebrew and Greek heritages combined to provide the proper precondition for the rise of art, culture, and science in the Middle Ages. Both history and nature were dependable orders under God and according to the laws of nature. Augustine's *City of God* gave main focus to Western man's thought concerning the meaning of history up through the Middle Ages, and Roger Bacon formulated one of the early statements to the effect that man trusted God's faithfulness in nature. Within such an outlook, intellectual, aesthetic, and scientific creativity burst forth.

Such faith in truth, however, was soon assailed. In effect, Isaac Newton reduced the historical order to the natural, thus helping to destroy faith in the God of history. David Hume separated both orders from the truth of pure reason, reserving truth for logic and pure mathematics, and introducing a radical skepticism as to any dependable and significant knowledge in the other realms. Instead of the knowledge of history and of nature belonging together under God and according to reason, there was for him no certain knowledge of either, especially not as wholes. More and more, thereafter, knowledge began to disintegrate into fragments of special sciences to the point where, as in modern linguistic philosophy, only abstract analytical meaning carried certainty, while this realm itself became totally divorced from the realm of fact, and all facts relegated by rigid, methodological rules to the special sciences. In other cases, the unity underlying history and nature was stated in terms of myths and symbols so loosely and thinly related to reality that they beclouded the mind and lamed the will.

We need, indeed, to return to a trusting of truth in both areas of history and nature. But such a return seems nearly impossible. We cannot will it. Mere reason is impotent to provide basic faith. What hope is there, then, for a new creative era to match the unprecedented demand of our day?

Our deepest need, we recall, indicates the nature of reality. Our evaluative response should therefore be in line with our deepest need as men. Clemens E. Benda, in his significant work, *Der Mensch im Zeitalter der Lieblosigkeit,* has pointed out that from within a false evolutionary presupposition we have defined need in the direction of what lies below man. Man's animal needs, so to speak, for physical survival and satisfaction have been made central: food, sex, and shelter, whereas man cannot be understood except on his own level, as a person and as a society in need most centrally of love. The Harvard Research Center in Altruistic Integration and Creativity, under Pitirim A. Sorokin, has amassed evidence to support this contention, and some social scientists are convinced that love is the context for the investigation of human behavior.

However significant such inquiry and such statements may be for theory, indicating evaluative responses to reality to be centrally love, the Hebrew Christian approach to love through acceptance and obedience is nevertheless the only way to know love as the power to transform life and to make possible the trusting of truth in history. If God is love and if love to be known must be obeyed, a century of lawlessness, crime, and wanton destruction in war should make it almost impossible for its generations to know him, at least not apart from genuine repentance and a change of ways. Only by the doing of the truth and even by the being of it can truth be known enough to be trusted; otherwise, it has to be known mainly by the breach of it as sterility, futility, and sense of guilt and meaninglessness.

Such obedience in history, however, can never take the place of trusting the truths of reasoned experiment in nature. The faithfulness of God in nature underlies the unity of the universe, which is the basic presupposition of science. The method of science is a sign of the trusting of truth. Higher education, to make possible full focus on the truths of history and of nature that can support and produce basic values, must rediscover a way to place our culture under obedience to God and under respect for reason, until combining and developing our Christian and our Greek heritages, we shall receive that sensitiveness to what is vital that shall let the values arising from our deepest needs spring once again to creative and robust life.

II

In addition to the trusting of truth a syndetic value is the freedom of fulfillment. No higher education can succeed if it fails to release the kind of freedom that is the foundation of a large cluster of secondary values like responsibility, initiative, and creativity. Our American culture has been cradled in liberty, nurtured in initiative, and it should mature in creative responsibility.

The denial of man's freedom is by now an old story. But our attention has usually been focused on the institutional and social denial of freedom. We have become increasingly aware of political totalitarianism and cultural conformism. Higher education, however, has contributed its share to the denial of freedom. By its absorption with the objective fields in the curriculum, whether in the natural or in the social sciences, higher education has turned man himself into an object. The natural sciences, of course, should study man as an object. But as a subject in the curriculum, the social sciences placed man under the control of predictable conditions, purporting to study the whole man but actually reducing him to an object. Thus was "the subject" made "subject to." Then philosophy (in large sections of its domain), as Paul Tillich pointed out in his Lowell Lectures (Boston, 1958), reduced the subject of man's thinking to a matter of linguistic analysis, and man himself to a sheer object for scientific verification.

Existentialism came as a revolt against this objectification of man. Søren Kierkegaard choked under the suffocating systems that made man an object. For him, subjectivity was truth, and choice was the only road to reality. Existentialism has now become a movement of revolt in literature and drama as well as in philosophy and theology. Central to this movement is its demand that man recognize his inescapable freedom. Such stress is one step on the return to reality, but most of the movement is guilty of the perversion or the belittling of freedom. The freedom advocated by existentialism is for the most part man's immature freedom of self-expression. Such freedom is rooted in man, not in his evaluative response to reality. Because it has no recourse to the conditions of the freedom of fulfillment, modern existentialism nearly always fails to find God, through whom truth can be trusted both for history and for nature. Freedom therefore becomes largely the despairing responsibility of a faithless generation.

The only adequate answer to existentialism is the fulfillment of its demand for the centrality of choice by the discovery of the kind of reality where choice not only is real and responsible but is capable of individual and social fulfillment. If freedom itself is not optional, as the existentialists rightly observe, the road to reality must lie through freedom. When freedom is conceived of as primarily for the self, there is no realm of reality in terms of which the freedom of the self can be fulfilled. Freedom becomes meaningless and frustrating. The reason existentialists like Jean Paul Sartre find all roads leading nowhere is that the goal toward which they start is already the self. They have nowhere to go with their freedom.

The freedom of self, at the least, must lie in our common humanity. Man must be an object of allegiance. Instead of other people "being hell," as Sartre dramatizes in No Exit, a fact for those who make their own freedom both ground and goal, other people should be understood and experienced as essential to self-fulfillment. Christianity and Hinduism join in affirming that other people, rightly understood and accepted, are part of our own body, not to be hated but to be loved. Martin Heidegger, we have seen, has expanded existentiell, or individual human nature, into existential, or common human nature. This way lies the truth of right existentialism. Freedom is real and decision is central both to knowledge and to reality, not as the freedom of the limited, isolated self, but as the freedom of the inclusive, social self. The glory of man is the glory of his common humanity; the responsibility of man is the inescapable freedom of man, the human community.

Moreover, as self-fulfillment comes only through the acceptance of others, in the grace of both common receiving and responsible doing, so the freedom of fulfillment comes only through the reaching of reality. Man's freedom is inescapably bound up with God's freedom, whose freedom is that of creative concern for the common good. Man is not alone even in the frightful choices of this day, except as he repudiates his Maker. Our own freedom is authentic, for it is the gift of a faithful God, but it need not become the freedom of frustration except as we ignore or defy the common good. We may have, for the receiving and the living of it, the freedom of fulfillment where freedom for self-fulfillment is liberated within co-operative community and where man's basic need for love is lifted up into the reaches of the ultimate reality of the freedom of God. A basic task for higher education, especially in our day of frustrating and dehumanizing conformism is to discover as well as to defend, to enlarge as well as to perpetuate, to sensitize as well as to make available, the total range of freedoms in all areas of life, without which man neither knows nor attains authentic existence.

III

The trusting of truth should lead to the fulfillment of freedom both by a larger view of God and by the acceptance of his universal will, and also by the fuller exploration and use of the natural order for the common good. For these values, as our evaluative response to reality at the center of our common need, are themselves consummated by the concern for community. It is unnecessary for our purposes to paint in large the conflict of our age between the surviving drives of a profane individualism and an obscene collectivism. Both are sins against God, for whatever else the Christian doctrine of the Trinity may mean, at its center it proclaims the truth of God's identifying himself conclusively with the individual in the Son, and with the community in the Spirit. In the biblical teaching, one cannot be had apart from the other. Man is neither free nor full apart from the self-acceptance which involves altogether the acceptance of the total human community under God.

To be sure, such community must begin at home. The wise know that the world will be changed in the family and that a new age must begin in the local community. There are those who grow eloquent concerning the breaking down of barriers and the building of bridges on a world-wide scale because they cannot govern themselves, because they have failed in their own family life, and because they are irresponsible in the concrete instances of social need. Beyond this obvious requirement of authentic life at home, however, there are three areas of critical demand calling for the creation of community: race, nation, and religion.

Whether in South Africa or in the United States, whether in London or in Fort Wayne, race comes as a curse because it expresses as well as symbolizes man's revolt against God. God created us with the glory of diversity; we fear what is different and defame

God's glory. For the problem of race there is no easy solution because it is not only rooted in our primitive passions but also intertwined with our relation to God. The only adequate solution for it is the power of God who created, contagious with the richness of our common humanity. Once when I was invited to address a law school in the southern United States, as I opened my Bible my eye happened to fall on two verses across the page from each other: "The courts are open" and "They were filled with the Holy Spirit." The values of God's diversity in creation by racial variety can become understood and appropriated only when the meaning and purpose of both law and love become effective in a new level of humanity. Higher education fails both God and man unless it can produce the power for the living of a new age in racial relations.

As our response to race indicates our fear of creative diversity, so our response to the urgent need for supernational loyalties and arrangements witnesses to our limiting of God to national regions. We have failed of the maturation that is now needed to keep pace with God's present summons. Nations have had their necessary day as the largest practical unity of human organization, possessive of effective sanctions. Some kind of world federation, keeping intact such regional and national freedoms as are consistent with, and enriching of, the common good, will have to come if the world is not to perish by its own hand, or at least not to bleed itself into ignoble and blasphemous impotence. Norman Cousins has prophesied the probable ending of our course of history unless man can rise with necessary speed from the age of barbarism, symbolized by war, to the age of civilization, symbolized by a new level of co-operative living. No education is high, let alone higher, unless it include as a contagious passion and a sober responsibility the values of one world in international relations.

Furthermore, as our negative response to race rejects God's riches in diversity and as our isolating or insolent response to nation indicates our limiting in our loyalties the effective reign of God, even so, our encountering of other religions is all too often an escape from the universality of God. Symmachus long ago, in discussing the relation of religion, informed Ambrose that so great a mystery cannot ever be reached by following one road only, and recently Dean Inge reminded us that there are many paths leading to the hill of the Lord and that the paths converge only at the top. Modern humanity has no choice except to face the fact that the world's religions will confront each other either for conflict or for fulfillment. If Christ is, as Christians claim, the symbol and the substance of God's universal love, Christians should surely understand and accept all religions at their best, working out with them, humbly and patiently, the common destiny of the many roads which men have started toward the hill of the Lord. There need be no guess that as they do so they will discern much new beauty and learn not a little of God's way in history and in nature. Higher education dare not accept any longer, on the penalty of sin against humanity as well as against God, what Ruth Benedict considers the absolutes of anthropological in-groupism rather than the true universal of a common humanity under God, united by its common need for universal love and creative community.

Higher education today confronts, at the center of its task of reconstruction, the nature and place of value. The crises of both civilization and of higher education converge here. If our analysis is right, the solution for both areas can come only as we learn to trust the truth, to find the freedom of fulfillment, and to release the creation of community. The trusting of truth requires the doing of truth. The will of God for the common good must be obeyed if it is to be convincingly known. Upon such doing of truth, the reliability of reason as a total context for the study of nature will once again begin to be restored to us. Upon such doing of truth depends also the finding of the freedom of fulfillment which makes the self whole, and releases the deeper freedom of our common humanity within the overarching reaches of God's concern for the total good. And the crowning glory of such trusting of truth and of such freedom of fulfillment will be the creation of community from the family circle of the local home to the whole family of God, in race, in world order, and in the richly diversified reaches of religion for one world.

The attention of America today is on her leaders of higher education as they not only inquire into the nature of value but labor to release the most authentic values both to satisfy the common need and to whet the appetite for that fuller craving for what is good, which lies at the center of what is best called the truly human.

Chapter 20

The Church-Related College and a
Mature Faith

THE Church-related college is of primary importance both for the Church and for education. *For the Church,* it can be pointed out that a main reason for the vigor of the American Church in contradistinction to the British and the Swedish, for instance, is the fact that, in both of these latter, leaders of thought in the Church have been generally overawed by the paralyzing power of secular thinkers. Both Britain and Sweden give their theological degrees through state-controlled institutions of higher learning. These secular institutions determine almost sovereignly what are to be regarded as criteria for truth as well as the patterns for what is properly accepted as legitimate knowledge.

In both instances, the leaders of science and philosophy, with few exceptions, have espoused theories of knowledge not only dampening to the faith but destructive of it. I have personally observed the blighting force of secular university influence. The point of view held by the secular university is regarded almost with religious reverence. It is final truth! In America, however, institutions of learning independent of such secular ones keep calling the bluff of these secular scholars, whose theories often spring out of their presuppositions and their presuppositions all too often out of their basic approach to life. Depth of learning and vigor of thought have helped the Church to accept the truth of its faith without the constant internal bleeding that results when it is secretly, at least halfway, assumed by the Church leaders that their faith, although good and high, is not in fact true.

For education, on the other hand, the Church-related college has helped the secular university. Surveys made of the background of scientists and of scholars generally in leading American institutions of higher education have indicated surprisingly that these come out of all proportion from the small Church-related colleges, if that term is taken to mean colleges with a general Christian background of contemporary concern. There is a motivation present in the Church-related colleges that gives the drive of seriousness to young scholars. Faith generates creativity. These scholars may later disavow the form of their erstwhile faith, but all the same, they owe to their background much of the drive which has put them in the position of leadership. This situation with regard to the small liberal-arts colleges, giving birth to prominent scholars who then generally stay in the secular institutions, parallels the raising up of the majority of the Christian ministry by the conservative churches. These persons then go on to become educated Christian leaders who generally hold a more intellectually mature faith than the communities which reared them.

To the fact of the demonstrated importance of the Church-related college must be added that now on a nationwide scale in America, even in secular education, there is an intensive focus of thinking and support directed to higher education. Along with this general undertaking to strengthen materially higher education, there is also right now intensive denominational and interdenominational emphasis on Christian higher education.

I

The role of the Church-related college is obviously twofold: It is an agent of the Church; it is a servant of higher education.

The Church-related college is nothing less than the Church in education. The Church-related college is the Church at work educationally. It is the Church learning; it is the Church expressing its faith in terms of knowledge and in relation to knowledge; it is the Church communicating its faith.

In the first place, the Church must find its faith. In one sense, to be sure, the faith of the Church is given once for all. In Jesus Christ, the Church has the abiding anchor of its faith. The Church that does not confess centrally that Jesus Christ is Lord is not Christian. Christ defines the Church and gives it reality. But in another sense, the faith must ever be discovered afresh. Gustaf Wingren, a weighty Swedish theologian, has said that the permanent task of the Church is to relate the Bible to the world, or as he puts it, the constant work of the Church in education is to carry on a dialectic between hermeneutics and anthropology. Hermeneutics, as he uses the term, expresses the constant requirement to look afresh at the basic interpretation of the Bible in the light of the needs of a concrete age; while anthropology, in his terminology, stands for the constant need to view man's understanding of himself in the light of the Bible. Thus, both the Bible and each age have need of continual confrontation of each other by the believer who participates both in the Christian community and in the thought patterns of his age. In this profound sense the Church is continually finding its faith, and the best place for so doing is within its own institutions of higher education.

But the Church needs also to confess its faith within the thought patterns which are most real to it; and within the forms that most clearly and forcefully express its faith. No believer or community of faith can be at its best until the reality by which it lives can be put into such natural expression and used so meaningfully in worship that the faith itself becomes its own best recommendation. In one sense, the faith should become such a sound background for study that it forms a context for thought, a context that is taken for granted.

Our highest faith is our presupposition; no presupposition, moreover, activates vigorous thought until it gives a steady perspective to our universe of knowledge. Faith should co-ordinate as well as motivate inquiry. Well has Goethe said that the believing ages are the creative ages. Even when Alfred North Whitehead maintains that, on the whole, it is the unstable ages that are the epochs most productive of high faith, he means not that such high-grade experience results from uncertainty or from confusion, but rather, that it results from the searing need to rethink what is assumed in the light of the welter of new evidence and new thinking. The task of the Church-related college is to facilitate the confession of faith. It is ever to reformulate the faith in terms of its foundation, with constant reference to the experience of the believing community. When this is done effectively, the foundation itself is understood afresh and the experience of the community of faith is cleansed and strengthened.

Besides finding and confessing its faith, the Church-related college must learn how to communicate it. No faith is mature until it knows how to live in its environment, however secular, without either hostility or conformity. Such maturity comes from the kind of security people have who know not only what they believe and why, but also how to communicate it to nonbelievers. Such communication depends upon an integrity of community experience within which it is possible to feel oneself into the very lives of those who reject the faith. The community must be able to become involved with the world, to enter into its inmost feelings of anxiety and self-assertion, without forfeit of its own confession. To do so, the Church-related college should learn how to make use of the signs and symbols that express the wider and the more basic faith of the outside world and to create symbols of communication of its own that will reach the nonbelieving community, whether this be the secular university or the more amorphous field of the general public.

To carry on this work of finding, confessing, and communicating a mature faith the Church-related college must be, to use Clarence Cranford's phrase, a fellowship of the unashamed. It must be a community of commitment to the Christian faith. The ideal, of course, is to have the whole of the administration and the whole faculty continuously aware of the commitment involved in being a Church-related college. The Church-related college is in purpose a community of Christian administrators and teachers. In any case, it is failing its distinctive task unless it has an administration definitely aware of its nature and committed firmly to its task, and unless a large group of the instructors are actively and intelligently concerned with the primary purpose of the college. A Church-related college without a Christian faculty fellowship is a misnomer.

But the Church-related college is not only the agent of the Church, the Church at work in education; it is also, on the other hand, the representative of higher education. Neither task can be subordinated to the other. The Church-related college must, by circumstance, serve two masters. Each master has full right over its servant. The Church-related college assumes inescapably this twofold task.

With reference to higher education, the college should have unswerving allegiance to truth. Its intellectual integrity needs to be beyond question. The task of higher education is to find, to formulate, and to communicate truth in general. It is to find truth for the sake of life. Knowledge must be sought with inviolable honesty; yet knowledge is also pursued with concern for life. Man is not in the educational enterprise for the sake of some unrelated, abstract ideal of knowledge; he is in education to solve his problems in the light of dependable knowledge. For this reason, in legitimate education, no bias can be presupposed that determines the conclusions beforehand. Whatever faith lays binding hands on truth is false. It is no use at all to say that all thinkers have presuppositions and that, therefore, the Christian has a right to his own. Mature faith is rooted and grounded in truth. Unless man has the capacity for some real measure of finding and bowing to truth not of his own believing or making, faith is the arbitrary shouting of seekers lost in the dark.

This integrity of service to higher education involves the requirement that the Church-related college enjoy freedom of inquiry, of thought, and of expression. No Church body or Church-appointed trustees should dictate the intellectual conclusions of faculty members. No faith is real that must live at the expense of truth. No creed is worth holding that can live only by the suppression or the distortion of facts. No confession is worth teaching that cannot endure hard reasoning. Even pressure, however subtle or indirect, on the faculty to conform to the Church's faith rather than to whatever truth it finds precludes a genuinely open inquiry.

The faculty must dare to criticize freely its own faith. At the same time it must be committed to the Church it serves. The Church-related college serves these two masters. Each is sovereign in its own sphere. There is a direct relation of the college as an educational institution to God. It does not need to serve God only as a part of the Church. It need not come to its finding within the presuppositions of its Church's theology. God has created the world and works in it. The Church-related college, *as college*, stands in a direct relation to God within the order of creation.

The Church, however, sees everything first of all in the light of Christ. Its temptation is therefore to telescope truth into a means of salvation. It tends to contract the order of creation into the order of redemption. But the college as an institution of higher learning deals with vast fields of knowledge, like chemistry and astronomy, where Christ and the Church have no direct relevance. Whatever ultimate relevance these fields may have is a task for theology to work out and is not the direct responsibility of the college. It finds and teaches the facts. When the facts of the order of creation, however, seem to do away with faith, the faculty must wrestle honestly with such a situation, with no compulsion from those who employ them, provided the faculty members recognize genuinely the primary purpose of the Church-related college to be the Church at work in education.

High religion and high education are basic needs for any creative culture. In the work of the Church-related college the two are wed. Marriage of independently influential partners offers occasion for strong tensions. Such tensions are altogether likely within the work of the Church-related college. They are, in fact, salutary, provided that the tension be constructive. Such crosscurrents should be the occasion for the growth of a zestful, creative community.

II

The role of the Christian college in its aim to produce a mature faith is therefore, basically, to be both a community with the Christian faith as its presupposition and a community of learning with a completely open method of inquiry. Such a commitment to two masters is impossible unless the Christian faith is also true. If it is not, there can be no authentic Christian colleges. My own conviction is that the Christian faith centers in the reality of Christ as God's universal love and in the Holy Spirit of truth. If Christ and the Holy Spirit are made central to the Church-related college, what results is a community of concern and integrity. The Christian faith stands or falls with the faithfulness of God for all and with the dependability of the Holy Spirit as the guarantor of freedom in the truth. My own experience is increasingly that discipleship and scholarship need not conflict but can give that background of constructive tension that makes it ever necessary to re-examine the faith and to keep it alive and fresh. The more the Church-related college becomes the community of integrity and concern, the more it will serve well both of its primary functions.

To be sure, this will involve a constant dialogue with the Church at large as to the nature of a mature faith. The Church-related college should serve as the mind of the Church. It should be the intellectual conscience of the Church. The mind by its very nature is restive. The feelings, on the other hand, flow in accustomed channels of satisfaction. They are basically conservative, while the mind transcends the present. It sees what can be and what ought to be. It sees different possibilities. It keeps the self unsatisfied, ever solving problems, ever adjusting itself to new situations. The mind of a community should stir that community out of its false self-satisfactions and self-securities. The mind of the Church stirs up the Church creatively and constructively. For those who live on the accumulation of the past, new ideas often come as the threat of the new and the untried. The Church generates much thought based on a false attachment to past ways of doing or of thinking. Much of its thinking is due to an uninformed devotional attitude that is not always wise. The Church therefore creates or constructs much thought that cannot stand the light of vigorous criticism. For this reason it needs the critical work of its mind, the Church-related college. The mind, if free to do so, insists upon a self-consistency that eliminates intellectual discrepancy or moral inconsistency, but, in fact, hurts as it helps. Then the Church-related college has a most important function to perform, however unpleasant its work may be for many in the Church.

To be sure, the Church-related college should also be willing to listen. Often, thought is advanced more lightly by those not in direct responsibility for the life of the institution. Often, the conservative feelings are right and need to be heeded. Thus, with regard to the need for arriving at a mature faith, the Church-related college and the Church need to carry on a constant dialogue. Because of the divergence of function there arises all too often a strong, if not bitter, anti-intellectualism in the Church and a determined anti-ecclesiasticism in the college. These are the false by-products of a necessary process of mutual co-operation within divergent functions.

The Church-related college must also, on the other hand, carry on a determined dialectic with the secular university. This dialectic is particularly needed with regard to religious data and religious interpretations. The secular university has its function within the general providence of God. The secular institutions of higher learning are of immeasurable help to the Church-related colleges because of their constant challenge of the theological bias on the part of those committed to the Christian faith. The world is better off for having secular universities, or at least for having public institutions of higher education not under any kind of Church control or dominating influence. But no subject is without presuppositions, and often the subjects taught in the universities have as their presupposition assumptions prejudicial to the Christion faith. Science, for instance, can be turned from a method into a metaphysics. When this is done covertly, the danger is great.

A naturalistic metaphysics often becomes a dominant theology, an idol, simply on some such false ground as that science is the only road to truth. Even when such a claim is made openly, it is dangerous, both to the faith of the faculty and to that of the students. When, however, it is simply assumed, the hurt is incalculable. The Church-related college in such a case needs to have representatives who, with utmost competence and integrity, will show the limits of efficacy on the part of the scientific method, without in any way appealing to arguments of ignorance in favor of religion.

Similarly, the social sciences may become messianic and pseudo-religious, claiming to be the main road to effective truth. Such claims put forward by able professors of university graduate schools who teach the instructors of the Church-related colleges and its graduate students, or who write the textbooks, may put the stamp of an ineffective religion on instructors or students for life. The Church-related colleges should then have the voice of the deeper wisdom, which appreciates and accepts all truth in science and social science, but which sees both the proper limits of their fields and the limited nature of their pronouncements. Psychology, for instance, may put forward a theory of determinism which is true for limited data and for definite purposes, but which becomes destructive of moral and social responsibility if really acted upon, and which contradicts the very meaning of the Christian faith, not because the claim of such a limited psychological pronouncement is the full truth, but because it has become falsely universalized either by the instructors themselves or by the students who fail to differentiate between limited operational efficacy and truth in general. Niels Bohr's advocacy of complimentariness is to the point in this case.

Or philosophy, by a false separation of life and logic, may rule that man's basic questions are meaningless, whereas it has pronounced most certain the metaphysical assumptions which underlie its whole approach. It is particularly important to remember that no knowledge of ultimates is neutral. Man either accepts or rejects God, through whatever circuitous routes. A large part of so-called secular knowledge is, in fact, the result of man's sinfulness and the rationalization of his disobedience. Such depth-conscious fighting of God takes place through the creation of false religions, by whatever name. Therefore, the Church-related college has a task staggering the imagination: to take every thought captive for Christ in the high places of man's secular learning.

In the Church-related college there should come together mature faith and mature learning, the synthesis of man's basic needs for a creative society. Such union of faith and of learning, however, cannot be had without much effort and pain. For the marriage of faith and learning to take place, the Church needs to raise up and to support its most competent representatives to man the Church-related colleges. Apart from such training and staffing, the difficult job of constant dialectic by the Church-related college with both the Church and the secular university is impossible. Needed, too, is the kind of Christian community of learning and communication which gives the support of a family warmth and a capacity for creative criticism.

III

In the case of a mature faith, however, we have to deal primarily with people. When this is done, usually most of the emphasis is put on the students. The Christian college should help the students find a mature faith. But if such mature faith is to be produced in the students, it must first be possessed and demonstrated by those more mature in years. Seldom is a mature Christian faith even understood, much less had, among those who man the Christian college; and therefore we start with them, where start we must.

A new movement, however, is already beginning to train trustees in their high and holy calling. Perhaps we must go back even further in responsibility to those who choose the trustees. The trustees should study to understand the dual role of the Church-related college, at least to the point where they become aware of the main issues on both sides and can put their influence behind every wind that blows toward a mature faith. In their selection of administrative personnel, the most careful and wise Christian judgment is required.

The administration ought to select faculty with the double function of the Church-related college in mind. Competence and integrity in one's subject are definitely not enough to qualify for such teaching; nor is it enough to add to these requirements a good character. Faith is of the essence, not only of the *bene esse*, of the Christian college. This fact makes staffing a most troublesome task. It cannot be shirked with immunity. Perhaps our Church-related colleges must select their own best products and persuade, yes, constrain, these students to prepare themselves for Christian college teaching, giving them all needed support. Such groups as the Danforth Foundation and the National Council on Religion in Higher Education stand anxious to help. The raising up of such Christian teachers should become a determined passion.

Possibly a truly great ecumenical Christian university of the highest competence and integrity would do more than anything else to change the scope and help provide top-level Christian teachers. We need such universities as well as the state-supported and privately operated ones. Besides, the administration can do wonders for a college by making available the right kind of outside resources that will more and more stand ready to help. Unless such Christian speakers of scholarly standing are found, increasingly, the administration will be handicapped. It should also, I believe, require unapologetically, Christian worship and Christian instruction. Certainly, regular worship by the whole college is part and parcel of the reason for the college's existence, and to be apologetic about required chapel services, required convocations, and required courses in religion is to call into question the very ground on which the college is built. These are required in the same sense in which any course requires attendance: if the students are not interested in pursuing such a line, they ought not to be in such a college. A strong administration, supported by a united faculty, and producing a sustained high level of worship and religious instruction is the key to a genuinely effective Church-related college. The answer is not a false freedom from religion but a fuller effectiveness of Christian worship and Christian instruction.

It goes without saying that the faculty members should know their subjects and maintain their professional competence. Usually, however, the need to teach and to do many other things puts a heavy drain on the time and energy of the faculty and impedes such achievement. But it should be an aim honestly accepted by the administration and faculty alike. Besides opportunity for such scholarly competence, time should be allowed for the continuous growth in the understanding and application of the Christian faith. A Christian Faculty Fellowship that is vigorous can help the faculty become mature in faith. Outstanding theological leaders can be called in, as available, to stimulate and to direct further growth. Some faculties take a long weekend and make a real job of finding such maturity, centered in some retreat led by graduate teachers of religion. Nothing, however, can take the place of discussions of contemporary theology by small groups of faculty members. In some places, such groups meet also for worship, even for prayer. This is good; but the danger exists that there may be a substitution of piety for intellectual vigor. Nothing of course, can be forced in the case of faith, but progress can be made whenever the strong few in the faculty who set the pattern for the rest acquire the vision and the drive to combine as fully as possible man's two great needs of intelligent education and intelligent religion.

I have written more about the administration and the faculty than about the students because I believe that the former are almost entirely the keys to a top-level Church-related college. Student generations come and go quickly. If students meet a staff Christian in faith and example as well as competent in teaching, they will usually take on the prevailing pattern. I know from experience that often those who teach the faith most powerfully actually teach a subject seemingly unrelated to the faith. The whole staff is therefore of top-flight importance. But the students are, of course, our central aim in producing a mature Christian faith.

Given a situation of Christian community, as real as we human beings can be without false piety or pretense, and given the environment of genuine and intelligent worship, the students, with some advice, will produce their own activities, both locally and with relation to national groups like the Student Christian Movement, the Intervarsity Fellowship, or like the YMCA and the YWCA. Effective programs can be integrated under Christian auspices in the Church-related colleges. But the crux of the matter comes in the teaching. The faculty, to produce a mature faith within the students, must have as its goal neither to shelter nor to shock.

Some institutions and some professors shelter students from the rough places of religion, either because of a false paternalism, even "momism," or because of a fear of the constituency. So to shelter the students is to keep them precritical and ineffective in the modern world. Deep faith thrives only on open truth. On the other hand, some institutions and some professors have grown so far away from the churches and from the faith that they delight in shocking their students. They care deeply and responsibly neither for the Church nor for its students. In such a case there is need for a few strong people to focus the faculty upon the genuine task and upon the distinctive nature of the Church-related college. The more independent a college becomes financially and in its manner of control, and the higher its academic standing, the more it is tempted to ape the secular university.

No high intellectual achievement, however, can in any way make up for the Church-related college that fails the students in the deepest needs of their lives. The students need the feel of reality. They need meaningfulness. They need a sense of purpose. They need to know what is true, and why. In other words, they need adequate authority that is not arbitrary, and they need strong motivation that is not drained by fear. When the faculty, instead of working off their own guilt feelings on their students, find for themselves a mature faith that combines high education with holy faith, then the students will have their best chance to grow deep in creative concern and to grow strong in co-operative community. A mature faith requires the fullest possible combination of integrity and faith, of truth and concern. This is the basic need of our world as well.

The Church-related college, then, stands at the center of the world's decision. It represents indigenously both education and religion. To dedicate ourselves not only anew, but within a far deeper seriousness and effectiveness, to the work of the Church-related college is to serve God and man where creation meets redemption. It is to minister to the world's needs where the mind and the heart meet in the whole man. God give all Christian educators wind in their sails.

Index